MW01127726

The International Library of Sociology

SOVIET YOUTH

Founded by KARL MANNHEIM

THE SOCIOLOGY OF THE SOVIET UNION

In 8 Volumes

I	Chekov and his Russia	*Bruford*
II	Educational Psychology in the U.S.S.R.	*Simon et al*
III	The Family in the U.S.S.R.	*Schlesinger*
IV	History of a Soviet Collective Farm	*Belov*
V	Nationalities Problem and Soviet Administration	*Schlesinger*
VI	Psychology in the Soviet Union	*Simon*
VII	Soviet Legal Theory	*Schlesinger*
VIII	Soviet Youth	*Meek*

SOVIET YOUTH

SOME ACHIEVEMENTS AND PROBLEMS

Excerpts from the Soviet Press

Edited and Translated by

DOROTHEA L. MEEK

First published in 1957 by
Routledge and Kegan Paul Ltd

Reprinted in 1998 by
Routledge
11 New Fetter Lane, London EC4P 4EE

Printed and bound in Great Britain

British Library Cataloguing in Publication Data
A CIP catalogue record for this book
is available from the British Library

Soviet Youth
ISBN 0-415-17816-9
The Sociology of the Soviet Union: 8 Volumes
ISBN 0-415-17836-3
The International Library of Sociology: 274 Volumes
ISBN 0-415-17838-X

PREFACE

A WHOLE library of books has been written on the USSR by outside observers, and the reader has a bewildering number of works to choose from. Most of the Soviet materials on the USSR, on the other hand, are published in Russian and therefore only accessible to the specialist student. For this reason I have tried to compile a volume which, as far as possible, allows the country to speak for itself, all the materials included coming from the Soviet press.

There are many different kinds of material on the USSR available to us: popular articles and letters to the editor in Soviet newspapers and magazines, more serious contributions in learned journals, speeches made by leading statesmen and others at congresses and conferences, laws and decrees, Soviet literature of every kind, and descriptions and accounts by foreign visitors and observers. It is only on considering all these materials that we can form a general impression about the country as a whole, or about a special field such as Soviet youth.

The method adopted by me in this volume has been to present the reader with some of these materials, which, with one exception, have hitherto been unpublished in English. They consist mainly of popular contributions to the press over the last ten years. These have been selected to illustrate the most salient features in the overall picture of Soviet youth obtained from readings in the various Soviet materials mentioned above, and supplemented by introductions in order to provide the necessary perspective. I am well aware that this approach is by no means perfect and that it is no guarantee of objectivity. It has the advantage of presenting the material in a lively form. But it must be borne in mind that the translations by themselves only tell part of the story. For one thing, in so far as they purport to reflect public opinion, the reflections are not necessarily strictly accurate.

In addition, the orientation of the materials themselves must be taken into account. It is quite wrong to suppose that there is complete uniformity throughout the entire Soviet press and that there are no differences of approach between the various magazines and newspapers I have used. Nevertheless, the great majority of articles published in the Soviet press have certain features in common. They all share a Marxist approach to the particular question with which they are dealing. They also have an educational aim. Many of the 'positive' articles in this volume are intended as examples to be copied by the reader, and many of the 'negative' items as illustrations of what the reader should *not* do. One of the problems here is that of deciding how typical the phenomena described, whether positive or negative, really are. This is made particularly difficult by the fact that the positive articles have a tendency to give a rather highly coloured account of Soviet achievements in a particular field and to understate the difficulties involved in a specific venture, while the negative articles tend towards exaggeration in the opposite direction.

Moreover, the negative articles and sketches, which criticise some defect or other, have in the past tended to be by far the most lively and interesting items in the Soviet press, while the more positive contributions have often been dull, conventional and wordy. In these circumstances the temptation to use *only* these critical articles was very great, simply because they were so much more readable. But a book consisting only of such articles would have had to be re-named 'Soviet Youth—Problems, Defects and Scandals', and not wishing to compile such a book, I have unfortunately been forced in some cases to include a fairly dull and conventional article in order that the picture as a whole should be more faithful to reality.

This method of allowing the USSR to speak for itself is of necessity an imperfect one, full of pitfalls for the compiler. If I have nevertheless chosen this method of presentation, it is because it seems to me to have at least one very great advantage. Few of us are able to meet and get to know the Soviet people. Even a careful reading of the Soviet press cannot, for the reasons mentioned above, be said to present the Soviet people to us direct. But it does seem to me that this method helps to describe the USSR primarily in human terms, and I feel that it may therefore serve the twofold purpose of teaching us more about Soviet society, while at the same time helping to bridge the gulf between our two countries.

My thanks are due to the members of the Soviet Institutions Department at the University of Glasgow for their advice and assistance. I should also like to thank Mrs. T. Minorsky and the Central

Asian Research Centre for their kind help with problems of translation.

A list of periodicals and newspapers, giving the equivalent name in English and the official standing of each, can be found in an appendix at the back of the book.

GLASGOW,
January, 1956. D.M.

CONTENTS

CONTENTS

I

PRE-SCHOOL PERIOD

INTRODUCTION

BRITISH and Soviet attitudes towards the upbringing of children in the first five or six years of their lives are very different. In this country, for instance, the child is looked upon, first and foremost, as a member of the family. In the USSR too the family unit is regarded as important, but there the child is seen above all as a member of the society in which it is growing up. This difference in outlook has found its expression, *inter alia*, in the respective attitudes adopted towards pre-school education in the two countries.

An important factor in shaping these different attitudes has been the relative demand for manpower in the USSR and in Britain. The USSR has needed an increasingly large labour force ever since the early thirties. From then onwards women's large-scale participation in industry became necessary from the economic point of view, and provisions for crèches and kindergartens had accordingly to be made. Britain, on the other hand, had considerable unemployment during the thirties, and it has only been during the war and post-war periods of full employment that more women have been drawn into industry.

Although the number of places in nursery schools has risen considerably during this period, it is nevertheless probably true to say that in Britain the domestic atmosphere of the home is generally regarded as that most suitable for the young child.

Educationalists in the USSR have always regarded the establishment of an extensive network of kindergartens and crèches as desirable and important. Some of the early statements in fact went so far as to relieve parents of responsibility for their children altogether.[1]

[1] N. K. Krupskaya, for instance, writing in 1899, thought that under socialism 'upkeep of children will be taken from parents, and society will not only provide the child with means of subsistence, but will also see to it that the child has everything necessary for its full, all-round development' (*Izbrannye Pedagogicheskiye Proizvedenia*, 1948, p. 23).

Soviet educationalists today, however, stress the joint responsibility of parents and teachers for the children's correct upbringing, while it is taken for granted that, except in some special cases, the parents alone are responsible for providing the 'means of subsistence' mentioned below by Krupskaya.

Before the revolution pre-school education in Russia was almost non-existent. During the last years of Tsarist rule local governments were starting to organise seasonal summer playgrounds in the countryside for children whose mothers were busy working in the fields. But nothing on any sizable scale was undertaken until 1917. By that year 5,000 children[1] were attending the 285 kindergartens and 14 crèches[2] then existing in the country as a whole. A few of these were in the hands of local authorities and worked as charitable institutions for the children of the very poor. Most of them, however, were in private hands.

The revolutionary government very soon took preliminary measures to improve this state of affairs. A long-term decision was taken to develop a network of crèches and kindergartens throughout the country, the former for children from the age of three months to two years, the latter for children between three and seven. These were to have a twofold purpose: to free the mother for work in some branch of the national economy, and to provide the child with a new kind of upbringing. A department of pre-school education was founded, whose main function was to be the training of teachers.

Then followed the years of the civil war. This was a time of general unrest and disorder; many homes were broken up and there was a general trend towards communal living. This may help to explain the fact that some progress in this field was made, even though pre-school education must have been fairly low on the list of priorities. By 1921, for instance, the number of crèches in the RSFSR had risen from the 14 mentioned above to 668.[3]

There now followed the period of New Economic Policy. The country had virtually been brought to a standstill after the prolonged period of war and civil war, and the immediate concern of the government was to set the economy in motion again. In these circumstances it was found necessary to give considerable scope to private enterprise once again, both in industry and agriculture, and capitalism as a whole was granted another lease of life. These years

[1] E. N. Medynsky, *Narodnoye Obrazovaniye v SSSR*, 1952, p. 43.

[2] A. W. Field, *Protection of Women and Children in Soviet Russia* (London, 1932), p. 28.

[3] Fediaevsky and Hill, *Nursery School and Parent Education*, 1936, p. 32.

were marked by poverty and unemployment. Some advances were made in the field of education during the period as a whole, but the country was still without sufficient primary schools at the time and it is hardly surprising that little attention was paid to pre-school education. At the beginning of NEP certain economy cuts had to be made, and in 1924 only 2 per cent of all children between the ages of three and seven in the RSFSR attended kindergartens[1]; in other republics the figure was probably even lower. There were great material difficulties: educational workers were anxious to use any available buildings and building materials for schools and classes in which both children and the vast masses of illiterate adults could be taught to read and write, and it must have been extremely difficult to persuade authorities to allocate their, very scarce, resources to kindergartens. In addition to obstacles of this kind, pioneers of pre-school education had to face a largely hostile and suspicious population.

We have an account of the setting up of a new kindergarten in the city of Tver[2] which illustrates the conditions in which many teachers were having to work. To begin with, it was decided to accommodate the kindergarten in the house of the former director of the local factory. The next problem was one of finding some children. The prospective teachers embarked on house-to-house visits persuading mothers to send their children along. At first only the very poorest responded. But the kindergarten was given assistance by the local factory, was therefore able to provide the children with food and clothes, in some cases of a higher quality than they would have had at home, and this no doubt helped to make it appear a more attractive proposition to the general public. Gradually the people's attitude towards it began to change, and it even became possible to organise a parents' committee. We are also told that the children themselves were having a good influence on their parents, teaching them, for instance, that it was wrong for the whole family to eat from one communal dish and, in some cases 'even getting their parents to supply them with a separate bed'.[3]

In the countryside conditions were more difficult still. There was

[1] *Izvestia*, Oct. 15, 1925.

[2] *Na Poroge Vtorovo Desyatiletia: Praktika Sotsialnovo Vospitania*, 1927, p. 87.

[3] *Ibid.*, p. 87. Social research carried on at this period revealed that 65 per cent of the children in this particular town had no separate bed, that 80 per cent had never cleaned their teeth and that, incidentally, 30 per cent of the households visited had icons. The latter percentage is likely to have been much larger in the countryside.

often no building in the village big enough to house a kindergarten, and here too the adult population was hostile. Teachers found their main allies in the children themselves, for whom the kindergarten provided a welcome contrast to their lives at home: they were not beaten, were provided with a hot meal and given interesting things to do. But the adult population still had to be reckoned with, and here the influence of religion expressed itself with particular force. People were afraid not that their children would be badly treated but, on the contrary, that they would be treated too well, spoilt and made unfit for eternity. They were also afraid that their children's crosses would be taken from them,[1] that they 'would be made godless' and that the family would be broken up.[2] While the kindergarten was not depriving the children of their crosses, it was teaching them to celebrate Soviet 'feast days' instead of the traditional religious feast days and was, therefore, bound to arouse the hostility of some of the parents. Here is an example of the impact which the kindergarten was having on the home:

> The child attending the kindergarten brought into the family many new things reflecting Soviet life: cultured habits which influenced those of the family, the little red flag given to the child in connection with revolutionary holidays, its own accounts of preparations for these and its constant requests for parents 'to celebrate them' at home, for cleanliness, hygiene and order—'like we have in the kindergarten'—all this brought a new element into the family and sometimes lifted parents out of the traditions of the old way of life.[3]

All through this period and until the beginning of the first five-year plan in 1929, pre-school education continued to cater for a very small minority only, even in the cities. The plan marked the beginning of industrialisation on a large scale. As a result the number of working women gradually began to rise and, by the early thirties, an extension of the network of crèches and kindergartens had become of paramount importance. Consequently, pre-school education now began to develop more quickly. The following table shows the growth of kindergartens up to 1939:

[1] It is customary for a member of the Russian Orthodox Church to wear a small cross round the neck.

[2] *Na Poroge Vtorovo Desyatiletia: Praktika Sotsialnovo Vospitania*, 1927, pp. 98 ff.

[3] E. Volkova, *Doshkolnoye Vospitaniye v Gody Stalinskikh Pyatiletok*, 1925, p. 28.

Year	*Number of kindergartens*	*Number of children in kindergartens*
1924–5	1,139	60,196
1928–9	2,517	129,256
1931	6,574	336,236
1936	—	1,230,000
1939	23,123	1,039,000

Sources: For 1924–5 and 1928–9—Volkova, op. cit., p. 25; for 1931—*Kulturnoye Stroitelstvo SSSR 1935*, p. 34; for 1936—Decree of June 27, 1936—(translated in R. Schlesinger, *Changing Attitudes in Soviet Russia: The Family*, 1949, pp. 275 ff.); for 1939—*Bolshaya Sovetskaya Entsiklopedia*, vol. SSSR (1947), p. 1218.

Pre-school education was also becoming more scientific in its approach. In 1928 the first number of a specialist journal, *Doshkolnoye Vospitaniye* ('Pre-School Education') appeared; a year later a special publishing house for children's books was opened and a children's programme started on the wireless.

As can be seen from the table above, pre-school education continued to grow at a tremendous rate until 1936, and then began to decline again. It looks as though this decline occurred only in the countryside,[1] while the number of places in towns continued to increase. This local decline may in part be attributed to the fact that kindergarten fees were introduced in 1935.[2] It is possible that these proved a deterrent in the countryside where ready cash was particularly scarce, but had less effect in the towns. By 1939 about 6 per cent of the total child population of pre-school age in the USSR was attending kindergartens.[3]

[1] According to the 1936 Decree, there were 400,000 places in collective farm kindergartens at that time. The 1941 Plan (*Gosudarstvenny Plan Razvitia Narodnovo Khozyaistva na 1941 god*, p. 622) has a target of only 140,400 places.

[2] Decree of July 6, 1935 (in *Narodnoye Obrazovaniye: Postanovlenia, Prikazy i Instruktsii*, 1948, p. 266).

At present payment varies according to the mother's income, and ranges from 40 rubles to 150r. a month in the towns, and from 30r. to 135r. in the countryside (V. Shavrin, *Gosudarstvenny Byudzhet SSSR*, p. 68). A kindergarten in Tbilisi which I visited in May 1954 charged 100r. a month for mothers earning between 600r. and 1,000r. a month, 30r. for mothers earning not more than 600r., and 20r. for mothers of three or more children, irrespective of earnings.

[3] F. Lorimer, *The Population of the Soviet Union: History and Prospects*, 1946, p. 143. Lorimer gives the following population figures:

Aged	
3	3,825,487
4	3,260,378
5–9	17,501,090

Since the Soviet child at this time started school at the age of eight, I have

As I have already mentioned above, Soviet pre-school education at this period was still very much in its experimental stages. Most of the teachers had only had very scanty training. No systematic network of teachers' colleges existed until the first five-year plan, and for a long time the training of most of the kindergarten teachers employed was confined to a short course of a year, six, or even three months.[1] It is only natural, therefore, that we should find distortions and exaggerations in their educational work. Their attitude towards 'labour' in the kindergarten was an instance of this. The idea that children should learn to respect labour and realise its importance has, of course, always been fundamental to Soviet education. But at this period there was a marked tendency to place too much emphasis on it and to overestimate the capacity of the children. In some kindergartens they seem to have been expected to do work which must have been quite beyond them. Here, for example, is a contemporary description of a kindergarten in Kuibyshev[2]: 'Our kindergarten has a special room equipped with benches, saws and a set of tools for woodwork.'

In other ways too children were treated rather as though they were already adults. For example, they were often expected to take part in political campaigns, form their own committees and hold general meetings of the kindergarten at which they would elect their chairman and discuss such topics as discipline and hygiene.

It would be quite wrong, however, to look at the development of Soviet pre-school education in this period merely from the point of view of these distortions. They were decreasing rapidly during the thirties, and the Decree on Pedology in 1936 (with which I will be dealing more fully in a later section) did away with them altogether. Pre-school education also came to take on many important positive features which had been advocated right from the beginning and which still form an integral part of education in the USSR today. The most important of these features is the emphasis placed on the social education of the children, teaching them to live and work collectively and to think of themselves as members of a community. Another very important feature of pre-school education (and indeed of Soviet education as a whole) is the importance it attributes to awakening in the child feelings of friendship towards other communities, and in particular, towards the peoples of other countries. With

---

calculated the number of children of kindergarten age (3–7) in 1939 by adding the figures for ages 3 and 4, plus half the number given for the 5–9 age groups. This is, of course, only a very rough estimate.

[1] Volkova, *op cit.*, p. 185.

[2] *Ibid.*, p. 66.

regard to capitalist countries this usually takes the form of solidarity and sympathy with the 'exploited' people there. Krupskaya gives an interesting illustration of what Soviet educationalists regard as the correct attitude towards the peoples in their own, sometimes backward, republics.[1] She has received a letter from an orphanage for Russian children in Uzbekistan. The children write that they know that the workers of all countries should unite and that they will therefore help to make the 'wild Uzbeks' living around them 'cultured'. This is Krupskaya's reply to the teacher in charge:

> You must tell the children something about the life of the Uzbeks so as to show that in some respects Uzbek children are at a higher level than Russian children. I am sure that Uzbek children have very interesting games. This is usually so with children who live in close contact with nature; they can probably run faster than Russian children. You must show them not that Uzbek children are backward but that, in some respects, they stand at a higher level.

As we have already seen above, pre-school education was also regarded as a vehicle for the spread of new political and cultural ideas. The population with which kindergartens and crèches now had to work was no longer as backward as it had been during the NEP period, but it still left much to be desired. Some kindergartens organised competitions for the best family. In one such competition[2] which, incidentally, throws some light on the general level of the population, parents promised to:

> Provide a separate bed, towel and toothbrush;
> see that the child's hands are washed before meals;
> serve meals at regular hours;
> let the child spend at least two hours daily in the open;
> provide a play corner to be kept tidy by the child itself;
> put the child to bed not later than 10 p.m.

With the beginning of the war, pre-school education became more important than ever. As the men left for the front, women took their places in industry and agriculture, and the number of hours spent at work daily were often very long. According to Volkova[3] kindergartens began to mushroom almost everywhere, and a policy of not refusing admittance to any child was apparently adopted. By 1943 a number of provinces had twice, and in some cases even three times

[1] Krupskaya, *op cit.*, p. 145. [2] Volkova, *op cit.*, pp. 75–6. [3] *Ibid.*, p. 34.

as many children attending kindergartens as they had had before the war. In Kinel, in the Kuibyshev province, for example, the numbers in one kindergarten alone rose from 75 to 120. The ruling that there should be not more than 25 children in each age group was now relaxed, and groups frequently contained as many as 35 or 40 children. Kindergartens and crèches had not merely to deal with the children of mothers who were now away at work for the greater part of the day. Many of them had to turn themselves into temporary hostels and accommodate those children from the war devastated areas whom it had not been possible to evacuate in time. And these had not merely to be fed and clothed, but taught anew to live relatively normal lives and to forget the horrors they had seen. The cultivation of an allotment by the kindergartens, which had previously been encouraged largely for educational purposes, now became a necessity in order to provide potatoes and fresh vegetables for the children. A number of kindergartens were evacuated to the east where they began to function as hostels. The duties placed upon teachers in these conditions were very heavy indeed. They had to take the place of the home completely. Children had to be accustomed to an entirely new climate. Since they were too young to write to their parents themselves, the task of maintaining contact with the latter also fell to the teachers.

Apart from these kindergartens in the rear, there were also a number working in some of the centres of the bitterest fighting. There are accounts of kindergarten-hostels in Leningrad which functioned all through the siege, often under the most terrible conditions —with water having to be fetched up in buckets from the Neva.[1] The reconstruction of kindergartens in these places as the Germans retreated is impressive. Volkova[2] reports that there were 73 kindergartens—most of them in dug-outs—functioning in Stalingrad in 1943. By the spring of 1945 the city had rebuilt 88.[3] An article written half a year later reports a total of 531 kindergartens for Leningrad.[4] Many of these war-time kindergartens were no doubt makeshift affairs, some of them of very poor quality indeed, and it is probable that large numbers of these closed down again at the end of the war. The building and staffing of new permanent kindergartens had, like everything else, been interrupted by the war.

Figures for the post-war period are few and far between. From the evidence available it appears that in 1949 the figure for the USSR

[1] Volkova, *op cit.*, p. 144.
[2] *Ibid.*, p. 166.
[3] *Pravda*, March 12, 1945.
[4] *Izvestia*, Oct. 10, 1945.

as a whole[1] stood at the 1936 level, with a total of 1,250,000 places.[2] It is obvious from this figure that many more kindergartens are needed. In 1949, for instance, there were about 900 mothers in one district of Leningrad alone who complained that they were unable to continue their work because they could find no vacancies for their children.[3] It also appears that plans for new kindergartens have not always been fulfilled.[4]

The situation in the countryside has been much worse. Here kindergartens are very largely financed by the collective farms themselves, and it is probably true to say that most of these have, at least until recently, been too backward, both economically and culturally, to organise them. In addition, the nature of agricultural work makes permanent kindergartens appear less necessary, and the majority of collective farms have merely organised seasonal playgrounds during the summer. As can well be imagined, the educational work carried on in these playgrounds is often of a very low standard, if indeed it is carried on at all. Conditions in rural kindergartens have generally tended to be much inferior to those in the towns.[5]

The last year or two have seen the beginnings of a considerable change in this respect, no doubt closely connected with the measures for improving conditions in the countryside which were announced in 1953. There have recently been several articles in the journal, *Pre-School Education*, describing the way in which new kindergartens are being organised in the collective farms. Two of these[6] provide a good illustration of the change that is taking place in the Leningrad province: in July 1953 there was only one permanent collective farm kindergarten in the province; by November of the same year the figure had risen to 10, and by June 1954 it stood at 30.

Pre-school education is in fact steadily growing. It has not yet reached a satisfactory level, but Malenkov mentioned a planned

[1] The *Bolshaya Sovetskaya Entsiklopedia*, vol. SSSR (1947), p. 1221, has figures for republics such as Georgia and Uzbekistan, showing a marked decline: in Georgia the number of places dropped from 36,400 in 1939 to 22,200 in 1946, in Uzbekistan, from 30,000 to 12,000.

[2] V. Zhirnov, *Razvitiye Sovetskoi Sotsialisticheskoi Kultury*, 1952, p. 33.

[3] *Literaturnaya Gazeta*, July 9, 1949.

[4] *Doshkolnoye Vospitaniye*, 1953, no. 12, pp. 11 ff. According to the first post-war five-year plan, 2,260,000 places should have been available for the USSR as a whole by 1950. In the RSFSR only 310 of the 702 new kindergartens planned for 1952 were in fact built.

[5] *Uchitelskaya Gazeta*, Feb. 17, 1954. The article also states that 'the number of permanently functioning collective farm pre-school establishments is still insignificant'.

[6] *Doshkolnoye Vospitaniye*, 1954, no. 3, p. 36, and 1954, no. 8, p. 2.

increase of 40 per cent over 1952 for 1953,[1] and in the industrial centres of the country a fairly wide network of crèches and kindergartens does exist already today. No figures for these centres are available, but a report to the effect that about 50 per cent of the seven-year olds starting school in the big cities of the country in the autumn of 1953 had previously attended kindergartens, gives us an indication of the considerable scope of pre-school education in these cities.[2]

And now a brief word about the nature of Soviet pre-school education today. As I have already said, its main function is, on the one hand, to provide the child with a social education which, it is maintained, cannot be provided by the home on its own, and on the other hand, to make it possible for the mother to carry on her trade or profession. A great deal of emphasis is now placed on the physical development of the child. Some of the games, for instance, are organised with a view to the physical movements they entail, and the necessity for play in the open, even during the very severe winters experienced in parts of the USSR, is recognised and stressed. The role of labour is still regarded as important. Children are taught from the earliest possible age to perform simple duties such as laying the table. They are encouraged to be as independent as they can, 'don't do anything for the child that it can do for itself' being the general motto. But, in contrast to the thirties, it is now realised that the child must on no account be overburdened. The kindergarten is divided into four age groups and it is not until the fourth group (five to seven years) that children are taught to count and read. On the whole, the kindergarten is a place where the children spend their time at play, both on their own and in an organised manner together with the teacher.

Most of the translations I have chosen for this section deal with problems of developing pre-school education and ways in which these problems are being tackled.[3] They give us an interesting glimpse of the manner in which broad sections of the population are drawn into this work, and introduce us to the institution of *shefstvo* (guardianship or patronage), whereby one community of people acts as 'patron' to another. This is something akin to our war-time

[1] Budget speech, *Komsomolskaya Pravda*, Aug. 9, 1953.

[2] *Doshkolnoye Vospitaniye*, 1954, no. 1, p. 33.

[3] A purely descriptive article (in English) on the normal everyday life of a Soviet kindergarten and of the educational work done in conjunction with parents can be found in *SCR Bulletin on Soviet Education*, vol. I, no. 2 (July 1954).

practice of a school or factory 'adopting' a ship or regiment, and we shall meet several instances of it in this volume.

In the account of kindergartens in the city of Kuibyshev, the active part played by the general public again comes out very clearly, although the pre-school education described here is greatly in advance of its counterpart in the countryside.

This brings me to the account of a kindergarten in a collective farm. This item is not intended as an illustration of what was typical for rural pre-school education generally in 1949. Indeed, if it were typical, the other items on collective farm kindergartens would make no sense at all. It does seem to me, however, to be typical both of the kind of activity carried on, and of the general atmosphere prevailing in already existing Soviet kindergartens. It should be remembered here, though, that these accounts of kindergartens by no means give an exhaustive picture of the activities carried on, or of all the facilities available for Soviet children below the age of seven.

The last of the translations in this section tells us something about Soviet attitudes to certain questions of upbringing. This item, strictly speaking, belongs to a later section, but I have included it here because it seems to me that fairy tales are more appropriate for this section, especially since children in the USSR do not go to school until they are seven years old. There was a time when Soviet educationalists condemned fairy tales as likely to encourage 'superstition' and an 'unhealthy imagination'.[1] This is no longer the official attitude, and traditional fairy tales are among the most beautifully produced books in the USSR today.

[1] Volkova, *op. cit.*, p. 65. Dolls too were regarded as harmful at this time. They were said to reflect the old way of life, and it was feared that the little girl playing with them would tend to think of herself as a future housewife.

ORGANISING KINDERGARTENS IN THE COLLECTIVE FARMS OF THE LENINGRAD PROVINCE

BY V. A. IVANOVA, HEAD OF THE PRE-SCHOOL SECTION, LENINGRAD PROVINCE EDUCATION DEPARTMENT

(*Doshkolnoye Vospitaniye*, 1954, no. 2, p. 17)

THE report of N. S. Khrushchov on 'Measures for the Further Development of Agriculture in the USSR', and the decision adopted in connection with this report by the Plenary Meeting of the Central Committee of the CPSU held in September[1] both point out that the raising of the material and cultural standards of the working people is something which must always be of concern to the whole nation, uniting the working class and the collective farm peasantry.

The plenary meeting draws attention to the immense part played by women working in collective and state farms, and also to our duty to do more mass-political, cultural and educational work among women in collective farms, MTS,[2] and state farms. More women must be drawn into collective farm work, and take an active part in striving to improve crop yields and livestock breeding.

To carry out these tasks successfully, it is very important that pre-school educational workers should combine with the general public in helping women to bring up their children and to give them an opportunity to work and study, free from anxiety about them. A permanent children's establishment—the kindergarten—must be set up in the countryside.

In the Leningrad province 76 kindergartens have been set up in state farms and four in industrial co-operatives. In 1953 there were

[1] Decision of Sept. 7, 1953. This decision marked the beginning of an important drive to improve the general level of agriculture and of the rural population.

[2] Machine Tractor Stations.

125 open air playgrounds for children in collective farms, and last autumn we started setting up permanently functioning collective farm kindergartens.

The province executive committee[1] decides each year on the children's establishments to be set up in collective farms. District[2] executive committees also submit their decisions based on what is needed and on what the collective farms are in fact able to do; this eventually becomes the plan for the district.

Although we began organising children's establishments in our province several years ago, there is still a great deal of explanatory work to be done among collective farmers, and public organisations and local soviets ought to give the matter their attention. This work is still not satisfactory in the Slantsy, Podporozhe Osmino and Lodeinoye Pole districts.

The organising of children's establishments in collective farms comes under the special commissions, attached to district executive committees, which are responsible for the organisation of recreational and holiday facilities during the summer. Each commission includes the secretary of the district executive committee (chairman of the commission), and representatives from the district education department, the department of health, the department of agriculture, the Red Cross and the district executive committee of the komsomol.[3]

The commission receives a great deal of help from the *aktiv* of teachers and pre-school workers in the province who have been carrying on explanatory and organisational work locally during the past few years.

The development of kindergartens has had many difficulties to contend with: still poor collective farms without suitable buildings; low remuneration per labour-day[4]; insufficient explanatory work

[1] Of the soviet (unit of local government). It is here referred to on both province and district levels. Each soviet has a number of 'permanent commissions' attached to it and giving special attention to such fields as health, education, etc. They are made up of about a dozen members who work together with an *aktiv* (the most active people, both party and non-party, in the community). In the towns there are sometimes up to several hundred such 'activists' doing voluntary work with a permanent commission. It is regarded as an important means of stimulating a general interest in local government among the population.

Descriptions of the regulations concerning these commissions and of the actual work carried on by them can be found in *Soviet Studies*, vol. II, no. 4, pp. 413 ff., and vol. III, no. 1, pp. 103 ff.

[2] Every province or county (*oblast*) is sub-divided into districts (*raiony*).

[3] Young Communist League.

[4] A labour-day is the unit of work used in calculating remuneration due to collective farmers.

among collective farmers on how important it is for their children to take advantage of the social education provided by the kindergarten; lack of qualified personnel to direct and teach in kindergartens, who would see to it that proper educational work was done; an underestimation by collective farm chairmen and leading officials in the districts of the importance of children's establishments.

. . . In the Leningrad province we are only just beginning to set up collective farm kindergartens. So far we only have 10. Here is the sort of work we are doing as a start: getting the general public to take part in organising collective farm kindergartens; propaganda work among collective farmers on the social education afforded by kindergartens; material aid to kindergartens; finding young people from among the komsomol in the collective farms to train as kindergarten teachers.

In order to draw the general public into this work of forming collective farm kindergartens, the deputy chairman of the province executive committee arranged a conference which was attended by representatives from the various departments of the executive committee, from the city education department, from 'patron' organisations and from the province committee of the primary and secondary school teachers' trade union. This helped to rouse the public into activity. The departments of culture, broadcasting and the cinema are helping us with visual methods of propaganda, and a short film about the collective farm kindergarten is being planned. The news broadcasts put out by the Leningrad wireless station make announcements about any new kindergartens which have been opened. At province and district branches of the Society for the Dissemination of Political and Scientific Knowledge, sections on the upbringing of children are being formed; there will be lectures by teachers from schools, kindergartens and orphanages.

A great deal of help is being given by some of the districts of Leningrad city which have 'adopted' collective farms in the province, each enterprise in the district taking on a particular farm. However, this work was begun without the help of education departments and did not envisage the actual organising of kindergartens, although 'patrons' can provide the necessary material support. They can also help with explanatory work among women collective farmers, making use of the kindergartens in their own enterprises to give advice on pre-school methods. The work of 'patrons' is directed by district party committees, and we have asked the province committee of the CPSU to draw the attention of 'patrons' to the need for including these questions in their contracts.

The city's pre-school workers responded to the decision of the September Plenum by undertaking definite obligations with regard to organising collective farm kindergartens.

The province committee of the komsomol held a conference attended by secretaries of komsomol district committees of the city, at which it was pointed out to them that they must take part in organising collective farm kindergartens. The Red Cross society in our province is also helping us: it provides medical attention in children's establishments on the farms and carries on explanatory work.

The province committee of the primary and secondary school workers' trade union has instructed all trades councils and trade union committees to take part in organising children's establishments in collective farms. . . .

The question of a network of collective farm kindergartens was raised in the province education department and at meetings of district education departments and heads of schools. We are thus drawing in the general public, and we intend to treat the matter as one of first priority.

But the kindergarten will never be really successful until the women in the collective farms themselves begin to realise and understand that it is necessary and important. For this reason our chief task is to carry on propaganda work for social education in pre-school establishments. On analysing this work, we came to the conclusion that our conversations with the women on the farms were frequently dry and uninteresting, often leaving the mothers quite unmoved. We therefore decided to help our *aktiv* in this propaganda work. We started by drawing up draft lectures on problems of organisation and teaching, and collecting illustrations. The province pre-school research centre[1] is holding a seminar for our propaganda workers. It is being run by specialists in the city and province, together with those heads of kindergartens who have experience in working with the population.

At lectures, photographs of kindergartens and work done by the children are shown. And the lecturer's words are brought to life by the children themselves, either in their normal, natural surroundings—the kindergartens of the province and city, or welcoming the collective farmers at the beginning of the lecture.

After the October celebration[2] in the district House of Culture,[3] the

[1] These research centres are attached to local education departments.

[2] Of the 'Great October Socialist Revolution'.

[3] Houses of Culture are centres for social and cultural activities. Most of them belong to trade unions, although some are run by local governments.

Red Partisan collective farm from the Pargolovo district held its account meeting.[1] This meeting had an unusual beginning. The curtain went up, the piano played and children from the senior group of Leningrad city's kindergarten no. 19 appeared on the stage. They performed excerpts from the programme they had prepared for a special morning of celebration. After the children's performance, O. I. Sirelius, head of the kindergarten, told the audience why kindergartens were being opened in our country and what they had to offer to the family. Criticising the farm management, women collective farmers pointed out that it was not giving enough attention to the children, and demanded the opening of a kindergarten.

A few articles on collective farm kindergartens have been published in the *Teachers' Gazette*, the *Leningrad Pravda* and in district newspapers. Articles by the head of the province education department, A. A. Andreyeva, appeared in the local newspapers of the Mga and Krasnoye Selo districts where hardly any open air playgrounds existed at all. The challenge contained in Andreyeva's articles has had a good effect. Wall newspapers of collective farms and rural soviets are also being used.

Together with specialists in Leningrad we are putting out leaflets to help collective farms in organising kindergartens.

It is very important for the teacher to talk with parents in their own surroundings, and hundreds of teachers have visited collective farm families in this way. As a result, the women have gained a better understanding of the importance of open air playgrounds and permanent kindergartens, and are beginning to want them for their children. It takes time to visit a collective farm. This is what E. V. Ryzhova, head of kindergarten no. 2 of the Krasnoye Selo district, told propagandists attending a seminar:

> If you want to set up a kindergarten in a collective farm, don't go there just for two or three hours. You will have a lot to do: talk with the women on the farm, raise the question of a kindergarten with the management, and also help with the actual preparatory work involved. When our staff were opening a kindergarten in the *Glyadino* farm, one of the teachers, A. I. Kivitar, spent a whole week down there. She had to make the place comfortable; with the help of the women she distempered it, and she also carried on explanatory work. She had already visited them

---

[1] An 'account meeting' is the annual general meeting of a collective farm, at hich rates for labour-days are fixed and plans for the following year discussed.

several times during the summer and this undoubtedly contributed to the management's decision to form its own kindergarten.

The decision of the September Plenum of the CC CPSU points to the need for building kindergartens and other social and cultural amenities in those collective farms which have now become more prosperous.

The availability of a building is a big factor in setting up a kindergarten in the collective farm. There are farms which have no suitable accommodation; four collective farms in the province have started to build special kindergartens, but they are still under construction.

The CC CPSU points out that, as the collective farms' general economies grow, they will be able to use part of their income to build kindergartens, crèches and maternity homes, creating better conditions for the women working on the farm and making it possible for them to play a more active part in public life. The Ministry of Agriculture should exert its influence to see that this type of expenditure is not neglected in the farm's budget.

The decision of the September Plenum makes it the duty of Gosplan[1] to allow for the necessary quantity of money, materials and equipment in its annual plans. In the Leningrad province this has not so far covered the planned supplies of building materials for collective farm kindergartens.

Pre-school workers from each district of Leningrad city (Leningrad has 16 districts) have undertaken to open one collective farm kindergarten in the province.

We are planning to open 30 new collective farm kindergartens during 1954. The help given by 'patrons' and the explanatory work carried on among the women on the farms may make it possible to open even more. The party and executive committee of the province have given us the task of making all new kindergartens good ones. In planning MTS settlements it is very important that plots to be used for kindergarten construction should be included in the general layout.

There are some collective farms such as, for instance, the *Bolshevik* farm in the Volosovo district and the *Victory* farm in the Roshchino district, which have shouldered all the expenses involved in maintaining a kindergarten. Here mothers do not have to pay anything at all towards the child's upkeep in the kindergarten. In some collective farms, fees to be paid vary according to the number of labourdays worked by the parents. In the Kirov collective farm in the

[1] State Planning Commission.

Sosnovo district, for instance, mothers who have worked a greater number of labour-days than those laid down as the norm[1] do not have to pay at all; those who have fulfilled the norm, pay 10 per cent of the actual cost of feeding the child, and the proportion to be paid by the mother grows in inverse ratio to the number of labour-days worked.

. . . New children's establishments in our province will be of a general type housing a kindergarten as well as a crèche. The collective farmers are quite happy with this arrangement and are mainly concerned that there should be a separate establishment for each brigade. . . .[2] The Ministry of Agriculture must give instructions to its province departments to exercise greater control in seeing that funds are spent correctly and that allocations for permanent kindergartens and seasonal playgrounds are included in the budgets.

Collective farmers will have difficulties in furnishing the kindergartens. There are no full sets of furniture to be bought, and the farms have no joiners; the carpenters they have can only produce rough tables and benches, and the chairs made by them are very crude and expensive. It is time we had factories producing children's furniture and supplying all children's establishments irrespective of the ministry responsible for them.

Tsentrosoyuz[3] must supply the rural trade network with linen, crockery and toys for collective farm kindergartens. All these things should be cheap, attractive and of good quality. The arts and technique council responsible for designing toys should plan an assortment suitable both for the activities carried on in collective farm kindergartens, and for the conditions in which they work.

Collective farmers are demanding satisfactory kindergartens for their children, and parents are not satisfied with the primitive kind of set-up where the children are merely looked after, but not given the right kind of upbringing. The standard of the kindergarten undoubtedly depends on the people working in it. Children's establishments in collective farms do not have a homogeneous group of

[1] The compulsory minimum for collective farmers in non black-earth districts and in high lying grain and livestock-raising districts was 100 labour-days annually (*Kolkhoznoye Pravo*, 1950, p. 254). This ruling was changed in 1954, and each collective farm now decides what the compulsory minimum for its members is to be.

[2] Collective farmers are organised into 'brigades' according to the different kinds of farming carried on. It is quite likely that each brigade is made up from people living in one of several villages scattered over the area of the collective farm, and that a separate crèche and kindergarten is therefore needed for each brigade.

[3] The central authority of consumers' co-operatives.

teachers. You can find young girls fresh from school, old women who are no longer strong enough to do physical work and mothers who have come to the playground because they themselves have small children. The level of education too differs widely, ranging from the semi-literate to people with a secondary-level teachers' training. The selection of staff is made more difficult by the fact that collective farms cannot offer a salary[1] to trained teachers from outside the farm, and that there are no qualified teachers among the farmers themselves. Farms should be given the opportunity of training their own teaching staffs.

In self-criticism, we must admit that we have not been making any special efforts to attract the children of collective farmers into the Sestroretsk training school for kindergarten and crèche teachers. During the past three years only 12 people from the farms graduated at the school, and the question of their going back to work in their native farm was never raised with them; on finishing their training they all went to work in kindergartens in towns and industrial settlements. In 1954, 18 girls from the farms will graduate at our school. If the komsomol organisation and the staff do the necessary educational work with these girls, they will go back to their farms to organise kindergartens.

Together with the province committee of the komsomol we approached the girls who have graduated from the school and appealed to them to go back to the collective farm; some of them—M. Minina, A. Filimonova and M. Sakman—warmly responded to our appeal. The training school is carrying on explanatory work in the seven-year schools in the countryside with the aim of getting young people from the collective farms to take up the profession of kindergarten or crèche teacher.

There is yet another way of building up teaching staffs. We are drawing in girls with a seven-year education to work in playgrounds and to study by correspondence at the same time. The trouble is that the collective farm cannot allow them to attend the course arranged for them by the training school, since this is held in summer when agricultural work is in full swing. A course should be held during the winter months for them.

The Leningrad province education department and the department of health are jointly organising seminars and practical training in

[1] Teachers employed by the collective farm are remunerated in labour-days' and the amounts paid, both in cash and kind, will vary from year to year depending on the prosperity of the farm. Trained teachers therefore generally prefer to work in the towns where they are assured of a more stable income.

kindergartens of towns and district centres for collective farm kindergarten teachers. In 1953, 85 people received such training.

School teachers are giving us a great deal of help. The Volosovo district, for instance, has a good tradition of teachers organising open air playgrounds and doing work with the children.

It must be admitted that the medical service in children's establishments in the countryside is inadequate. The Ministry of Health must improve its medical inspection in children's establishments in collective farms. There should be definite standard rules for buildings and for the sanitary conditions in them, and these rules should be distributed to all collective farms.

The XIX Congress of the CPSU gave instructions for an increase of 40 per cent in the network of kindergartens. A considerable proportion of these should be made up of collective farm kindergartens.

THE WORK OF A COLLECTIVE FARM KINDERGARTEN WITH THE FAMILY AND THE PUBLIC

BY E. I. KRUGLOVA

(*Doshkolnoye Vospitaniye*, 1949, no. 7, p. 14)

KINDERGARTEN no. 5 in the village of Khvatovka (Arzamass district, Gorky province) was opened in April 1946. Until then the village had only had seasonal children's playgrounds which functioned while work in the fields was in full swing.

The village of Kamenka, about two miles away, already had a kindergarten, and so our collective farm applied to the education department for one to be opened in our village too.

The prestige of our kindergarten with the collective farmers is very high. This is what F. P. Nikitin, the farm chairman, had to say about it at the farm's annual meeting in 1947: 'Our kindergarten is making it a lot easier for us to get our agricultural work done. Both parents can now go out to work in the fields without having to worry, knowing that their children are in reliable hands.'

This is what collective farmer, A. I. Frolova, said about our work: 'I have three children, two of them at kindergarten. My husband was killed at the front. Before we had a kindergarten I wasn't able to spend much time working for the collective farm; I would all the time be worrying about the children. I never used to earn more than 100 labour-days, but this year I've earned 230. I've the kindergarten to thank for that. My children are growing up healthy, strong, intelligent and cultured.'

We often hear such statements, at meetings of the farm management, and also at brigade meetings.

The kindergarten enjoys this prestige because it has been constantly improving its work, both from the educational and the economic points of view, and because it has established close contact with parents and with collective farm members in general. . . .

INDIVIDUAL WORK WITH FAMILIES

At the beginning we made a lot of mistakes: we tended to visit mainly those families where children were often absent from the kindergarten without a good excuse, or where parents were not paying their kindergarten fees on time. Our visits to homes where children were not being brought up properly were very much rarer.

We discussed and analysed this problem at a teachers' meeting and realised our mistakes.

. . . Here is an example of the work we do. We found the mother of Vitya and Galya to be a retiring sort of person of low cultural level. There are four children in the family; the father was killed at the front. For a long time the mother refused to let the children come to the kindergarten. During the winter they would sit by the stove and hardly ever go out into the street. One of our teachers, Comrade Maisova, explained to her how she should go about applying for her pension. The parents' committee and the kindergarten together helped to provide clothes and shoes for the children. As a result of their efforts the childern were able to attend the kindergarten free of charge (the collective farm paid for them). At first they used to come in ragged and dirty clothes. We in the kindergarten decided to launder and mend all their underclothes, and to wash the children themselves. Later, the collective farm agreed to assign two women to put the family's house in order. They worked under our supervision and reset the stove (it smoked) at the cost of the collective farm. The mother was very pleased to have our help and began to keep the house clean herself. When the kindergarten head or one of the teachers came to see her she would cast a quick glance around the room and apologise if there was anything left lying about.

The change at home made itself felt at school too: the children were tidier and more disciplined. In the past Vitya's and Galya's brother, Vova, would pull up a flower, turnip or carrot as he passed the kindergarten plot. Now he helps us on the plot and guards over it.

Vitya, was a shy, quiet boy. He loved drawing, and listening to fairy tales, but would never say anything about them aloud. We gave him some paper and coloured pencils to take home with him. He enjoyed drawing at home and started bringing his drawings to the kindergarten. His elder brother has begun to read to him. Vitya has developed considerably, both mentally and physically, and he now has a much healthier complexion.

This is what the mother of these children said at a meeting of the parent-teacher association:

'I'm not a very educated woman; I grew up in poverty and there wasn't anything in my own childhood that I'd want to remember. Until my children started to go to kindergarten they were always being naughty, and I used to be terribly worried wondering how I was going to bring them up on my own without a father to help. It does my heart good to see them now. Last night Vitya said "good night" to me as he went off to bed. When I took no notice, he said: "Why don't you answer me, mummy, when I say 'good night' to you, like they teach us at the kindergarten?" I felt ashamed and at the same time happy that my children were growing up sensibly, not the way I'd been brought up. That's what the kindergarten has done. And we owe all this to our beloved Stalin who cares about our children. Under his leadership nice kindergartens are being opened.[1] And the kindergarten doesn't only have an influence on my own children; it also influences the children who don't attend kindergarten. I'd feel quite helpless without it.'

We do not only visit the families; we also invite separate groups of parents to the kindergarten where we give talks on various problems of upbringing. Here are a few examples of the kind of topic we deal with: 'How to Look After the Child at Home', 'How to Deal with Stubbornness and Temper in Children', 'What Toys to Choose for Children', and 'How to Teach Children to be Independent'.

. . . We also arrange for a doctor to talk to parents, and we have found that these talks bring the kindergarten closer to them; after listening to the doctor they often come to us of their own accord and ask our advice about their children. We also hold individual consultations—informal and friendly talks. Sometimes we arrange 'open days' for parents, when they can come and watch their children in the kindergarten. As a result they tend to adopt the teachers' methods,

[1] There are several references of this kind to Stalin, both in this section and in the other sections of the volume.

This kind of thing is no longer found in the Soviet press today, and there is no doubt that it was carried to extremes, particularly at the time when the above article was written. It would, however, be wrong to regard it purely as something turned on from above (and now arbitrarily turned off). It is much more likely to have been in part a reflection of the level of the people themselves. It seems to me quite natural that a relatively uneducated peasant woman should think of the Soviet régime in terms of personalities.

using them as and when they can be profitably applied in the home. Parents enjoy visiting the kindergarten festivals; they are sometimes moved to tears to see how gay their children are and what a good time they are having.

In the summer we arrange special matinée performances on the kindergarten plot; many people in the village come to these even if they are not directly connected with the kindergarten, simply because it is popular with the villagers. Seventy-six year old collective farmer and member of the farm management, Ivan Nikolaevich Zotov, for instance, is a frequent guest of ours. 'I've come to you to unburden my heart,' he says to us. 'What a pity I've no grandchildren when life for children today is so good and cheerful. To think how we grew up!' Then he usually turns to the head of the kindergarten and asks her whether there is anything she needs or wants.

One day Ivan Nikolaevich came to 'unburden his heart'. The children had just gone home, and we were about to start a staff meeting to discuss preparations for the New Year tree. Ivan Nikolaevich asked to be allowed to stay, pleading that everything in the kindergarten was of interest to him. This is what he said at the meeting: 'If you don't mind, I'd like to be Grandfather Frost[1] and give the children a treat.' We accepted his suggestion with pleasure, and Ivan Nikolaevich started coming every day to help us with the New Year tree.

At last the long awaited day arrived. The children came in their best clothes, happy and excited. The mothers too were there, proudly watching their children. The children danced, skipped and sang around the tree and then waited for Grandfather Frost who they were sure would come, listening with bated breath to every knock. The time was getting on, and still he was not there. So we decided to set out together with the children and with our guests to meet Grandfather Frost on the road. Clothes were quickly put on and everyone went out. Our kindergarten stands at the end of the village, on a little hill. A mile or so from us in the direction of Gorky the forest begins. We suddenly caught sight of Grandfather Frost emerging from it as we were going along the road. The children rushed towards him with joyful shouts and helped him to pull along the beautiful sledge, heaped with presents. On the way back Grandfather Frost explained to the children why he was so late: he told

[1] Grandfather Frost is the Russian equivalent of Father Christmas. Soviet children, however, are taught to celebrate New Year's Day instead of Christmas Day. This New Year's Day is, of course, completely secular, but the children have a tree and presents as ours do at Christmas.

them about the New Year tree in the kindergarten of the neighbouring village where he had just been. And once again there was joy around the New Year tree together with Grandfather Frost. . . .

WORK WITH GROUPS OF PARENTS

We hold group and general parents' meetings at which we discuss questions such as the annual plan of the kindergarten, how to teach children to be industrious and courteous, to prepare them for their first year at school, and to harden them physically. The doctor has given a talk on the prevention of diarrhœa in children during the summer.

Talks on political subjects too, such as the local elections, Soviet Army Day, International Women's Day and the elections of people's judges have been given at general parents' meetings. But there are many problems of upbringing which are of special interest to parents of children in a particular age group. These can be discussed in greater detail in group meetings. At one of the meetings, for instance, . . . Nina's and Galya's mother spoke of how she had taught her children to look after their books and toys. Vova's mother told the meeting of the work she was doing with him, on the advice of the kindergarten teacher, to correct faults in his speech; she also spoke about the literature she was using for this purpose.

Parents attend these meetings regularly. We usually hold them in winter; in summer when parents have no time to visit the kindergarten we go into fields and talk with them during the lunch-hour break.

At parents' meetings we show exhibitions of the children's work, demonstrate toys and books suitable for children of the various age groups, model play corners for the child at home and children's clothes for summer and winter.

The kindergarten has a parents' corner. Here we exhibit children's work, recommended literature, patterns for children's clothes, material for the various festivals, our plan of work and time-table, and menus and recipes for a few dishes. All this is changed from time to time.

The parents' committee, which consists of five people, gives us a great deal of help. It works according to a plan and in co-operation with the kindergarten staff. Many a time the parents' committee has been able to find a favourable solution of our economic difficulties through the collective farm management. The parents helped us to lay out a plot, to plant 30 apple trees, 65 strawberry and currant bushes and 25 bushes of ornamental plants. Thanks to them we have a lovely flower bed on the plot every year, as well as a kitchen garden from which we harvest several tons of potatoes and cabbages. The parents' committee insisted that the collective farm should equip the plot, provide a shelter and a special cookhouse and furnish a large room for group activities. The parents' committee helps children of needy families and brings up the cases of such families before the collective farm management or the village soviet. Our staff is in close contact with the farm and the village soviet; the head of the kindergarten and the two teachers all work as agitators.[1] We are helping cultural workers to put out a wall newspaper and are taking an active part in the amateur groups of the club.

The chairman of the village soviet and the collective farm often visit us at the kindergarten, and all the economic side of our administrative work is carried on under their close supervision. Once we were not supplied with firewood in time and had nothing for the stoves. I went to the village soviet chairman, Comrade Stalnov, and told him that the kindergarten would have to be closed on the following day owing to lack of firewood. 'You can have as much as you need,' the chairman answered me. 'Don't close the kindergarten; we'll let you have some firewood by tomorrow.'—We have never had to shut the kindergarten. In winter it is attended by between 53 and 55 children, in summer by 160 children.

But our work with parents also has its defects. We do not always make sure that the decisions reached at parents' meetings are in fact carried out, there are not enough talks for parents from the doctor, we are not holding group and general parents' meetings regularly, and we have not yet arranged for mothers to be on duty.

At the moment the kindergarten is doing a great deal of broadcasting in connection with its work with families and with the general public.

Shortly before March 8[2] the province pre-school research centre broadcast a talk entitled 'Love your Mother' from our Arzamass wireless station, and children from our kindergarten recited verses over the wireless about their mothers and about our leader, the great Stalin.

In future we will be giving regular broadcasts at which we will talk about our achievements and our shortcomings. We will invite men and women collective farmers to the microphone to tell the

[1] An agitator (*agitator*) is a person doing active explanatory work among the population with a view to stimulating political activity.

[2] International Women's Day.

public about their children's upbringing in the kindergarten, and about what they themselves are doing to provide a correct upbringing for the child at home.

The province research centre is helping our staff to disseminate pedagogical knowledge among wide sections of the population.

We share responsibility for the upbringing of children together with parents. For that reason, it is our duty to help the family, while at the same time drawing from its experience. Together with the family we are bringing up the young generation which will be capable of fighting selflessly and victoriously for the triumph of communism.

PRE-SCHOOL EDUCATION IN THE CITY OF KUIBYSHEV [1]

BY V. D. ZOTOVA, HEAD OF PRE-SCHOOL SECTION, KUIBYSHEV CITY EDUCATION DEPARTMENT

(*Doshkolnoye Vospitaniye*, 1952, no. 3, p. 13)

This article is based on my report to a meeting of heads of pre-school sections in territory and province education departments and ministries of culture of autonomous republics.

THE city of Kuibyshev has 112 kindergartens attended by over 8,500 children. During 1951 the number of places in the city's kindergartens increased by 1,005. Seventy-six kindergartens have groups where children can stay at night as well; these groups cater for mothers who are working night or evening shifts. The increases in the network of kindergartens and of places in them envisaged for Kuibyshev by the national economic plan have been fully achieved.

Last year we had great difficulties in trying to accommodate children in kindergartens. In the spring of 1951 the education department had more than 400 applications which it could not satisfy. The city education department approached the city executive committee to see whether an economy made in the budget could not be used to increase the number of places in kindergartens. The executive committee approached the RSFSR Council of Ministers on this question, and their request was granted.

The city soviet decided to allocate to the education department space for 175 places, representing 5 per cent of the new big dwelling houses being built by enterprises.[2] As regards day-and-night nurseries, eight groups which had been closed down in 1949 were re-opened.

[1] A city of some 400,000 inhabitants.

[2] I have met several articles (e.g. in *Doshkolnoye Vospitaniye*, 1953, no. 12, pp. 11 ff.) which mention a law according to which 5 per cent of the space in

Supplementary groups of 150 places have been formed in kindergartens attached to institutions. In addition, one kindergarten with 100 places has been opened and two with 200 places are about to be opened.

As a result, our most difficult problem, that of finding sufficient places for children in the city's kindergartens, has been solved and no child whose mother goes out to work is now refused a place.

Each new kindergarten or group is supplied with textile goods, furniture, crockery and teaching appliances, and the city education department has also helped kindergartens run by institutions in this respect. We obtained an increase in our grant from the city department of trade which enabled us to acquire this equipment through our bank account.

In order that we should continue to be able to accommodate the children in future too, we have taken an account of all dwelling houses under construction: the plans for these include space for kindergartens of 300 places, to be run by the city education department. There are six such buildings (all of them owned by institutions).

Measures have also been taken to speed up the erection of standard kindergarten buildings. As a result, three of the five buildings envisaged in the plan for 1951 have been completed; the other two will become ready for use during the first quarter of 1952.

The city education department has made an application for 12 kindergartens to be built in 1952 (attached to enterprises where a bigger network is needed).

The number of kindergartens in the city will thus increase by 14 in 1952, and this will make it possible to accommodate all the children for whom a kindergarten is needed.

The city and district education departments of Kuibyshev did a great deal towards creating satisfactory conditions in kindergartens. Last year repairs had been finished by the end of August and were really well done.

In most of the kindergartens the repairs are being done by 'patron' factories. Twelve kindergartens belonging to the Ministry of Education and two belonging to other departments, have built covered balconies this year so that the children can spend their midday rest in the open air.

A great deal of attention is being given to tools and plants for the

---

newly built large blocks of flats must be reserved for pre-school establishments. I have not been able to find the actual text of this law.

kindergarten plots. 'Patrons' and parents are drawn into this work, and all the kindergarten plots are well equipped. In the spring and autumn of 1951, 31,000 trees and bushes were planted.

The plot belonging to kindergarten no. 117 which had been short of plants and equipment last year, has now been transformed into a comfortable little garden; it is well laid out and has the necessary equipment for games and other open air activities.

During the past year pavilions and summer houses have been built for 14 kindergartens; this made it possible for the children to spend the whole time in the open air during spring, summer and autumn. There are six kindergarten plots where bathing pools and fountains for water games have been installed.

This year the city of Kuibyshev has for the first time opened a park for pre-school children which is visited by pupils from kindergartens and by other children in the town. On the request of the city education department, an attractive garden was allocated to the park. It also has all the necessary games equipment (provided from the funds for general extra-curricular work).

The 'patrons' attached to all the kindergartens under the Ministry of Education are giving us a great deal of help in creating good conditions. Individual factory shops act as 'patrons' to these kindergartens, the work being organised by the factory committees.[1]

The education department's kindergarten no. 40, for instance, has the Water and Sewerage Board (head, Comrade Makarov) as its 'patron'. The administration and the party and trade union organisations of the Board never lose sight of the interests and needs of the kindergarten.

The management is systematically helping us to repair town buildings and *dachas*[2] in the country belonging to kindergartens, by providing materials, labour and transport.

The kindergarten staff is carrying on educational propaganda among the workers of the administration. Articles on the role of the kindergarten in the upbringing of the child, and on the best working mother at the Water and Sewerage Board have been published in the administration's wall newspapers. Other kindergartens too are doing similar work.

[1] Of the factory trade union organisation.

[2] A *dacha* is a house in the country built for use in the summer only. It is, as a rule, a wooden cottage or hut. Many city dwellers in the USSR spend weekends and summer holidays at one of these, sometimes their own personal property. The *dacha* has become quite an institution, and 'going to the dacha' sometimes simply means 'going on holiday', although many city dwellers move to the *dacha* for the whole of the summer and travel in to work every morning.

The city authorities are also doing a great deal of work with 'patrons'. Last year a conference of representatives from 'patron' organisations was held to discuss health measures for children, as well as the preparation of kindergartens for another year's work and for the winter.

Two conferences have been attended by directors of enterprises, party secretaries and factory committee chairmen; the participants discussed their experience of working as 'patrons'.

Our contact with the general public as well as the work done by 'patrons' helped us to make our summer recreational and holiday facilities for the children a success.

According to the national economic plan we should have provided holidays for 8,000 kindergarten children. This plan was overfulfilled: 66 kindergartens with a total of 5,020 children went to stay in *dachas* during the summer, and 44 (3,280 children) were put on to a special health régime in the town.

Three hundred and fifty children attended open air playgrounds. A total of 1,190,000 rubles (provided from economies in the budget) was spent on these health measures.

Our town has a tradition of very careful health work for children. This is assiduously supervised by executive committees and party organisations. The city education department has done a great deal of work with heads of kindergartens, teachers and cooks, while the city health department has worked with doctors and with medical personnel who have graduated from specialised secondary-level colleges.[1]

In summer kindergartens move out to *dachas* specially set aside from them; these are rented from the *Dacha* and Gardens Department.[2] Local stores with provisions have been supplied by the city trade department.

These holiday places are provided with medical inspection and other services for the prevention of disease.

All the summer buildings and plots were distinguished by their freshness, cleanliness and comfort. Wholesome food, daily medical supervision and other health measures all contributed in improving the children's health (on the average they gained between 2 and 5½ lb.).

One of the most important tasks of the education department in

[1] *Sredny meditsinsky personal*, i.e. people with a 'specialised secondary education' in a medical school or college.

[2] *Sadovodachnoye upravleniye*. I have not been able to find a recognised translation for this authority.

1951 was to raise the qualifications of heads and teachers in kindergartens.

There are 702 people working in the kindergartens of Kuibyshev city. Of these 96 per cent have either had a university-level training or have graduated from specialised secondary-level training colleges; 29 people have incomplete secondary education[1]; four teachers, all with between 20 and 25 years' experience, are not studying on account of their health; these are working three hours per day.

The Kuibyshev kindergarten workers are actively improving their knowledge of Marxism. Four people are attending advanced evening courses in Marxism-Leninism, 415 people are attending courses on the *Short History of the CPSU(B)* (260 of these are in the second-year class), and 257 people are studying on their own.

The city education department and the city committee of the primary and secondary school workers' union have jointly organised lectures for pre-school workers on the following subjects: 'Lenin and Stalin on the Communist Upbringing of Children', 'Comrade Stalin on Linguistics',[2] 'The Place of I. P. Pavlov in Soviet Science', 'The Great Construction Schemes of Communism',[3] 'The Great Ethical and Ideological Qualities of Soviet Teaching on Education'.

Three lectures on the international situation were given. Each of these was attended by between 150 and 200 people.

During the school year 1950–1, 45 pre-school workers completed refresher courses for heads and teachers. Forty heads of kindergartens are about to finish these courses. The institute for teachers' refresher courses[4] is being attended by 45 people. All the music teachers (there are 37) have been through refresher courses.

. . . Research groups specialising in a study of the different age groups in the kindergarten have been organised in all the districts of the city. In making up the programme of study for these groups,

[1] I.e. have passed through the first seven grades of the secondary school.

[2] Stalin's work on linguistics, *Concerning Marxism in Linguistics* was published in 1950.

[3] This was the name given to a number of ventures entailing the building of large-scale canals and hydroelectric stations which it was decided to embark upon in 1950. The planting of afforestation schemes to act as shelter belts is also regarded as a 'Construction Scheme'.

Some of these, such as the Volga-Don Canal, have already been completed. Others, like the Turkmenian canal, are going ahead in a somewhat modified form.

[4] *Instituty Usovershenstvovania Uchitelei.* These are research institutes which work in close contact with schools. They provide courses of study in educational and political subjects, and organise teachers' conferences. They have existed in the USSR since 1938.

teachers' requests, and difficulties encountered in educational work were taken into consideration.

At the Frunze district section for teachers of the youngest kindergarten group, for instance, inspector Comrade Tikhonova discussed the teaching of drawing.

A. V. Grigoreva read a paper for kindergarten teachers of the second and third age group on the role played by didactic games in enriching the child's vocabulary and teaching it to speak grammatically. Teachers watched some games of this kind, and were able to see for themselves how valuable these didactic games are in improving the children's grasp of the Russian language.

The section for teachers of the senior groups discussed ways of teaching children about the world around them. Plans for the year's work were analysed, and the character and content of this work, which includes the use of literature and illustrations, was made clear.

City conferences of kindergarten heads were held monthly. At these conferences organisational problems were discussed, lectures on educational subjects were given and individual heads of kindergartens related their teaching experiences. . . .

All these measures are helping to improve the educational work of the kindergarten . . .

ABOUT CINDERELLA AGAIN

BY E. YACHNIK, FRUNZE CITY[1]

(*Komsomolskaya Pravda*, Oct. 4, 1951)

THE simple preparations for the fim show did not take long. The lights were turned out, and the children sitting on the sofa in the dining hall impatiently waited while eight-year old Igor, the operator, was focusing.

A girl appeared on the screen. A mop in her hands, she stood submissively before the haughty mistress of the house. Third-former, Nina, read out the caption:

'Once upon a time there was a woman who had two daughters, one diligent and beautiful, the other slothful and unsightly. But the woman loved the slothful one more because she was her own flesh and blood.'

The next picture flashed on to the screen, and Nina read further:

'The other, who was only a stepdaughter, had to do all the work in the house.'

'Boring! We know the story already,' a few dissatisfied voices complained. The schoolchildren watched the film *Grandmother Snowstorm*, without interest. . . .

The colour film, *Cinderella*, was one of the new productions which the children thought they would like. 'This'll be good,' they all declared.

But the children were soon disillusioned. The lights went out and a Cinderella 'of unparalleled humility and goodness' appeared on the screen. 'Once upon a time there lived a squire. When his wife died he married a woman so haughty and proud as none other in the whole world,' the caption read. 'She had two daughters.'

The beginning of the next film, *The Daughter and the Stepdaughter*, was surprisingly familiar. It read: 'Once upon a time there lived an

[1] Frunze is the capital of the Kirghiz Republic.

old man, his wife and their daughter. When his wife died, the old man married a widow who had a daughter of her own. A hard life now began for the old man's daughter, for her stepmother took a dislike to her . . .'

A story savouring of religious non-opposition to evil, about an unprotected, innocently persecuted and long-suffering girl called Zamarashka is being widely advertised by the *Diafilm* studio.

The humble young working girl who submissively bears the mockery of her evil stepmother is served up to the children in every possible form. Here we find the girl in *Grandmother Snowstorm*, the merchant's daughter, Vasilisa Prekrasnaya, the orphan Tiny Khavroshechka and other young martyrs.

Why do film producers find this subject so attractive? Take *Khavroshechka*, for instance. The film begins with a pronouncement of deep moral significance:

'Some people are good, some are not so good, and some are quite shameless. It was to this third kind that Tiny Khavroshechka happened to come.'

Naturally, the mistress of the house has lazy daughters 'who do nothing but sit and look out at the street'. After suffering a great deal of mockery, the orphan nevertheless finds a rich and, of course, handsome bridegroom through the active aid of a magic cow. And the idle daughters—serves them right!—stay unmarried.

What do these stories teach the children? Love of work? Nothing of the sort. The only Cinderella who really loves her work is the girl in *Grandmother Snowstorm*. Tirelessly she spins, and shakes out the grandmother's featherbeds, and finally receives a generous reward for her diligence. The other girls do no work at all. *Khavroshechka's* daily tasks are all carefully done for her by a speckled cow, and Vasilisa's, by a caterpillar given her by her mother before she died; the old man's daughter has a mouse to do her work for her.

Perhaps these films teach children to love their parents and respect their elders? I doubt it: the fathers in these stories appear in a most unattractive light. As a rule they are spineless people incapable of defending their own daughters even and quite undeserving of any love. And the stepmothers and other personages not directly related to Cinderella are presented in such a way that they merely—quite wrongly!—arouse feelings of hostility in the children.

During the hard years of the Great Patriotic War many orphans found a home with Soviet families. Here they were given a mother's tenderness and a father's protection. No difference whatever was made between them and the parents' own children. Then why persist in teaching children that there are good people who are your own flesh and blood, and bad and cruel ones who are not?

Instead of this persistent repetition of the same old misfortunes of poor orphans, they would do better to produce a film which told children how an ordinary Soviet family had taken a little girl into its home and was bringing her up—without the help of handsome bridegrooms waiting on her.

What do the stories put out by the *Diafilm* studio teach? They teach religious non-resistance to evil and the petty bourgeois moral, 'be good and you will get a rich husband'.

Children are glad of every new film and book. Judging from the advertisements, the subjects of the films are very varied indeed. . . . The trouble is that the responsible work of editing all these films is almost entirely left to one man, a certain L. S. Gurevich. He has to edit films on every kind of subject: geography, agriculture, industry, and so forth; and Comrade Gurevich obviously has no time to worry about the content of all these films or to form an opinion of the, frequently dull and primitive, drawings provided by the artists. Nor is he able to give careful attention to the captions, some of which one hesitates to read aloud.

So you see, the editor has a great deal of work to do. And there are no magic caterpillars, Grandmother Snowstorms or speckled cows to help him.

II

SCHOOL AGE

INTRODUCTION

IT is easy enough to define where school age begins in the USSR—quite simply when the child enters school at the age of seven. It is much more difficult to determine when the young boy or girl ceases to be of 'school age'. In the large cities many children now stay at school until they are seventeen. In the smaller towns and in the countryside on the other hand it is more usual for children to leave school at the age of fourteen, and either to go straight into industry and agriculture, or to spend the next two or three years at a technical training college. For this reason the age groups represented in this section, and in the following section dealing with the young worker, will tend to overlap.

The history of Russian education may be said to date from the eighteenth century when Peter the Great first introduced schools not directly under the authority of the church. In 1764 the first secondary schools for girls were opened in Moscow and Leningrad, the famous Smolny and Ekaterinsky schools. These and other similar schools were however very exclusive and attended by only a small minority. For the general population two types of primary school existed: one providing a course of two years, and the second providing a five-year course. These had been introduced towards the end of the eighteenth century, and by 1913–14 there were 63,425 such primary schools in the Russian Empire, attended by 5,115,586 pupils.[1] But this network of schools was far too small to provide the population as a whole with an elementary education, and the revolutionary government in 1917 was confronted with a population 64 per cent of which was illiterate.[2]

The newly formed People's Commissariat of Education began to lay the foundations of what was to be a socialist education. A number of important decrees were issued between 1917 and 1919 which made certain sweeping changes, and set out some of the immediate tasks

[1] *Bolshaya Sovetskaya Entsiklopedia*, vol. SSSR (1947), p. 1210.

[2] G. T. Grinko, *The 5 Year Plan of the Soviet Union* (1930), p. 261.

of Soviet education. It was decided to establish a 'single, secular school for all citizens' in place of the many different types of school which had existed before the revolution and which had frequently been under the influence of the church. It was hoped that all children would eventually be provided with a secondary education. Until such time as this would be possible, access to all higher grades of education was to depend solely on the ability of the child. Corporal punishment was abolished, and it was decided that non-Russian nationalities should in future receive their education in their own native language. The most immediate and urgent of all the tasks facing Soviet educationalists, however, was that of eliminating the appalling illiteracy of the population, and in 1919[1] it was made compulsory for all illiterate persons between the ages of eight and fifty to attend courses in reading and writing. These courses can only have been moderately effective however, since 42 per cent of the population was still illiterate at the beginning of the first five-year plan.[2]

The new Soviet school, 'the unified labour school' as it was called, was to be of two kinds: a primary school for children from the ages of eight to thirteen, and a secondary school for children between thirteen and seventeen. Education in both these types of school became free immediately. It was to become compulsory for all children of school age as soon as sufficient schools had been built and staffed.[3] Education departments were asked to obtain lists of all children between the ages of six and seventeen, and to prepare estimates of the cost of the necessary building, furniture and staff for the schools, as well as of food, clothes and textbooks for the children. It is, however, doubtful whether this kind of work could have been carried out in the conditions prevailing at the time, and the acute shortages of almost everything would have made it very difficult to act upon such information.

All schools were to be polytechnical, i.e. 'the basis of the life of the school should be productive labour'.[4] Polytechnical education had been advocated already by Marx who regarded the education of the future as one which

> will, in the case of every child over a given age, combine productive

[1] Decree of Dec. 26, 1919 (in *Bolshaya Sovetskaya Entsiklopedia*, vol. SSSR, p. 1215).

[2] *Summary of the Fulfilment of the First Five-Year Plan for the National Economy of the U.S.S.R.*, 1933, p. 236. By 1939 the number of illiterates had fallen to 19 per cent (Medynsky, *Narodnoye Obrazovaniye*, 1952, p. 25).

[3] Decree of Oct. 16, 1918 (in *Direktivy VKP (b) i Postanovlenia Sovetskovo Pravitelstva o Narodnom Obrazovanii za 1917–1947 gg.*, p. 121).

[4] *Ibid.*, p. 122.

labour with instruction and gymnastics, not only as one of the methods of adding to the efficiency of production, but as the only method of producing fully developed human beings.[1]

It was also favoured by Lenin and by leading Soviet educationalists such as Krupskaya. Schools were to be equipped with workshops. Children were to acquire elementary skills and to be 'brought up as future citizens of the socialist republic'.[2]

Within the next few years, however, and especially with the arrival of NEP, it was realised that many of these measures could only be regarded as part of a long-term plan. It became clear, for instance, that polytechnical education could not be introduced in NEP conditions. At that time little modern machinery was available, and the children were merely taught the rudiments of joinery and sewing.[3] The introduction of compulsory education up to the age of seventeen was another measure which must have seemed utopian at that time. In 1922 when local authorities were made responsible for the financing of education, the number of schools actually dropped.[4] In 1925 it was decided to begin the systematic introduction of compulsory primary education for children between the ages of eight and eleven, and it was hoped that by 1933–4 primary education would have become compulsory throughout the RSFSR.[5]

School life at this time tended to be interesting and exciting for the pupils, at any rate in the cities, but not very likely to give them much theoretical knowledge. Both schools and pupils were poor, and the most elementary necessities were often unobtainable. Lunacharsky, the then Minister of Education, speaks of children not going to school because they have no boots, and of one textbook having to be shared between four pupils.[6] In addition, there were still some hostile elements among the teachers, and some of the organisational work in the school had at times to be carried out by the children themselves. In some cases, for instance, they collected money and food from the local population and arranged for hot meals to be served at the school.[7] Children were, on the whole, taking a very

[1] K. Marx, *Capital*, vol. I (Foreign Languages Publishing House, 1954), p. 484.

[2] *Direktivy . . . (op. cit.)*, p. 123.

[3] N. K. Krupskaya, *Izbrannye Pedagogicheskiye Proizvedenia*, p. 194.

[4] *Bolshaya Sovetskaya Entsiklopedia*, vol. SSSR, p. 1223. The situation was apparently at its very worst during 1922–3, especially in the villages.

[5] Decree of Aug. 31, 1925 (in *Direktivy . . . (op. cit.)*, p. 92).

[6] *Izvestia*, Oct. 10, 1924.

[7] *Na Poroge Vtorovo Desyatiletia: Praktika Sotsialnovo Vospitania* (1927), p. 111.

active interest in the general life of the country, frequently doing work which would hardly be regarded as suitable for children in the USSR today. We have a description, for instance, of a school in the countryside trying to improve sanitary conditions in its particular village.[1] The children here seem to spend most of their time outside the school: trying to teach the local inhabitants not to throw dirty water and refuse out into the street, organising rubbish clearing work and helping with the spring sowing.

As regards the theory of education, the Soviet school was going through a period of experimentation, while no one official theory to be followed in all Soviet schools had been worked out in any detail. In some cases this experimentation took on extreme forms: the children virtually ran the schools and all school work was done collectively, a brigade of four to six children apparently being made responsible instead of the individual child.[2] There was a tendency to provide the child with an education in Marxism in terms which it was hardly likely to understand. Krupskaya,[3] for instance, mentions a tiny girl from an orphanage who, when asked what she was being taught at school, gravely answered that she was 'studying Leninism'. But despite this general tendency, educationalists like Krupskaya were advocating a more realistic attitude as regards both the theory and practice of education. Speaking in 1926 at a congress on physical education in primary schools, she stressed the fact that the children who were now at school had lived through years of shortages and even famine, and that many of them had suffered in health as a result. In the prevailing conditions, she maintained, it was useless to talk about introducing such amenities as shower baths into all schools. It was a question, first and foremost of providing children with food, seeing to it that they had enough sleep and that they were kept clean.[4]

The achievements, problems and distortions of Soviet education during this period are summed up very well in a conversation between Lenin and Klara Zetkin.[5] Lenin is speaking:

> I must tell you something more which ought to give you particularly great pleasure. Recently I received a letter from some children in a village school. This is what they write: 'Dear Uncle Lenin, we can already read and write a bit, we can do all sorts of things, and we wash our faces and hands every day now.'

[1] *Na Poroge Vtorovo Desyatiletia: Praktika Sotsialnovo Vospitania* (1927), p. 129.

[2] B. King, *Changing Man: The Soviet Education System* (1936), p. 20.

[3] *Op. cit.*, p. 117.

[4] Krupskaya, *op. cit.*, p. 121.

[5] Quoted from *ibid.*, pp. 105 ff.

> . . . We do a terrible lot of talking about such things as eugenics, eugenic-economic principles, the ideological process, athletics, motor cycling and so on and so forth. But we say extremely little about how we with our beggarly resources can get parents and economic organisations willing to act as 'patrons', etc., to help us to arrange school meals, obtain instruments for shaving the children's hair, convince parents that this must be done, get rid of lice, and clean the children's clothes at school . . . Altogether we completely ignore all those details which, in their sum total, determine the cultural level of the population, and which are so important and must be changed.

Another educational problem confronting the Soviet authorities was the phenomenon of large masses of vagrant children, *besprizornye* as they were called—a heritage of the war years. Some of these children were simply homeless orphans roaming the country; others were active juvenile delinquents, often working together in gangs. Orphanages and camps for these had to be organised. The work done with these juvenile delinquents at this period throws considerable light on Soviet attitudes towards education and children. One of the basic ideas underlying this attitude is that there are no 'morally defective' children. A. S. Makarenko, the famous Soviet educationalist who spent a considerable part of his life as head of a colony for juvenile delinquents,[1] maintained that 'once you put a child into normal conditions of life he will become normal himself within a day'.[2]

NEP was a period of tremendous difficulties, both material and ideological, but despite all these difficulties there was a considerable increase in the number of children going to school. By 1928 the number of pupils attending primary and secondary schools was double what it had been in 1913–14.[3]

The thirties brought tremendous advances in education. By 1931–2 the introduction of universal compulsory primary (four-year) education had been 'on the whole' completed.[4] Schools were now subdivided into three grades: grade I (primary) for children from eight to eleven; grade II (incomplete secondary or seven-year school) for

[1] Two fascinating accounts written by him and describing his work in one of these colonies exist in English: *Road to Life*, 1936, and *Learning to Live* (Foreign Languages Publishing House, Moscow, 1953).

[2] Makarenko, *Learning to Live*, p. 645.

[3] *Bolshaya Sovetskaya Entsiklopedia*, vol. SSSR, p. 1210.

[4] *Summary of the Fulfilment of the First Five-Year Plan*, p. 237.

children between twelve and fourteen; grade III (secondary or ten-year school) for children between fifteen and seventeen.[1]

Methods of education now gradually became more stabilised. Elementary technical skills still continued to be taught as a subject in the schools, but an increasing emphasis was being placed on the importance of theoretical knowledge, and in 1937 polytechnical education was finally discontinued.[2] Industry was developing at a very great rate, but it was still not possible to equip schools with the modern machinery needed if pupils were to be given an adequate grounding in industrial techniques. There was altogether a tendency for schools to become more conventional in character. In 1936 the science of 'pedology', which had acted as a basis for many of the various experimental schools, was officially condemned.[3] It was attacked, in particular, for its 'fatalistic determination of the child's future according to biological and social factors, the influence of heredity and an unalterable environment'. The decree went on to characterise it as a 'profoundly reactionary "law" in glaring contradiction to Marxism and to the whole experience of socialist construction which is successfully re-educating people in a spirit of socialism and eliminating survivals of the past both in the economy and in people's minds'. The system of intelligence tests to which children had been subjected at the age of six or seven to determine their 'pedological' age and their future mental capacities were also abolished, and intelligence tests have been frowned upon by Soviet education ever since. As a result of these tests a great many children had apparently been classified as 'retarded' or 'difficult', and had been placed in special schools. The decree maintained that the majority of the children in these schools were perfectly normal, and transferred them back into ordinary schools. A year later all 'model schools', as some of the experimental schools had been called, were also discontinued and turned into ordinary schools.[4] As time went on, it was becoming more and more important that the rising generation should have an all-round, general education.

But the school was not solely interested in academic standards. It has always been one of the most important aims of education in the USSR, just as of education in the West, to bring up what each society respectively regards as 'good citizens'. The Soviet child was accordingly taught to be 'an active builder of communist society'. It

[1] Decree of May 16, 1934 (in *Direktivy . . .* (*op. cit.*), p. 169).
[2] Decree of April 1, 1937.
[3] Decree of July 4, 1936 (in *Direktivy . . .* (*op. cit.*), pp. 190 ff).
[4] Decree of April 20, 1937 (*ibid.*, p. 195).

was recognised now that some of the 'social work' children had been doing was most unsuitable for their age. But this did not mean that children were henceforth expected to confine their activities to school work and live in isolation from the outside world. It was maintained that children should be made aware of and take some part in the general life of the society. Here is a description of the kind of work a school child might have been expected to do at this time:[1]

> You may see, for instance, that there is a kindergarten in the house in which you live, but that there are no toys and that the little ones are bored. Organise a group of a few people, and make some toys for the little children, and take turns in playing with them. Or you may see that there are illiterate young boys and girls in your village who for some reason or other were not able to go to school when they were younger. They would like to study, but there is nobody to teach them. Organise some work with them, get them paper or exercise books and various school books, and teach them what you yourself are being taught. This is very necessary sort of work. Or perhaps there is a school for adults in your village. Perhaps they study geography in the school, but have no maps. Make maps for the school for adults. You are being taught how to, and many of you love doing them; discuss among yourselves how best to go about it. How grateful the pupils in the schools for adults will be to you!
>
> Or perhaps you see terrible dirt all around; begin a campaign for cleanliness—in the reading room, the dining room, the crèche and the kindergarten.

	Pupils in forms 1–4 (ages 8–11)	*Pupils in forms 5–7 (ages 12–14)*	*Pupils in forms 8–10 (ages 15–17)*
1928–9	10,349,000	1,437,000	164,600
1932–3	17,674,000	3,515,000[2]	67,000[3]
1939–40	20,471,000	9,715,000	1,870,000

Source: Bolshaya Sovetskaya Entsiklopedia, vol. SSSR, pp. 1210 and 1225.

---

[1] Krupskaya, *Pismo Pioneram* (1938), reproduced in Krupskaya, *op. cit.*, p. 316.

[2] The figures given in the *Summary of the Fulfilment of the Five-Year Plan* vary slightly from those given in the *Entsiklopedia:* it gives the number of pupils in forms 5–7 in the autumn of 1932 as 4,298,000. The original plan, incidentally, provided for 1,843,000 pupils in these forms by 1932–3.

[3] The temporary drop in the number of pupils in the last three forms may

During the whole of this period the school network continued to grow. By 1939 the spread of education in the USSR could be regarded as one of the major achievements of the new régime, particularly when it is remembered that it had assumed power at a time when the total number of pupils in all schools had been just over seven million.

Apart from this general increase of education, the proportion of girls in the schools, and in particular in the higher forms, had changed considerably: only 37 per cent of the pupils in secondary schools in 1928 were girls; by 1939 the figure had apparently risen to 51·6 per cent.[1]

So far, all education had been free. In October 1940, however, it was decided to introduce fees for the last three years of the ten-year school, and for universities and university level institutions.[2] School fees amounted to 200r. a year in Moscow, Leningrad and capitals of republics, and 150r. elsewhere. (The average industrial wage at the time was 250–300r. a month. Today it is somewhere around 700–900r.) The school fees were introduced the same year as the Labour Reserve Schools with which I will be dealing later, and presumably both these measures were intended to divert young people into industry. The only reason given by the Soviet authorities was the one which I quote later in the volume and which merely suggests that the private individual should now pay some of the cost of education direct. Several categories of children were exempted from these fees in subsequent years. At the time when they were introduced, however, these fees must have proved a strong deterrent in many cases, and there can, I think, be no doubt that at the time the introduction of fees represented a considerable blow to the principle of equality of opportunity. At the worst, a family with three children aged fifteen, sixteen and seventeen respectively would have had to pay 50r. a month, although the amount would presumably have decreased at the end of the first year when the eldest left school. The same school fees are still in force, but with a much higher average wage, they present a far smaller obstacle to secondary education today, and according to the draft directives of the sixth five-year plan (1956–60), all school fees are to be abolished.[3]

---

have been due to the fact that a large number of pupils between the ages of fifteen and seventeen now entered specialised secondary schools. The number of pupils in these schools had increased very rapidly during this period, from 206,000 in 1928–9, to 723,700 in 1932–3.

[1] Medynsky, *op. cit.*, p. 83.

[2] Decree of Oct. 2, 1940 (in *Narodnoye Obrazovaniye: Osnovnye Postanovlenia, Prikazy i Instruktsii*, 1948, p. 456).

[3] *Pravda*, Jan. 15, 1956.

The most important and, in my opinion, retrograde development in education during the war period which now followed was the decision in 1943 to abolish co-education.[1] Here are the reasons officially given at the time. It was maintained that separate education for boys and girls would be better able to take into consideration the differences in development in the two sexes and the correspondingly different activities which ought to be carried on in physical training classes. It was stated that, now that the school network had grown to such an extent and equality of the sexes was established, co-education had served its purpose and was no longer necessary or desirable. In general, it was hoped that separate education would cater for 'certain differences in the preparation of each of the sexes for practical life.'[2] One mitigating feature of this measure was that it applied only to schools in the cities and that most schools, which were in the countryside, continued to be co-educational.

That same year a decree was issued lowering the school age from eight to seven years.[3]

The war had caused great destruction and dislocation, and there had been a consequent deterioration in the level of schools. Towards the close of the war it was therefore found necessary to take measures to improve the standard. In the summer of 1944[4] examinations for pupils at the end of their fourth and seventh years at school were introduced, and a 'Certificate of Maturity' examination was instituted for pupils graduating from the tenth form. Pupils who received 'very good' (5) in all subjects in this examination were henceforth to be awarded a gold medal, those with 'good' (4) in not more than three subjects and 'very good' in the rest to be awarded a silver medal. Holders of gold and silver medals were exempted from university entrance examinations.[5]

School buildings had also suffered greatly during the war. Eighty-two thousand[6] out of a total of just over 171,000 schools[7] had been destroyed during the war, and in 1945 the Ministry of Education, and indeed the whole country, was faced with an immense task of reconstruction. But by 1948 already the pre-war figure had been

[1] Decree of July 16, 1943 (in *Direktivy . . . (op. cit.)*, p. 203).
[2] Medynsky, *op. cit.*, p. 85.
[3] Decree of Sept. 8, 1943 (in *Direktivy . . . (op. cit.)*, p. 117).
[4] Decree of June 21, 1944 (in *Direktivy . . . (op. cit.*, p. 218).
[5] Decree of May 30, 1945 (in *ibid.*, p. 220).
[6] *Bolshaya Sovetskaya Entsiklopedia*, vol. SSSR, p. 1227.
[7] Medynsky, *op. cit.*, p. 30.

more or less reached again.[1]

Since then there has, I believe, been a remarkable increase in the number of pupils attending secondary schools. The overall number of pupils in schools does not, however, appear to have risen at all. This may well be due to the fact that the children starting school at about that time were born during the war, when the birth rate, at least in certain parts of the country, might possibly have been rather lower than normal.

The first really important step taken in education after the war was the decision of 1946 to introduce universal compulsory seven-year education within the next five years.[2] Seven-year schools had already existed for some years in the larger towns, though most of these schools were working in two or even three shifts.[3] Where the schools already existed, it was largely a question of recovering school buildings that had been used by other organisations during the war, and getting existing schools repaired.[4]

In the countryside, however, the four-year school was the rule, and it was here that the greatest difficulties lay. The village tended on the whole to be poor and backward, and funds, building materials and fuel were hard to obtain. Great distances between fairly small settlements meant that children often had to walk a long way every day, frequently along very bad roads. Apart from these difficulties, the older children were sometimes needed at home to look after their smaller brothers and sisters, and there were also cases of children working on the farm instead of going to school.[5] The first item ('Into the Fifth Form') translated in this section illustrates some of these problems and the ways in which they are being overcome. It also shows to how great an extent improvements in rural education seem to depend on local initiative.

The following item ('School and Life') also describes education in the countryside at roughly the same time. It was obviously not intended as a characteristic picture of education in the village. In the majority of schools children were probably not made to feel that collective farm life was thrilling, partly no doubt, because collective farm life in actual fact was often anything but thrilling. As a result, there was a general tendency for young people to drift into the towns upon leaving school, and even a local party official in a rural area

[1] *Pravda*, Nov. 23, 1948.

[2] First Post-War Five-Year Plan (1946–50), in *Direktivy . . .* (*op. cit.*), p. 75.

[3] *Izvestia*, June 6, 1950. The two-shift system is still continued in many Soviet schools today.

[4] *Pravda*, Aug. 18, 1946.

[5] *Uchitelskaya Gazeta*, Oct. 10, 1953.

is said to have asked; 'Do you think people study just to stay in the collective farm?'[1] 'School and Life' was no doubt intended as a picture of what rural education could be, and what in the best schools it already was now. It was published as an example to be followed.

Judging from several statements made in the press after 1950,[2] it does not look as though seven-year education had been completely introduced as planned by the following year (1951). But it is probable that it has by now been established in most areas.[3] A transition to free and compulsory ten-year education throughout the whole country has recently been announced,[4] and it is planned that by 1960 every child in the USSR between the ages of seven and seventeen will be receiving its education in a ten-year secondary school. This will undoubtedly be one of the major achievements of the Soviet régime, particularly if it is remembered that in 1939 still only 7·7 per cent of the population had had a secondary education.[5] This measure has already been carried through to a considerable degree in the large cities. It was reported last year that in Leningrad every tenth worker in industry had had a secondary education.[6] By the beginning of the school year 1955–6 it will already have become compulsory and free in 117 towns of the RSFSR.[7]

All this is beginning to create its own problems. Formerly secondary schools, like our grammar schools, were regarded as a stepping stone on the way to a higher education at a university or institute. As recently as 1948 an article in the *Teachers' Gazette*[8] stated that it was the main function of secondary schools to 'prepare cadres of students for higher educational establishments'. As more and more children attend secondary schools, this can obviously no longer remain its chief function. The proportion of young boys and girls who will leave school at seventeen and will fail to pass the competitive entrance examinations to a university or institute may be expected to

[1] *Ibid.*, April 14, 1954.

[2] *Komsomolskaya Pravda*, Oct. 22, 1953, which complains of insufficient seven-year schools in the Voronezh province; *Uchitelskaya Gazeta* (Oct. 10, 1953) on the Rostov province; *Komsomolskaya Pravda* (Sept. 12, 1953) on the Kirov province.

[3] It was stated that during the last years of the first post-war five-year plan more than 90 per cent of the pupils finishing the fourth form went on into the fifth (V. Zhirnov, *Razvitiye Sovetskoi Sotsialisticheskoi Kultury*—1952—p. 27).

[4] At the XIX Party Congress (*Pravda*, Oct. 10, 1952).

[5] *Bolshaya Sovetskaya Entsiklopedia*, vol. SSSR, p. 1235.

[6] *Uchitelskaya Gazeta*, Aug. 21, 1954.

[7] *Ibid.*, Feb. 9, 1955.

[8] June 17, 1948.

increase in the next few years despite the steady expansion of higher education.[1]

It is obvious that the vast majority of pupils will have to go into industry or agriculture on leaving school in much the same way as they do now. But with this difference, that they will have had the same training as those pupils who go on to a university and that they will be most reluctant to become ordinary workers. It is already becoming very obvious that school leavers feel that it is a waste of their training and somehow 'beneath them' to become manual workers. There are apparently quite a number of cases where young boys and girls from reasonably prosperous homes who have failed the university entrance examinations simply stay at home for a year and then have another shot at them.

The Soviet authorities have been trying to counteract this feeling in a variety of ways. In the past various institutes used to hold 'open door days', as they were called, on which pupils in their last year at secondary school were shown round the building and its various departments, and given some sort of an idea what the various professions taught by these institutes were like. This practice is now being adopted by factories too. There has also been a spate of articles in the press during the past year stressing the importance of having a skilled and well-educated worker at the bench, and trying to combat the idea that a person who has gone on to a university upon leaving school is in some way a 'superior being'.

'Choosing a Career' is an example of an article of this kind. It is published in the form of an open letter from the well-known Soviet novelist, V. Kochetov. It shows how the gulf which used to exist between a person with a university education and an ordinary factory worker is becoming narrower. Naturally, when the ordinary worker had no more than a seven-year education, the status of the man who had been to a university was relatively much higher than it is today when an increasing number of young workers have full secondary schooling and when additional facilities for acquiring high-grade skills are being provided.[2] All this in its turn will have an effect on industry, and as Kochetov puts it, a man will now have to attend special courses even just to be a shepherd.

But the impact of universal secondary education is of course

[1] Moscow University, where competition is probably greater than in most other Soviet universities, has 30 applications for every vacancy in some of its departments (*Narodnoye Obrazovaniye*, 1955, no. 2, p. 29).

[2] New technical schools are being set up to provide training for pupils with a full secondary education. I shall be dealing with these in the next section.

greatest on the school itself. I have already mentioned the principle of polytechnical education which had been advocated by the Marxist classics. The question was brought up again by Stalin in 1952.[1] He stresses the need for the bulk of the workers to raise their 'cultural and technical level to that of the engineering and technical personnel'. And he looks forward to a time when what he calls the 'essential distinction' between physical and mental labour, 'the difference in their cultural and technical levels, will certainly disappear'. At the XIX Congress, that same year, it was decided to re-introduce polytechnical education and to equip schools with workshops.[2] But very little was said about the specific forms which this instruction was to take. Would the school curriculum become very much more technical? Would the children be divided into various streams at a certain age, some carrying on with the present 'grammar school' programme, the others following a 'modern' course? Or would all the children be expected to take the fairly academic secondary school course which had been in operation so far? These were some of the questions uppermost in one's mind.

In August 1955[3] certain changes in the curriculum were published. (They had already come into effect by the beginning of the school year 1955–6.) These changes provide an answer to some of these questions. The new programme intends to give more attention to physics and mathematics and to teach the children less 'pure theory' undiluted by any practical experiments and practical skills. Most important of all, the new teaching programme represents the first really serious and practicable attempt at the 'unified labour school'. Polytechnical instruction will consist of one handwork lesson per week for the first four forms, two lessons of more advanced practical work in forms V-VII, and two lessons of practical studies in such subjects as electrical engineering, principles and handling of machinery, agriculture and basic industrial techniques, in forms VIII–X.

With the exception of these new subjects and of logic which will no longer be taught at all, there is to be very little change, and the new curriculum is remarkable in its similarity to the old one, with its insistence on 'grammar school' standards.

[1] *Economic Problems of Socialism in the U.S.S.R.* (1952), pp. 33–4.

[2] *Pravda*, Oct. 10, 1952. For an interesting review of a recent book on the subject, see E. Koutaissoff, 'Recent Data on Polytechnical Education', in *Soviet Studies*, vol. VI, no. 2, p. 145.

[3] *Pravda*, Aug. 27, 1955. *Narodnoye Obrazovaniye*, 1955, no. 7, p. 4, contains a detailed table of the new curriculum.

Another change inside the Soviet school was brought about by the decision reached in 1954[1] to re-introduce co-education in all schools. Co-education had been abolished in 1943 without any prior discussion in the Soviet press. But as the years passed, it became increasingly obvious that a considerable section of the population was bitterly opposed to separate education. This opposition made itself felt in many different ways: articles against separate education appeared in the press from time to time[2]; a famous writer of short satirical sketches, S. Narinyani, attacked it in one of his stories[3]; and letters and articles spasmodically appeared in magazines. The decision of 1954 did not, therefore, come as a surprise. The whole co-education issue was, at first sight, of only limited importance in that only the schools in the towns were affected.[4] It becomes rather more significant, however, when one considers that these city schools had largely provided the intelligentsia of the country.

One cannot write about Soviet education without mentioning the propagation of a materialist world outlook and the part played in this by the two youth organisations: the Young Communist League (komsomol) for boys and girls between the ages of fourteen and twenty-six; and the Pioneer organisation for children between nine and fourteen. Both movements have grown steadily over the past thirty years. By 1954 most children belonged to the pioneer organisation, while about 60 per cent of eligible schoolchildren were komsomol members.[5] The article entitled 'It is Your Concern' describes some of the activities of a komsomol group at school and the kind of moral values which it is trying to foster. Anti-religious work plays its part in this, but it is interesting to see how much the problems are oversimplified here. In fact the work seems to be much the same as it was in the twenties and early thirties[6] when the

[1] Decree of the USSR Council of Ministers, July 18, 1954. It was decided to re-introduce co-education in all except the tenth form (ages sixteen to seventeen) where it was felt that a big upheaval would cause bad results in the school-leaving examinations.

[2] *Literaturnaya Gazeta*, April 18, 1950, May 4, 1950, and June 28, 1950 (translated in *Soviet Studies*, vol. II, no. 2, pp. 180 ff). Also *Literaturnaya Gazeta*, Aug. 6, 1953 (translated in *Soviet Studies*, vol. V, no. 3, pp. 316 ff.).

[3] Narinyani, *Feletony* (1952), especially the stories on pp. 24 and 29 ff.

[4] According to I. A. Kairov, RSFSR Minister of Education, only 13·8 per cent of all pupils in the RSFSR had been going to separate schools (*Pravda*, July 20, 1954).

[5] Speech by A. N. Shelepin at the XII Komsomol Congress, reported in *Komsomolskaya Pravda*, March 20, 1954.

[6] A plan of anti-religious discussions included such topics as 'The Universe and its Structure', 'Origin of Life on Earth and of Man', and 'Miracles and the

scientific explanation of 'miracles' was regarded as evidence against the validity of religious beliefs. The attitude to the religious child at school seems to be much the same as ours would be to someone who insisted that the earth was flat and who, we felt, could be *proved* wrong. There is an episode, similar to the one described in this article, in a sketch about children in a secondary school in Dnepropetrovsk.[1] Here it is discovered that one of the girls, Vera, is religious. Worse still, she fails to turn up for the celebrations of the October Revolution, apparently because she is afraid of being late for the practice of the church choir in which she sings. This is what one of the children says about Vera at a meeting of the form:

> Vera has been going to school for eight years, three of them at our school. She gets 'very good' for biology, physics, history, geography and other subjects which prove to you, as plain as a pikestaff, that there is no god. So why does Vera still go on believing in one?

The item entitled 'It Concerns the Whole Community' is of particular interest in that it shows the kind of demands made by the school on its pupils. It also manifests the somewhat rigid attitude towards divorce which some Soviet people seem to adopt and which was certainly that of Makarenko.[2]

Every Soviet school is supposed to have a parent-teacher association, and this elects a committee which meets once a month. But many schools also have another link with the outside world in that a factory or institute in the vicinity may 'adopt' them. Such a 'patron' factory or institute does much the same kind of work as the parent-teacher association does, and in fact the two frequently merge, as in 'When a Club takes the Initiative' (translated on p. 91), where the workers of the 'patron' factory are also the parents of the school children involved.

There are many aspects of school life which I have not touched upon. I have said nothing about examinations or textbooks, for

---

Laws of Nature'—all topics which might appear in a similar plan today (*Anti-religioznoye Vospitaniye v Shkolakh Povyshennovo Tipa*, 1930, pp. 47 ff.).

It has, incidentally, been estimated that in 1930, 40 per cent of the children from 10 seven-year schools chosen at random were religious (*ibid.*, p. 10).

[1] B. Tartakovsky, *Starsheklassniki* (1951), p. 57.

[2] In assessing Makarenko's views, it is important to take into account the fact that much of his thought was formed in reaction to the very Bohemian ideas about love and marriage held by some sections of the population in the twenties and early thirties. An example of Makarenko's views on the matter can be found in his *Book for Parents* (Foreign Languages Publishing House, 1954), pp. 134 ff.

instance. A comprehensive description of all the important aspects of life in Soviet schools belongs to a work on education and would be out of place in this volume. I have nevertheless included an item ('The Strength of the Community') dealing with school discipline. This particular article describes the kind of treatment advocated by Soviet educationalists for a particularly difficult child.

The actual teaching methods used in Soviet schools have moved away from 'modern' trends. These had been associated with the 'pedology' theories and were dropped soon after 1936.

So far I have dealt solely with the Soviet child at school. Let us now see how Soviet children spend their leisure, both in term-time and during the holidays.

Among the institutions which cater for children during their leisure time are the Houses and Palaces of Pioneers. These are vast children's clubs in which anyone of school age can work at a large variety of hobbies under expert guidance. At the Pioneer Palace in the Georgian capital of Tbilisi, for instance, which I visited in May 1954, there were groups for 70 different hobbies, and we saw children working a puppet theatre, learning folk dancing, taking classes in sculpture, rearing silk worms, etc. The first Pioneer Palace was opened in Moscow in 1923. Since then many more have appeared, and by 1951 there were over 1,200 in the USSR.[1] At the present time there are 1,269,[2] but it is unfortunately impossible to tell exactly how many children visit these. They can obviously only cater for a small proportion of the child population, and they probably only exist in the towns. I have nevertheless included a description of these Pioneer Palaces; although there are relatively few such Palaces, they do seem to me to be typical of a general attitude towards children. The article, 'A District House of Pioneers', shows us how an undertaking of this kind is organised and maintained in a small place like Novozybkov which has a population of no more than 10,000 and is not even the centre for the province.

These Pioneer Palaces and the children's theatres[3] and cinemas which exist are a step in the right direction. But since there must be many children who remain outside these institutions it is worth our while to see in what other ways Soviet children spend their leisure. As a rule, they spend either the morning or the afternoon at school. The other half of the day the child is left to itself. Some of this time

[1] *Bolshaya Sovetskaya Entsiklopedia*, 1952, vol. 13, pp. 497 ff.

[2] *VOKS Bulletin*, 1954, no. 6, p. 19.

[3] In 1950 there were 30 children's theatres in the country (*Izvestia*, April 30, 1950).

is, of course, filled in by homework. After that the child is free to do as it pleases. In many Soviet families both father and mother have full-time occupations, while they frequently have a grandmother living with them who keeps house and looks after the children during the day. But often there is no grandmother to keep an eye on the children, to see that they do their homework properly and that they do not get into mischief playing in the street. This is a very real problem to many Soviet parents and is frequently voiced in the press. I have therefore included several items in this section which illustrate the way in which the problem is seen by Soviet people, and the kinds of measures which are being taken to solve it.

I have also included one item dealing with juvenile delinquency. Some of the more sensational articles which appeared in the Soviet press during the last year have been made much of in the West. I have chosen the article, 'Do Not Pass By, Comrade', because it avoids sensationalism and describes ways and means of preventing delinquency. Apart from the reasons for delinquency given in the article, I was told at a people's court in Moscow that the amnesty of 1953 had been too sweeping and had brought back undesirable elements who were having a bad effect on the children. The fact that many of the children now in their early teens will have lost their fathers during the war must also be taken into consideration.

Summer school holidays in the USSR are fairly long, lasting from the beginning of June until the end of August. A number of children spend part of this time at pioneer camps. (These camps exist for schoolchildren generally and are not confined to members of the pioneer organisation.) Although they are called camps, they are not as a rule under canvas. It is more usual for them to consist of small chalet-like wooden buildings situated in some picturesque spot in the country. The children come in three shifts, each shift staying for about a month. A substantial number of these camps are run by the trade unions which usually pay part of the cost. Of the 5,000,000 children who visited pioneer camps in 1949,[1] for example, just over half (2,550,000)[2] were in camps run by trade unions. There are also holiday excursions some of which are organised by the schools.

There are, however, many children who spend the summer at home. For these, pioneer camps in the cities have been organised, and one of the items in this section describes the kind of activities which are planned for the children.

[1] *Trud*, May 31, 1949. The figure now stands at 5,500,000 (*Pravda*, Jan. 21, 1955).

[2] *Trud*, May 6, 1949.

There must also be many children who go on holiday with their parents or are sent to stay with relatives. Many of the city dwellers still have some roots in the countryside, and a number of children probably spend the summer with grandparents, aunts or uncles in the village. I have included an article describing a holiday of this kind, partly for its picture of a city child in the country, and partly because of the light it sheds on life in the countryside itself.

So far I have not dealt specifically with problems and achievements in the Eastern republics. The situation there, particularly with regard to girls, warrants separate treatment, and I shall be dealing with it more fully in the last section of the volume.

1. WORK

INTO THE FIFTH FORM

BY D. NOVOPLYANSKY, TOPKI DISTRICT, KEMEROVO PROVINCE (WESTERN SIBERIA)

(*Komsomolskaya Pravda*, July 20, 1949)

AFTER the abundant June rain, the roads were beginning to dry up, and the driver from the collective farm set out for the railway station to fetch wood for building purposes. Collective farmer, Koroleva, asked him to call in at the shop and to see what school books they had.

'For Shurik? But he's already left school, hasn't he,' the driver asked. 'No, he hasn't; he's moved up into the fifth form,' Koroleva corrected him. She had firmly decided that Shurik was not going to leave school even though the school in Sergeyevka only went up to the fourth form. She had made him felt boots and a coat and was determined to send him to the seven-year school in Simonovo.

Anna Sovetova too told us that her younger sister, Manya, was going on into the fifth form, and suddenly added:

'You know, I'm sorry I didn't stay on to the end of the fifth form—can't forgive myself for leaving. But this year's lot won't drop out!'

No, this year's lot won't. The women on our collective farms want and can give their children an education. Since the revolution 76 schools, including 22 seven- and ten-year schools, have been opened in the Topki district. At the end of the war these schools had 260 teachers; now they have 462. Last year already expenditure on education in this ordinary agricultural district reached four and a half million rubles. This year almost six million rubles have been allocated to the schools. Expenditure on education for the children of collective farmers now makes up two-thirds of the total budget for the district.

It was not possible to introduce compulsory seven-year education in the countryside immediately. The way for it was paved by the development of schools and of culture in general—by the growth of our whole country. In 1947, 436 pupils reached the fifth form in the schools of Topki; in 1948, the number had risen to 731. This year, according to calculations made by the komsomol organisation, there should be a total of 1,365 pupils—almost twice as many as last year—in the fifth forms of the district. These will be split up into 42 forms. (There are 24 working at present.) This step is being carefully considered and efficiently prepared for; but it is by no means an easy task to undertake.

Speaking at a komsomol meeting in the *Free Labour* collective farm in Sergeyevka, Denis Yakovlev, secretary of the farm's komsomol organisation, said:

'We have a great deal of work to do, my friends, if we want all children finishing the fourth form this year to go on to the fifth.'

There was only one item on the agenda: a discussion on how to help the schools. Among those present were many young boys and girls with a seven- or ten-year education. But there were also those among the young collective farmers who had had no more than four years at school and who were continuing their studies in evening classes. Fifteen komsomols took part in the discussion. Some of those present were criticised for not paying sufficient attention to their younger brothers and sisters; it was decided that Seryozha Svintsov, for instance, must go back to the fourth form from where he had dropped out. The resolutions which were finally adopted filled four pages of an exercise book. They included the following points:

One active komsomol to undertake responsibility for every 10 households, Yakovlev, Lyutikova, Vershinina, Golovin and Korolev being entrusted with this work. They should visit all the cottages, talk to parents and explain the law about compulsory education to them.

Within the next two weeks to help school heads in listing all children who have left school early and to examine each case individually in order to see what needs to be done to enable the child to go back to school.

To find out which of the schoolchildren will need financial aid during the autumn and winter months.

To raise the question of an education fund with the farm management.

To arrange a komsomol and youth 'Sunday'[1] to repair the school and clean up the plot of land around the school playground.

To call a meeting of parents and discuss compulsory seven-year education with them.

On the following day, Galina Vershinina visited four households, Denis Yakovlev five, and Evdokia Lyutikova, two.

Four miles away lies the village of Shishino. Here too the komsomols called at the cottages and made a note of all children of school age. Alexander Postovoi, a coung combine operator, had a long conversation with Anna Spiridonovna Korneichuk, one of the older collective farmers. They arranged for her daughter, Elena, to start going to the seven-year school and for Dunyasha to go back to the third form from which she had dropped out during the winter. . . .

In every collective farm we visited, the secretary of the komsomol branch there had a list of the children of school age. Everywhere we found komsomols taking responsibility for 10 households each and talking to parents. But merely registering the children with the school will not make compulsory education a reality. At the teachers' conferences which will soon be held, komsomols will ask teachers to make a careful study of the experience gained by their colleagues in charge of fifth forms and of their methods of work. Teachers taking charge of fifth forms this year will be able to gain useful knowledge from those teachers who were in charge of them last year.

By the spring of 1948 Vera Krivtsova and Olya Kolosova had completed the primary school course in the village of Shishino. The nearest settlement with a secondary school was too far away and too difficult to get to. But they did not want to leave school, and so the two friends stayed on in the fourth form for another year. Vera and Olya have recently passed their fourth year examinations for the second time. And what is to happen now? After all, they can hardly go back into the fourth form again! Vasilii Afanasevich Krep, director of studies[2] in the Stantsionna secondary school, briefly put the most immediate and essential task facing us: 'We need a hostel,' he said.

Last year we had no hostels. This year teachers and komsomols have been concentrating their attention on getting some. . . . In

[1] The tradition of 'Sundays' or 'Saturdays' as they were sometimes called, dates back to the early days after the revolution. The idea is that people should from time to time voluntarily spend their day off on some special job, usually for the direct benefit of their own community.

[2] Soviet schools have a headmaster or headmistress and also a 'director of studies' (*zaveduyushchy uchebnoi chastyu*). The latter concentrates entirely on the children's work, leaving the administration of the school to the head.

Glubokoye a large four-roomed cottage is being built. Similar cottages are going up in Sosnovo, Topki, Kokui and other villages.

The komsomol committee and the education department have sent a large number of activists, such as pioneer leaders, komsomol secretaries and teachers from the district centre, into the countryside. These will help village schools and komsomol branches in the collective farms to put compulsory seven-year education into practice and, above all, to furnish the hostels. The teacher and komsomol activists will also give talks at parents' meetings.

'My Shurik will go on to the fifth form,' Klavdia Koroleva tells us confidently.

Yes, Shurik and thousands of other children of his age will soon be going into the senior forms of seven-year village schools. In fact the country has already begun to introduce universal, compulsory seven-year education everywhere.

Here is something for the komsomols to do, to put their hands to. The komsomols of the Topki district are helping teachers to enforce general seven-year education. They are setting us all an example.

SCHOOL AND LIFE

BY K. LESNICHY, HEADMASTER OF TREBUKHOV VILLAGE SECONDARY SCHOOL, BROVARY DISTRICT, KIEV PROVINCE; DEPUTY TO THE DISTRICT AND VILLAGE SOVIETS

(*Izvestia*, Oct. 10, 1948)

I HAVE discovered a remarkable and encouraging fact: half the collective farmers of the village have had a ten—or seven-year education. The people who drive tractors or work on the collective fields and livestock farms now also play their part in raising the level of Soviet agriculture.

Most of the collective farmers are former pupils of our secondary school. Here are a few of our former pupils who have become famed for their high yields throughout the Brovary district: link leaders, Nadezhda Potapenko and Galina Prudkaya from the *October* collective farm, link leader, Olga Kuzmenko from the Lenin farm and Maria Korniiko from the Stalin farm. Polina Solodkaya, also a former pupil of ours, is deputy chairman of the *October* farm, and a talented organiser. Ivan Lukyanenko who has only recently left our school is one of the best tractor drivers in the district.

The school has taught them, from childhood up, to love agriculture and to take an interest in it. Under our Soviet conditions the school is indissolubly bound up with the life of the collective farm. Our staff is trying to strengthen this bond with life in all their teaching and educational work in the school as well as in extra-curricular work.

At geography, literature and history lessons and when studying the Stalin Constitution the teachers stress the superiority of socialism over capitalism. When studying the works of T. Shevchenko, M. Kotsyubinsky and I. Franko[1] and acquainting the children with the peasant heroes of their books, the teacher compares the bright and

[1] Three Ukrainian revolutionary poets of the nineteenth century.

cultured life of our Soviet people, and in particular of the collective farmers here in Trebukhov, with their joyless existence of the past.

Pupils have written compositions on such subjects as 'Our Collective Farm', 'My Village' and 'What I Want to Be', and these showed the children's burning love for their native land and their patriotic striving to become better socialist citizens.

Extra-curricular work too serves to encourage these noble feelings. The history circle has started to compile a history of Trebukhov village. How many interesting facts the children have unearthed! All of them now know that the land around the village used to belong to a landowner called Galagan before the revolution and that the peasants worked for him as hired farm labourers. There was only one sower in the whole village at that time. The children also know that only eight of the 1,000 head of cattle which Trebukhov had before the war, were left after the fascists took the village. The pupils are able to see for themselves how the collective farms, helped by the party and government, are repairing the damage caused by the enemy during the war; they can see, for instance, that three of our four farms have already regained their pre-war level both in livestock farming and in other branches of agriculture.

At arithmetic and geometry lessons the teacher Maria Petrovna Kolesova sets the children problems taken from actual farm life: the children estimate amounts of arable land, capacities of silos, and so forth. At chemistry lessons the teachers tell the children about mineral fertilisers; geography and physics lessons are accompanied by experiments at the small meteorological station which has been equipped by the pupils themselves under the supervision of the physics master, Viktor Mikhailovich Levitsky.

This year the physics master will combine his lessons on mechanics with practical work in the garage of the *October* collective farm; the children will be working together with Fyodor Lukyanenko, head of a tractor driving brigade.

In the teaching of biology contact with collective farm life is particularly important. Studying the elements of the biological sciences should make pupils want to be active themselves transforming nature like real Michurinists.[1] The school experimental plot is used for this purpose. Here, the children take their first steps towards becoming experts who will harvest high yields in the future. Supervised by the biologist, Nina Karpovna Bozhko, the children planted yarovised[2]

[1] Michurin was a famous Soviet biologist.

[2] The seeds are subjected to a special process which makes it possible for the subsequent plant to grow and mature more quickly.

potatoes on this plot and had a record harvest. Their experiments at growing Russian dandelion[1] and long-fibre cotton under our local conditions were also successful. . . .

Work on the school plot awakens pupils' initiative and makes them want to take an active part in collective farm work. Many of our pupils started growing various crops on small plots belonging to the farm, this year, and have brought in excellent results. Raya Khavro, for instance, a girl from the sixth form, grew a record crop of red pepper. Others harvested rich crops of millet, potatoes and vegetables. Sofia Kovbasinskaya, also a sixth form pupil, reared 20 pedigree hens at home and presented them to the poultry section of the *Peremozhets* collective farm. Our pupils reared a total of 250 chickens for the collective farms, and the pioneer links[2] have 'adopted' the young collective farm cattle.

The pioneers who had 'adopted' the orchard of the Lenin farm, loosened the soil round the trees on over 49 acres of land, planted 1,500 saplings, helped to exterminate pests, to guard the harvest and to pick the fruit. During the summer the children weeded 1,700 acres of collective farm land.

During the spring and summer the schoolchildren earned 2,145 labour-days working on the collective farms. Seventh form pupil, Olga Solodkaya, has 150 labour-days to her credit, and her name hangs on the board of honour in the October farm together with those of other outstanding workers.

Our school takes an active part in the whole life of the village, and the village soviet has great helpers in the older schoolchildren.

The school wireless circle has made about 500 crystal sets as well as a radio network for the whole village.

On the initiative of the school, a monument to the great Lenin has been set up in the centre of the village, and flowers and ornamental trees have been planted.

The village club has been decorated with posters and placards made by Ivan Oznakh, Leonid Rogach and other young artists from our school. At home the children read papers and interesting new books from the school library to their parents.

The teachers of Trebukhov take a most active part in the agricultural work of the village and in its social problems. On the initiative of the school, the first village lecture centre in the whole of Kiev

[1] *Kok-sagyz.* This plant is used in the manufacture of synthetic rubber.

[2] Every school has a pioneer group (*druzhina*). This is split up into detachments (*otryady*) of up to 40 children of the same age group. The detachment, in its turn, is subdivided into links (*zvenya*) of between 10 and 12 pupils.

province was organised in our village. Over a hundred lectures and talks on such subjects as the evolution of the universe (by school teacher Levitsky) and on current affairs (by school teacher Zinchenko) have already been given. The lectures continue to be popular with the collective farmers.

The school shares the life of the village and its collective farms. Our teaching staff feels that this practice will lead to a general improvement in the work of teaching and upbringing carried on by the school.

IN ONE SCHOOL FAMILY AGAIN

BY F. V. VIGDOROVA

(*Literaturnaya Gazeta*, Oct. 21, 1954)

'LET'S SIT TOGETHER!'

HOW many heated discussions this vital question of co-education has aroused! Last year people were talking about it in trams and trains, parents and children argued about it—everybody in fact was concerned.

'It's grand and quite right too that they're going to go to school together again,' said a middle-aged man in spectacles sitting in the carriage of a long-distance train, as he carefully folded the paper he had just read.

The woman sitting next to him put down her knitting, the youth standing by the window shut his book, and a minute later everyone was busy talking about this vitally important question and the way in which it had been settled: 'They're together at home, at college and at their work, so what's the point of keeping them apart at school?'

'Oh dear,' sighed the nine-year old girl sitting by the window watching the fields and woods of the Moscow countryside go by. 'If only these was someone like Egor in our new form!'

There was such genuine enthusiasm in her voice that everyone involuntarily turned towards her, interested to know about this Egor who possessed such great virtues.

'What's so wonderful about him then?' asked the man with the spectacles who had begun the conversation.

But it is obviously not always easy to explain why somebody seems so charming to us. So we merely learnt that the mysterious Egor 'never starts any quarrels and doesn't show off'. All in all, it appeared that Egor was the only boy she knew who did not 'start quarrels'. To her all boys were ruffians.

This view is also shared by some of the parents. At the parents' meetings held in the schools of Moscow last spring 6,000 people expressed their points of view. Of these only 230 were against co-education, and almost all of these were mothers and fathers of girls. Both they and their daughters feared that boys would bring an atmosphere of violence and disruption into the schools.

As to the boys, I heard one ninth-form pupil remark in passing on 'how lucky the tenth forms are'.[1] This was to show that he despised girls and envied those boys who would not be going to school together with them. But I should add that both the statement as well as the scornful tone in which it was made by the 'unlucky' ninth-former had a false ring about them.

Second-form pupil Yura, on the other hand, said with the whole force of his inner conviction:

'Another nine years to have to stick girls!'

And then came September 1.[2] Muscovites will remember how brightly the sun shone on that day and what noise and hubbub there was in the school playgrounds. The older boys and girls were shy and would only steal a glance at one another. The boys pretended that they were completely indifferent to it all, while the girls were noisier than usual. All the same it was quite obvious which of the children were at their old school and which had come to their new school for the first time: those whose old school it was were cheerful and uninhibited, while the 'guests' stood around frowning. It was not so easy to get used to a new school and new comrades and to make new friendships, after seven or eight years in another school.

Complete agreement and trust was found only among the youngest children. They were holding one another by the hand. Looking out from under the skip of his school uniform cap, the woman-hater Egor saw a blue-eyed little girl to whom he suggested a minute later: 'Let's sit together!'

Then the bell went and the school doors were opened. The second day followed and then the third. And now September is already past and we are at the end of October. For almost two months boys and girls have been at school together. What have these months shown?

JOINT WORK AND MUTUAL JOYS

In essence the impressions gathered by the teachers in the school courtyard on that first day in September have been confirmed by each

[1] Co-education was not introduced in the tenth form in 1954. It was felt that the sudden change during the pupils' last year at school would have a bad effect on their school-leaving examinations.

[2] The school year begins on Sept. 1 in the USSR.

successive day. With the youngest children everything went satisfactorily right from the start. It was here that we saw how right and natural it is for boys and girls to go to school together. In the senior forms things were more difficult. A schoolgirl in Kiev told me that she was 'even frightened to talk to the boys'. Two weeks later that same girl said to me:

'If only you knew how interesting and nice everything is! First of all, we're going to build a wireless station for the school, and then we're going to put on a play. And I'm no longer afraid of boys either.'

These words are worth a whole educational tract. All the causes and effects in this case are perfectly clear: as soon as there was work to be done together and the children experienced mutual feelings of joy the first shoots of the future community sprang up, and it was no longer possible to separate the form into hostile groups. It is obvious that the teacher in charge of this form has a very good grasp of his task, realising that he must form his pupils into a community and that such a community will not come into being through pious talk, but through activities carried on together, and joys and anxieties experienced in common.

From every side you can hear favourable comments about the good effect co-education is having. But how steady and calm is the school's pulse-beat at present? Are there any symptoms that demand our attention and thought?

It is over and finished with now, but it must nevertheless be admitted that some even among the most respectable of school heads tried to get rid of their most incorrigible ruffians when asked to transfer some of their pupils to another school. In school no. 618 in Moscow, for instance, everyone was shocked because some of the boys persisted in entering the school building by the window for the whole of the first week, even though their form room was on the third floor. They would climb up the drain pipe, poke their heads through the window, greet the teacher, and then jump into the room. And one can hardly blame the teacher for not insisting that the pupil who had arrived in the form in this unusual manner should leave it again at once by the same route!

Those people who feared that boys would only bring an atmosphere of violence and disruption into the school can say that they have been right; formerly your neighbour did not pull the girls' hair, disturb them during lesson time or tease them during break. And in spite of all this, these people are wrong, for the boys are not the only cause of the quarrels in schools today.

The children sit before the teacher and he diligently tells them that they must behave themselves, and not fight or pull the girls' hair. Every boy knows all that by heart. He knows it well enough, but nevertheless does not act accordingly. As Makarenko said: 'No matter how persistently you tell a person what thoughts and what knowledge he should possess—if you do nothing else but that, you will be wasting your time or, at best, turning the person into a hypocrite and automaton.'

The boys and girls in question are between thirteen and fourteen years old. One must understand this age, its burning thirst for activity and its insatiable energy. It must be provided with something to do, something interesting and attractive that arouses feelings of comradeship among both boys and girls, knits them into one family and gives them something more interesting to do than pulling people's hair.

It cannot be denied that it is difficult to create a community when the form is a new one made up of children from three or four, and sometimes as many as six, different schools. And the older the children are, the more difficult and knotty does the problem become. With some trepidation, I am now about to touch on a subject which is bound to bring down upon me the wrath and indignation of certain teachers.

In spite of the fact that, far from condemning it, separate education regarded a co-educational upbringing for children as something to be taken for granted, boys and girls lived as though on different planets. In the pioneer camps they were divided into separate detachments and even had their meals at separate tables. And when they tried to arrange something to do together in the town, they found themselves wading in a sea of troubles. I know of a girl from the seventh form of one of the Moscow schools, for instance, who tried to arrange an evening of humour together with the seventh-form pupils from the neighbouring boys' school. The first reaction to this plan came from their form mistress who had the following comment to make:

'I was just waiting for that—an evening with the boys! What next!'

The girls then approached the head of the school from whom they received a similar reply. The district komsomol committee admitted that it would be a good idea to arrange a joint evening of humour, and told the children to go back to school and to try to persuade their head mistress once more. The latter, however, refused to be persuaded, and the evening of humour and satire never took place.

I have not recalled these instances in order merely to harp on our difficulties of the past, but because a great deal of hypocrisy has grown up on the soil of separate education. Hypocrisy is a plant with deep roots, and you do not destroy it by merely tearing off its leaves.

'YES, BUT WITHOUT THE GIRLS!'

In school no. 182 a questionnaire was passed round the senior forms at the beginning of September: pupils were asked what new and interesting things they wanted the school to do during that year. The replies contained all kinds of suggestions.

'I should like to have some cheerful music played during every break,' somebody suggested. This is hardly practicable, but there is something very charming and buoyant about the idea.

'I should like us all to have a lot of things to do together and to be really responsible for the school. In my old school nobody ever trusted us with anything. We even had the teacher to turn us out of the classroom during break as though the boys on duty couldn't have done it without them.'—This reply contains the very important embryo of something which can unite all these boys and girls from their different schools in one community: love towards their school, mutual responsibility for it, and common interests.

'I think we ought to have a discussion about friendship and comradeship. But without the girls; you can't speak your mind when they're there.'

That was the reply from a boy in the tenth form. Nine years of separate education have taught this young boy to mistrust half the human race to such an extent that he does not want to discuss any problems in their presence, not even when these problems worry boys and girls alike.

The pupils of school no. 618 did not receive any questionnaires but they in fact replied in the same way as the tenth former from school no. 182 had done.

The senior pupils in school no. 618 were to be given a lecture on friendship and comradeship. Everyone was interested and eager to come. Finally the day of the lecture arrived. The speaker went up to the platform and saw—100 girls and not a single boy. Her face expressed such bewilderment that the girls all started to talk at once, explaining why they were here alone. It transpired that the boys had at the last moment raced downstairs and on to the street, and that it had been quite impossible to halt them:

'They're embarrassed! They haven't got used to us yet!'

Suddenly the door opened and in came—two boys. These desperate heroes were met with laughter, but the path of retreat had already been blocked and they sat down on the nearest empty seat, blushing and keeping their eyes averted. And so only two boys ventured to come to a lecture which the school had been looking forward to so much. The rest were simply afraid. Of what? Of a lecture on such a straightforward, important and interesting subject?

'SURELY IT ISN'T RIGHT?'

They were not given a lecture, but a simple and sincere talk, such as people rarely succeed in giving when they speak on this subject to an audience of young people.

'It's very bad that you've got into the habit of doing things separately—the girls on their own, and the boys on their own,' the speaker told them. 'Imagine what would have happened if the Young Guard had acted like that, if Ulya Gromova, for instance, had refused to keep an appointment with boys, or if Sergei Tyulenin had refused to work with Lyuba Shevtsova!'[1]

'Yes, but they were going to school together; they would never have thought of saying things like that,' the girl sitting next to me—an eighth-former with attentive blue eyes—replied. And she was right. This proportion of 100 girls to two boys at a talk on a subject which really worries both the sexes, had only been made possible by 10 years of separate education.

And when the speaker had finished, many notes were sent up to her. It was obvious that the girls were all worried about their school. They wanted to know how they could form a single community out of the particles of different school communities which had now been brought together. What work did the speaker think they should do together?

There was a whole stream of other questions, such as 'is it possible to fall in love for life at our age?', and 'my mother doesn't want me to go out with boys; how can I persuade her that there's nothing wrong in it?', which obviously seemed equally important to those who were asking them.

And the mothers are not the only ones who have sometimes to be persuaded that there is nothing wrong in friendships between boys

[1] The 'Young Guard' was a group of komsomols in the Krasnodon region who carried on an organised underground resistance against the Germans. They were eventually captured and executed. Their courage and heroism have been described by the well-known Soviet writer, Fadeyev, in his novel, *The Young Guard*. Ulya Gromova, Sergei Tyulenin and Lyuba Shevtsova were members of this 'Young Guard'.

and girls. I am sorry to say that there are some teachers and heads of schools who have to be reminded of this fact.

In school no. 636 a teacher caught a boy misbehaving during break, and started to tell him off in a loud voice. Finally she said to him: 'If you don't start behaving yourself I'll have to make you sit with the girls!'—This queer threat was made in front of everyone and shook the whole edifice of co-education; it might indeed have tottered had the boy himself not come to its rescue: 'I don't mind,' he said. 'I like sitting with them!'

One careless word can sometimes destroy the inner world of an adolescent: 'You're too young to be going out with boys', 'why aren't you doing your homework, you haven't fallen in love, have you?', 'with whom were you at the cinema last night? And don't try to tell me it was your brother'.

None of this questioning and scolding has been thought up by me; it could be heard in the schools, and it immediately destroyed all trust in the teacher and substituted feelings of contempt, suspicion and secrecy. More than that, such words taught adolescents to be hypocritical and petty bourgeois themselves and gave them a narrow and mean conception of human relationships.

There is no doubt that the teacher is now faced with many difficult problems which have yet to be solved. He has once again to get to know a new form with only a few familiar faces, while the rest have come from other schools. And some of those on whom he has spent so much work and energy have now left. The community has to be formed anew, and the children have to be taught to love their new school, to think of it as their own. None of this is easy, and it will take many months to accomplish. But there is yet another problem which we must not forget. After an interruption of 10 years our schools have once again become co-educational. There is a great deal here which the teacher must watch carefully. He needs sensitivity, sincerity, tact and a real understanding of the people entrusted to him.

I have a letter here. This is what it says:

'Surely it isn't right, is it? I share a desk with Vitya V., and every lesson our form mistress starts saying: "I'll have to separate you two or you'll start flirting and not work properly." Surely it isn't right to talk like that?'

No, it is not right to talk like that. The teacher must never forget his own youth when he too was vulnerable, impressionable and sensitive to every unjust word.

It is very important and right that co-education has been re-introduced in our schools. And the first month and a half have shown that school life now is different, attractive and interesting. But it is now, at the very beginning, that we must discover anything that hinders this wonderful work of joint education and upbringing; we must listen carefully for any unevennesses or false notes in the beat of the school's pulse. And we must, right from the very start, remove all obstacles in the way of a healthy community where boys and girls will be friends and comrades in one school family.

THE STRENGTH OF THE COMMUNITY

BY V. LYALIN, HEADMASTER, UPPER ELTSOVKA VILLAGE, ISKITIM DISTRICT, NOVOSIBIRSK PROVINCE

(*Uchitelskaya Gazeta*, Aug. 5, 1953)[1]

VALERII NEVZOROV entered the fifth form of our school. His father brought him to school, and it was evident that he was very worried over something. Before he left he turned to all the teachers:

'I'd like to ask you to give special attention to my boy,' he said. 'He is really impossible. So if he does anything, be as severe with him as you like.'

During the first few days while he was getting used to his new surroundings, Nevzorov did not appear any different from the other schoolchildren, and even showed some interest in his work.

But then it started. First he left his exercise book at home, then he did not bring his penholder, and finally he played truant. Zoya Antonovna, the form mistress of 5A, often heard comments in the staff room such as 'your Nevzorov hasn't done his homework', 'your Nevzorov won't do any work during lessons', and 'your Nevzorov has played truant again'.

'Mine, mine, always mine,' Zoya Antonovna flared up one day. 'He's not only mine, is he? He's mine exactly as much as he's yours. I think we need the joint efforts of all of us to bring him up.'

At first Nevzorov got on well with Zoya Antonovna. But soon the following incident occurred.

Zoya Antonovna came into the classroom to take a lesson. The pupils stood up—all except Nevzorov.

'Why are you sitting down?' the teacher asked. 'The children are standing waiting.'

[1] Reprinted, with a few alterations, from *Soviet Studies*, vol. V, no. 3, by kind permission of the editors.

'Let them stand for me,' the boy answered insolently.

'Sit down, children,' Zoya Antonovna said, quite calmly as though that were the end of it.

The children sat down. The teacher turned to Nevzorov:

'Valerii!'

Valerii got up. The teacher, pretending not to notice him, began to take the lesson. Embarrassed, Valerii asked:

'What, Zoya Antonovna?'

'Nothing. Now you can stand for everyone else.'

We had plenty of opportunities to convince ourselves of Zoya Antonovna's wonderful tact in dealing with pupils. The punishments which she meted out never humiliated the child's personality, though they would make it acutely conscious that the teacher was in the right. But Valerii took punishment badly. He began to avoid Zoya Antonovna, and stopped doing his homework in her subjects.

The teachers of 5A decided that they would have to train Nevzorov to work properly, and that they would have to use a skilful, pedagogical approach and to be stubborn, persistent and at the same time gentle, if they were to be successful.

The first term Nevzorov had a 'two' in Russian language, Russian literature, arithmetic and history. However, he was doing well in geography. During geography lessons he worked very hard. It was characteristic of his lack of self-control that he would react vehemently to other pupils' replies:

'He hasn't answered it properly. I'll tell you!' he would shout out.

Maria Naumovna, the geography mistress, would quietly stop him:

'You're quite right, Valerii. But you must only speak when I ask you to: that's necessary to keep the lesson orderly.—Well then, let's hear the complete answer.'

'Why don't you just order Nevzorov to do things?' we asked the teacher.

'And how can I give him orders when he hasn't yet acquired the habit of obeying orders right away? We've still got to train him to do that.'

The teachers paid attention to what Maria Naumovna had said; so this was how Valerii should be approached!

We soon noticed that Nevzorov knew how to speak the truth: While 5A is having a gym lesson, I find Nevzorov wandering unconcernedly through the school corridors.

'Why aren't you at the lesson?' I ask him.

'I didn't obey Nikolai Stepanovich and was made to stand out. So I walked off.'

'It's good to see you tell the truth.'

The boy blushes. Who knows, perhaps he does not always tell the truth. But it is so pleasant to hear someone who has a good word for you.

'You're a good lad to tell me the truth, but it's bad that you don't obey the teacher,' I continue. 'A pity you're not doing gym just now, like the others.'

The boy guiltily hangs his head, and that already is a good sign.

From his first days at school Valerii had kept himself apart from the other children. At first the pioneers tried to get friendly with him. One of them volunteered to help him with arithmetic and another with Russian. But Nevzorov refused all help, and when he felt that they were 'bothering' him too much he became insolent, and that would be the end of the friendship.

They tried to attract him into the young fishermen's circle. What do village children love more than the river and fishing! We knew that Nevzorov was an ardent fisherman. He had spent the whole summer fishing on the Ob, not only with a line but also with a drag-net and other nets.

Nikolai Stepanovich, the gymnastics master, who was in charge of the circle, asked Nevzorov:

'Are you going to enrol in our circle?'

'What would I do there?'

'Learn about the importance of the fishing industry and study the fish,' Nikolai Stepanovich explained.

'Not very interesting,' Nevzorov replied, though he was obviously keen to hear what else the circle would do.

'We'll teach you how to use a line and how to catch perch, pike, turbot and white salmon with a special net.'

'I know all that.'

'And how to make ordinary nets and drag-nets from threads, and snares with twigs.'

'I know how to.'

'That's good. You can teach the others. Shall I enrol you?'

'All right.'

But Nevzorov did not come to the first meeting, apparently to discourage the teachers from their attempts to draw him into the life of the child community. It looked as though nothing would come of it. But that is never so. Everything positive the teacher does sooner or later shows itself in some good deed done by the schoolchildren. Only one must not be naïve and expect the seeds to grow and bear fruit immediately.

It is not so very long ago since Nevzorov went over to the fourth-formers during break: the children are crowding around and watching something with concentration. It is Tolya Bagrov who only started learning how to make nets yesterday; he has brought to school some fishing tackle and a drag-net he has started to make. Onlookers who are no doubt keen to learn the art themselves have gathered around him. But the first loop is not a success; it has got firmly stuck in a tangle, and the inexperienced netters are vainly trying to straighten it out.

'Oh, you fishermen!' Nevzorov laughs good-naturedly and takes the net from Tolya.

In a flash he has got rid of the useless loop and has begun to use the needle so quickly and with such confidence that he has everybody's admiration.

'Jolly good!'

Valerii tells the children which threads are strongest, and explains to them the whole process of net-making.

We learnt later that Tolya had been to the Nevzorov's flat several times to watch him making nets. Then it somehow happened that Valerii and Tolya became inseparable: they went about together during breaks, and went skiing together.

Nevzorov has felt himself particularly drawn towards the other children ever since the day when he had to face a general meeting of the school and felt the full force of its indignation at his behaviour.

Although the meeting was held in the largest of the classrooms, there were three or four people sitting at each desk. Nevzorov sat in the front row. On one side sat Naumov, the editor of the school wall newspaper, on the other sat Tatarintsev, a member of the pupils' committee.

Everyone was listening attentively to the report of the chairman of the pupils' committee; only Nevzorov was looking around with indifference. But then the speaker began to talk about him. Valerii pricked up his ears; he looked surprised. Drawing in his head between his shoulders, he growled out:

'I've always played up and I'm not going to stop now!'

'Sit still!' Naumov nudged him lightly with his elbow.

Valerii shifted in the direction of Tatarintsev, intending to leave.

'Listen, listen,' Tatarintsev whispered seriously.

With even more determination Nevzorov quickly turned in Naumov's direction.

'Where are you off to?' Naumov asked, raising his brows at him. 'Sit still!'

Nevzorov was at a loss. The speaker was still talking about him. The boy suddenly blushed, then went pale, and darted under the desk in the hope of slipping away, but Naumov and Tatarintsev, as though by previous arrangement, both caught him by the arms and gently sat him down in his place.

At first the children did not say anything about Nevzorov, but then it all came out as almost every speaker mentioned him. Bratchikov, a boy from the sixth form, spoke carefully, without hurrying:

'There is not one pupil in any of the forms here with a bad conduct mark; only Nevzorov in 5A has a "three"!'

Belova, a girl from the fifth form, indignantly turned to Valerii:

'You ought to be given a reprimand by the general meeting so that you'll understand and remember!'

'In my opinion,' Sharov, a boy from the seventh form, said with determination, 'the teachers ought to be asked to expel him from the school. He won't learn himself and he is hindering others!'

The secretary of the komsomol branch said:

'We all protect the honour of our form and our school; only Nevzorov lets us down. But it won't bring us much honour if we chase him away. In my opinion the teachers ought to be asked to have him up before a joint meeting of teachers and parents.'

Most noteworthy of the speeches was Naumov's:

'At the beginning of the year we had some children who played up and were working badly. There was Perelazov from 6B, Vyatkin from 5B, Pavel Bessonov, and others. We summoned them to a meeting of the pupils' committee, wrote about them in the wall newspaper, helped them as well as we could, and they understood us and did their best to start working and behaving better. Nevzorov works badly and behaves badly. We have asked him time and again to come before the pupils' committee, but he has never turned up, refuses all help from the pioneers and runs away from the general meetings of the form. We want to help him to get himself straight, but he won't accept any help from his comrades, the pupils' committee, the wall newspaper or anybody. Why waste our time with him for nothing? I think he should no longer be regarded as a pupil of the school.—That's all.'

'Aren't we to be friendly with him then?' someone asked, puzzled.

'What good would that do?' Naumov made his meaning clearer: 'We are not going to turn away from him, but we'll regard him as a member of the school only when we see that he behaves as a pupil should, when he begins to respect the pupils' committee, the school organisations and our meetings.'

Nevzorov was listening attentively now, though it did not look as though he understood at all clearly what Naumov was saying. But there is no doubt that at home, away from everyone else, he very much took to heart what had been said at the meeting. . . .

Examination time has come. Ermila Sergeyevich and an assistant are marking 5A's arithmetic papers. Zoya Antonovna is looking out of the window as though it was all the same to her.

Suddenly Ermila Sergeyevich looks up at everyone with satisfaction:

'That Nevzorov of ours has got a "four"!'

Zoya Antonovna breathes a sigh of relief.

'Ours,' she says smiling. 'Valerii was the only one I was worried about.'

Nevzorov successfully completed the examinations and was moved up into the sixth form.

IT IS YOUR CONCERN

BY V. BENDEROVA, GIRLS' SCHOOL NO. 11, KAZAN

(*Komsomolskaya Pravda*, March 20, 1948)

SEVEN komsomols were sitting at the table, trying to think what the new komsomol committee should do to start with. . . . After a heated discussion it was decided to institute 'Thursdays' at school. These were to consist of a meeting held once a week in the evening, and were intended to widen the school's horizon, and to tell the girls about the kind of life people led in the distant parts of their Motherland.

The committee members started preparing for the first evenings to be held. Dilyara Saidasheva sat up until late in the city library, deep in a book about the Soviet North. At the school 'Thursday' she spoke about the intrepid explorers who had hacked their way through ice in the darkness of the polar night, and about the wealth which lies hidden in the icebound earth.

Lyusya Shebarsheva made out a large map of the southern arid regions. And on the following Thursday her young audience studied the map with interest, and listened to her account of the bold venture of Soviet man to transform this land. . . .

The girls grew accustomed to their 'Thursdays' and looked forward to them impatiently. They longed to do independent work, and asked to be given subjects for talks.

Raya Paisina, the secretary of the committee, felt that they were working in the right direction.

And all the time life itself was suggesting new, important and urgent work to be done. One day Raya heard that one of the girls in the fifth form was wearing a cross. The girl was superstitious and afraid of various 'unlucky' objects, and was often seen at dusk exchanging 'news' with her friends in whispers: someone she knew had been in church and had seen how the candles had lit up on their own accord while the prayers were being said; someone else she knew had witnessed another 'miracle'—an old icon had become as good as new before her very eyes.

Raya was worried. She could hardly stand by idly and do nothing while this absurd nonsense was being peddled around, fuddling everyone's mind. Klavdia Ivanovna Loginova, the chemistry mistress, was invited to a meeting of the committee, and a joint plan of action was worked out. Soon the vestibule was studded with posters inviting everyone to an 'Evening of Miracles'.

To begin with, there was an interesting and lively talk on the origin and growth of life on Earth. This was followed by the 'miracles' themselves: candles burst into flame of their own accord—not a soul was near them—and tarnished metal tracery suddenly grew bright and sparkling. But the young chemists were soon showing everyone how it had been done: the candle must be dipped in a solution of phosphorus and bisulphide of carbon beforehand; the bisulphide of carbon evaporates, leaving the phosphorus which is self-igniting in air—that is why it is stored in water. The icon 'miracle' had just as easy an explanation: simply the action of mercury on metal.

Not a day passed without new joys, sorrows and anxieties. One day Raya saw some seventh form girls during break, spellbound by a tattered book from which they were reading aloud. . . . She went up to the girls. They were eagerly reading a novel by Charskaya. A heated argument followed. The girls defended their 'idol' and simply could not understand why Raya should attack it and call it sentimental, petty bourgeois poison.

It was a new signal for action. The committee had a long and serious discussion about the ideas and tastes of their school mates. A good, intelligent book about real life and real people would, they felt, be an effective antidote for many bad influences. The girls asked their form mistresses to advise them on books to be read together in the forms or detachments, and colourful posters which said: 'Read this Book!' began to appear on the walls. . . .

IT CONCERNS THE WHOLE COMMUNITY

BY I. G. TKACHENKO, HEADMASTER, BOGDANOV SECONDARY SCHOOL, ZNAMENKA DISTRICT, KIROVOGRAD PROVINCE[1]

(*Semya i Shkola*, 1954, no. 8, p. 15)

I SHOULD like to stress how very important the community is for the happiness and successful upbringing of the child. Some parents either cannot or do not wish to understand this. Preoccupied with their own narrow interests, they lightheartedly destroy the family community, tear the child away from its school, deprive it of the joy of friendship, loyalty and comradeship it had found there, and substitute the selfish joys of petty, personal pleasures.

We teachers should take a firm stand whenever we find parents adopting such an attitude. It is also our duty to teach the child community to defend the true happiness of each of its members.

I should like to recount an incident experienced by one of the form masters in our school.

'Why is Galina absent?' asked Nikolai Pavlovich, mustering the children who had come to help the collective farm.

All eyes turned to Vera, the komsomol organiser of the form.

'Galina has gone off to visit her father,' Vera replied. 'She left two days after the exams were over.'

Nikolai Pavlovich was surprised. 'That's very strange,' he said. 'Galina has lived and worked together with us as friends for many years; and now she has suddenly violated the decision of the komsomol meeting. I wonder why she didn't even ask us? After all, we wouldn't have stopped her from visiting her father.'

'Of course we wouldn't,' the children agreed.

Nikolai Pavlovich remembered a letter he had written to Galina's father three years ago when the latter was a student in his final year at the medical institute. Nikolai Pavlovich had concluded his letter

[1] In the Ukranian SSR.

with a plea that he should consider the following statement by Makarenko:

> I should like to add that where a father or mother leaves the family, that family ceases to exist as a community, and the child's upbringing is made more difficult. If therefore you have a feeling of duty towards your child, think carefully before you do this. I have left some things unsaid in my book, but I will tell you this in secret; if you have two children and you cease to love your wife and fall in love with another woman, stifle your new feeling. It will be hard and difficult, but it is your duty. You will remain father to your family. This is your duty because your child is a future citizen, and you must sacrifice a certain measure of your own personal happiness for it.

But when Galina's father became a doctor he did not return to his children. Galina's form had to take the place of the broken family. And now she had suddenly left without telling anyone, ashamed to let her comrades know what she was doing.

And so the form went to work on the collective farm without Galina.

On returning from the local hospital where she worked as an assistant, Galina's mother was surprised to see the teacher in her room waiting for her. After all, these were the holidays, what could have happened?

'I've come to see you,' Nikolai Pavlovich said to her. 'I should like to know why you ignored our komsomols' decision to help the collective farm, and allowed your daughter to go off to her father without even asking the school's advice. You have lost your husband; do you want to lose your daughter too?'

Galina's mother was embarrassed.

'Her father's been asking for her all this time,' she said. 'It's very interesting at the resort where he works. Why shouldn't Galina see a bit and have a holiday? What's wrong with that? Here, read her letter.'

'I'm having a lovely time here,' the teacher read. 'I go for walks in the park or out boating, and in the evenings there are concerts. There's a photographer here who keeps taking my photo and who says that I'm beautiful.' Nikolai Pavlovich read the letter and looked up at the girl's mother.

'Yes, Galina is beautiful,' he said. 'But there's not one word here about the school or her comrades; she doesn't even ask you how you are. Her father wants to make up for what he's done, and so he allows his still immature daughter to lead a "gay life"; he's ruining her.

Boats, concerts and photographers—none of that will last. She'll have to come back to school, into the ninth form where there'll be a lot of work to do. It won't be easy for Galina to keep up with the form. The poison of the "gay life" she has known has harmed her mind already and may corrupt it completely.'

Galina's mother was silent, distressed by the teacher's frank and severe words.

'Never mind,' he encouraged her. 'We'll hope for the best. Ask Galina to come home.'

But after the teacher had gone, Galina's mother changed her mind and did not ask her daughter to come home.

At the school celebrations of 'the first bell', certificates of honour were presented to those who had worked best in helping the collective farm to bring in the harvest. To the smaller children they appeared like 'Heroes of Labour'[1] as they stood there in front of the whole school holding their certificates of honour and their flowers.

'We were given a job to do,' began tenth-former, Alexander Borodin. 'We were asked to help our collective farm in its most important duty—to provide the country with bread. The damp grain had to be dried, cleaned and sent to the collecting stations. That was the job we did. The komsomols helped to clean and supply the country with 400 tons of grain. We worked day and night, in fact we trained our characters. But there are some komsomols who didn't take part in this important work for the country. I hope they feel ashamed of themselves! The school and farm are our own flesh and blood. We shall always strive to keep our komsomol banner and our komsomol honour unsullied!'

Alexander's words were drowned by applause. The school orchestra played and the joy of those with certificates was shared by everyone.

Galina stood in line feeling lonely and sad. She would have to explain her conduct to the komsomol meeting. Galina's mother was there together with the other parents. What was she thinking?

Term began. Galina was rebuked at the komsomol meeting. After that she shrank into herself and gave up the komsomol work she had been doing with the pioneers. She began to receive her first 'twos'. She was living a separate life of her own, more and more losing touch with the community. Something had to be done. But what?

While the form master was still worrying about what to do, Galina's mother unexpectedly came to see him. She told him that she had left her work earlier than usual the previous day, and had found

[1] An official title awarded by the Soviet government for outstanding achievements in industry or agriculture.

her daughter sitting at home. When she had asked her why she was not at school, Galina had simply said she was ill.

'I didn't believe her,' Galina's mother continued. 'And I found out that she had in fact lied to me. We had a row, and Galina's saying now that she'll go away to her father because everybody here—both at school and at home—has a down on her. What am I to do? Surely I haven't lost my daughter!'

'So Galina wants to go away to her father? Let her go then!' was Nikolai Pavlovich's first reaction. But it soon gave place to other thoughts: 'It's easy enough to evade difficulties; but that's no solution. We must ask the help of the community. But is it right do discuss a question like this at a komsomol meeting at all?'

Nikolai Pavlovich turned to his comrades for advice. Some said that it was definitely right, and that one must have faith in the wisdom and strength of the community no matter how difficult the position was. Others said that it would be wrong to arouse the children's attention and interest in a problem concerning a broken family. 'It doesn't concern them,' these people said. 'You would do better to talk with Galina on her own.' Others again refused to express any opinion 'for' or 'against', and suggested that nobody do anything at all because these things always 'solved themselves'.

'Which is right?' the teacher wondered. He remembered a passage from a book he had recently read: 'Every man should go out into life armed against bad influences. People should not be protected from bad influences but taught how to fight against them. That is Soviet education.' These words come from Makarenko. Nikolai Pavlovich called to mind what this great and original educationalist had said about the child community and about the necessity of settling conflicts carefully but boldly and without evading them.

And Nikolai Pavlovich decided to take the risk. He called a meeting which Galina's mother too was invited to attend.

First of all the floor was given to Valya Pavlova, a close friend of Galina's. She spoke with warmth and sincerity of their friendship which had lasted three years, and which was now being destroyed because Galina had taken offence in a petty way.

'I wish Galina would stop avoiding us. After all, we are her comrades in spite of everything that's happened,' she said in conclusion. Then she turned to Galina and said simply and sincerely: 'Stay with us Galina, it's nicer together.'

The komsomol organiser, Vera, criticised Galina for her conduct and turned to her with the following question:

'I'd like to ask you this—what do you think is better, an album of photographs or a certificate of honour for excellent work from the collective farmers?'

After her Volodya Dubov went up to the platform. 'We went out in a boat too,' he said. 'But not until we'd got the harvest in. We earned our holiday, while Galina went off without asking her komsomol branch first. Who gave her permission?'

'I did,' her mother replied.

For a second Volodya was at a loss what to say; but he soon recovered himself and said to Galina's mother:

'You too should have discussed the matter with us. You didn't, and now Galina is threatening to go away to her father. Well, let her go! Only she ought to know that people who leave their home, their mother and their comrades for an easy life are just rolling stones and not real people at all!'

A hush, like the calm before a storm, fell over the meeting. And then the storm broke. Everyone started to talk at once, excitedly interrupting one another, and the discussion grew heated. Galina's fate had become something of really vital importance for the whole form. Finally the teacher spoke:

'Galina went off to the south without telling anyone. She deceived our community and abused our trust in her. Not long ago she lied to her mother. Now she's going to leave us in search of an "easy life". But Galina is a komsomol; she should have the courage and honesty to tell her comrades what kind of a life she is going to live.'

Galina went up to the platform hanging her head. For a long time she stood there, painfully silent and obviously finding it very hard to control herself.

'I'm—not going to go away,' she finally said, and went back to her seat.

And so the komsomol meeting ended. It was decided to write a letter to Galina's father and to invite him to come on a visit to the school.

Soon after the meeting, Galina asked the senior pioneer leader to allow her to take up her work with the pioneers again. The wall newspaper published an article on Galina's conduct, written by Valya together with Galina herself. Galina apologised to her mother and promised never to tell lies again. All these were the outward signs of the fundamental change which was taking place in the girl's mind as a result of the influence of her teacher and her comrades.

The making of a man, the forming of his personality and character, all this is a complex process full of conflicts. And the teacher needs great insight, sensitivity and courage if he is to be a steady guide, confidently leading his pupils through childhood and adolescence. . . .

PARENTS AND EXTRA-CURRICULAR SCHOOL ACTIVITIES

BY I. MARENKO, CANDIDATE OF PEDAGOGICAL SCIENCES[1]

(*Semya i Shkola*, 1952, no. 2, p. 20)

EXTRA-CURRICULAR activities for children play an important part in education and upbringing. They widen and improve the knowledge acquired by pupils at their lessons, raise their general level of culture, develop their artistic tastes and teach them to be practical and to become good organisers. This work is of very great educational importance, and helps to create a greater degree of consciousness in the children.

Unfortunately this work is unsatisfactory in some of our schools. The heads of these schools often maintain that they have not got sufficient specialists in technology, art and other branches, who could organise and take charge of the corresponding extra-curricular work.

The best schools solve this problem by making extensive use of parents. In this way it is almost always possible to find the necessary specialist willing to devote a few hours per week to organising extra-curricular activities in his particular field. . . .

In secondary school no. 48 in the city of Borisoglebsk (Voronezh province) and in school no. 7 in Golitsyno (Moscow province) the children's parents work on the railway. They take a very active part in the technology circles of these schools. With the help of parents the wireless circle of school no. 48 had a wonderful time making valve and crystal sets which were then put into railway guards' huts. The pupils made a powerful valve receiver for the club of the *Red October* collective farm just outside the city; the school is 'patron' of this farm. In school no. 7 parents who are specialists in these particular branches are teaching the children about radio-telegraphy, the system of

[1] 'Candidate of Sciences' is the name given to the lowest post-graduate degree.

signals and automatic blocks in railway transport and about the industries making steam engines and electric engines.

In this same school Arkadii Alexeyevich Shelkin, the father of a seventh-form pupil, organised a music circle with which he worked during the whole school year. The members of the circle can now play brass instruments, and Comrade Shelkin is teaching them new works. The brass band has become the pride of the whole school.

In Borisoglebsk secondary school no. 5 the drama circle had been doing badly for a long time even though the pupils were very keen on it. Finally the teachers asked Comrade Iskrin, the father of one of the pupils and an actor at the local theatre, to help them. Iskrin agreed with pleasure and began to direct the pupils' drama circle. The pupils were attracted by Comrade Iskrin's professional skill and his love of the theatre, and the circle began to flourish. During the easter holidays it performed excerpts from Pushkin's *Boris Godunov* and Fadeyev's *Young Guard* at the city's junior amateur drama festival. The young actors were warmly received by the audience, and the festival judges described the drama circle as one of the best school circles.

The drama circle directed by Comrade Iskrin is having a considerable educational influence on its members and on the rest of the school. The poignancy with which he expresses emotion, his excellent diction and his beautiful deportment are having a marked influence on the appearance and conduct of many of the pupils.

Parents who have no educational experience but possess sufficient knowledge in one or other subject, should be asked to help with individual tasks connected with the circle. They might, for instance, be asked to organise small libraries for each circle, to collect materials for its activities, help to find visual aids, make costumes and draw sketches and drafts.

The success of the pupils' 'research societies' in school no. 110 in Moscow was due in part to the extensive organisational and material help given by the parents. The 'Young Chemist' society, for instance, which is directed by chemistry mistress L. I. Rozina, obtained reagents for its work, arranged to have typed copies of the necessary material, prepared visual aids and started a small chemistry library.

Some schools follow the commendable practice of doing systematic work to improve the pedagogical knowledge of the parents who work with circles. Parents are given talks on problems of method in extra-curricular activities and are asked to carry out individual tasks in connection with these problems; they are invited to attend open meetings of the circles followed by a discussion of their activities. All this helps the people in charge of circles to improve their work.

The institutes for teachers' refresher courses in Stalingrad and Sverdlovsk have set a good example in this respect. They analysed parents' experience of work with pupils, and demonstrated ways in which parents could be attracted to extra-curricular school activities.

Naturally, only parents with a certain amount of previous training can be asked to work independently with the circles. Most parents can, however, find suitable work to do in connection with the extra-curricular mass activities carried on. Those among the parents who are specialists in one field or another, distinguished people of our country, heroes of the Civil or Great Patriotic wars, old inhabitants of a district and knowledgeable people in general are all welcome guests with the children.

They can take part in school festivals, social evenings, readers' conferences and discussions of films and plays; they can also give talks on literature, science and politics. In addition, it is possible for them to be active in organising museums of exhibits of local interest for the school, teaching the children the history of their town or village, arranging excursions and trips into their native district, as well as pioneer assemblies and komsomol meetings.

In school no. 3 in Borisoglebsk parents often give talks. One of the most successful of these was a concert-lecture on the life and work of Chaikovsky: one of the mothers gave a talk on Chaikovsky's work; another played a number of his compositions on the piano; this was followed by a further talk by one of the mothers, this time about her visit to Chaikovsky's house in Klin. This concert-lecture organised by the mothers was very popular with the children.

Parents' participation in pioneer and komsomol assemblies is of great educational significance. Parents' eye-witness accounts of great and memorable moments in the nation's history make a very deep impression on the pupils. The seventh form pioneer detachment of Golitsyno school no. 7 held a pioneer meeting devoted to the Chinese People's Republic. Leva Khlyupin's father (Leva is a pioneer in the detachment) told the pioneers about the time when he met the leader of the Chinese people, Mao Tse Tung. The latter had visited the factory where Khlyupin works and, as the best Stakhanovite, he had had to welcome Mao Tse Tung on behalf of the many thousands of workers at the factory.

The pioneers listened to Leva's father with great attention and interest. He was able to make the Chinese people's leader live for the children.

Another pioneer meeting was devoted to the heroic Korean people. Here the speaker was a retired colonel, the father of Valya Rumyantseva. He had taken part in the liberation of Korea from the Japanese imperialists in 1945.

The pioneers learned many interesting facts from Valya's father about the ways of life of the Koreans. Rumyantseva also told the pioneers how the people had begun to build a new democratic Korea after they had been liberated by the Soviet Army from Japanese slavery. This meeting aroused great sympathy among the pupils for the Korean people, who are today staunchly and heroically defending the freedom and independence of their country against the American imperialists.

The next meeting was devoted to the Stalin Plan for Transforming Nature.[1] An engineer from the local afforestation scheme, Zhenya Yerusalimsky's father, was the speaker.

Engineer Yerusalimsky told the pioneers something about the Stalin Plan for Transforming Nature, and described the idea of creating a green belt around Moscow. The children were particularly attracted by the project for improving the forests in which the engineer Yerusalimsky was himself taking part. He told the children of the plan for 'reconstructing' the forest belts by uprooting various types of useless trees and planting more valuable species in their place. This process, he told them, would be carried out according to the method advocated by academician Lysenko. When these trees grow up they will crowd out all useless species. The engineer also mentioned the many valuable trees growing in the countryside around Moscow. On the following day the pioneers set out into the forest and collected branches and leaves of 30 valuable tree species. They also gathered seeds, which they handed over to the afforestation scheme.

The pioneer meeting on 'The Western Railway' was most interesting. The speaker was the father of Galya Filatova, station master at Golitsyno. The pioneers learnt about the outstanding workers on the Western Railway. They were particularly attracted by the Stakhanovite engine drivers who had been able to speed up their train services, thus achieving a great economy in the state's resources. The pioneers acquired a better idea of the part played by railway transport in the life of our Motherland.

The meeting was followed by an excursion to the station itself,

[1] This refers to the Great Construction Works of Communism (already mentioned on p. 32), and in particular to the large afforestation schemes which have been planned.

where Comrade Filatov showed the pioneers its complicated workings.

Pioneer meetings of this kind, in which parents take part, leave a lasting impression with the pupils. The authority of their fathers and mothers grows in their eyes as they see them as builders of communism in our country. The children feel proud of their parents, and this feeling in its turn improves their work and conduct.

Comrade Dovbysh, a form master, found that parents' participation at pioneer meetings helped him to achieve a marked improvement in the entire work of the form. Everyone in the seventh form finished the school year successfully: at the annual examinations 80 per cent of the pupils received 'fours' and 'fives'.

In attracting parents into extra-curricular activities Comrade Dovbysh systematically teaches them how to work with children. He helps them to gather the necessary materials for talks, looks over the plan for each talk, gives advice on how to speak with children, what to give one's chief attention to, and so forth. He invites parents to pupils' extra-curricular activities. Many parents come gladly and then begin to take part in the work themselves, helping the teacher.

All the parents came to the end-of-term celebrations. They sat at one table together with their children and the teachers, celebrating the end of the school year.

The experience of parent participation in extra-curricular activities deserves to be studied from all angles, analysed and generally applied. There are many schools which do not make use of parents as much as they ought to. In that same Golitsyno secondary school no. 7 even, which has the excellent example of Comrade Dovbysh, the other teachers have not followed up his valuable initiative.

The parents themselves speak very favourably of their participation in extra-curricular activities. And they have, of course, reason to do so. Take, for instance, the father of Lenya Norkizov, a pupil in the fifth form of the Golitsyno secondary school. Lenya's work was weak, and his conduct not particularly good. S. A. Norkizov had taken part in the storming of Berlin in 1945. He gave a talk about it which made a big impression on all the children, including also Lenya. He began to respect his father's authority, and his work and conduct improved.

The Soviet family and school share the same task—to rear and educate all-round, highly developed, active and conscious builders of communism. It is therefore the teacher's duty not merely to maintain contact with parents, but to attract them into extensive participation in the whole life of the school.

WHEN A CLUB TAKES THE INITIATIVE

BY T. KORMILITSYNA

(*Rabotnitsa*, 1953, no. 9, p. 24)

DURING the lunch-hour break Kirillina, one of the workers, went up to Androsova, the controller of assembly shop no. 2. Androsova was known for her interest in welfare work, and so Kirillina told her about her difficulties: her 13-year old son, Slava, had begun to do badly at school. He was not doing his homework properly and there was nobody at home to keep an eye on him, since his mother was away at work all day.

'I thought I'd come and discuss it with you, Maria Nikolaevna; I know you take a lot of interest in the children and do a great deal of work for them in the club. If only you could think of something for children like my Slava!'

Androsova thought for a moment.

'You don't just want advice,' she said. 'What you need is help. I'll have a word with the factory committee.'

She found the chairman of the factory committee, Eryomin, busy talking to a young worker. When he had finished, he turned to Androsova:

'You again, no doubt wanting me to do something or other for the children?' he said.

Maria Nikolaevna told him about Kirillina.

'Yes, it's an important problem,' Eryomin agreed. 'I've had women coming to me too with the same trouble. Perhaps we ought to find a special room where the children could do their homework, but I don't know where we could accommodate them.'

'Where?' Androsova repeated, warming up to the subject. 'In the club, of course!'

And that was how the study room for children came to be opened in the club of watch factory no. 1 last year.

*

It is cosy, light and quiet in the room; there is a rustle of exercise books; children's heads are inclined over the table. A dark-eyed little boy is fixedly looking in front of him trying to think very hard, and wrinkling his forehead with the effort. A teacher sits at a separate table. She is carefully watching the boy and when she sees that his efforts are proving fruitless, calls him up to her.

'What don't you understand?' she whispers. 'Let me see the problem.'

The study room for the workers' children at watch factory no. 1 is open all day long. Not only children who have nobody to look after them at home or are backward at school come here. Valerik Romanov, for instance, does well at school, but he too comes here to do his homework: it is easier to do your problems and to learn your rules of grammar in the quiet atmosphere of the cosy room where there is always a teacher who can explain anything you don't understand.

The club director, Ekaterina Ivanovna Toropchenko, and club committee member Maria Nikolaevna Androsova take great care that the children should do their homework properly.

One day Androsova went into machine shop no. 1 where Kirillina was working.

'Why does Slava no longer come to do his homework?' she asked her.

'I'm very grateful to you,' was Kirillina's embarrassed reply. 'My Slava's alright now—even brought home a "four" yesterday.'

'And do you want him to get out of hand again, left like that without supervision?' Maria Nikolaevna retorted. 'Send him tomorrow without fail; it's best for him to do his homework in the club.'

And Slava started coming again. Androsova met him in the vestibule of the club, sat him down on a sofa and asked him how he spent his time after school until his mother came home from work.

'You can come to the club whenever you like, not just to do your homework,' she said. 'You can do your drawing and modelling here as well.'

School examinations drew near, and the children were busy revising for them. The workers now tried to go past the children's room as quietly as possible, and if somebody dared to raise his voice, he was at once reminded:

'Quiet, the kids are working!'

The club workers felt for each of the children: they were pleased over every examination passed by Alla, every good mark received by Vasya Arkhangelsky.

Eryomin, the factory committee chairman, would ring up and ask: 'Well, how're your kids getting on?'

Ekaterina Ivanovna Toropchenko knew at once what he meant. 'So far so good,' she would answer, sometimes adding that she was a bit worried about Sveta, or Gena.

And then the examination worries were all over. The children solemnly brought their reports to the club, and the club workers looked at their marks as strictly as any father would. Sometimes one would hear remarks such as: 'You could do better still you know; we'll help you to get a "five" next year.'

But Ekaterina Ivanovna was pleased with them. 'Good work!' she said. 'You've done very well. Congratulations! We'll have some prizes for those with the best results.'

Slava, Valerik, Alla and many of the other children left the club with large, neatly tied parcels—the prizes they had received for good work.

The children do not just do their homework in the club of watch factory no. 1. They have interesting talks to listen to, they sing in a choir, learn to recite, and give their own matinée performances which they thoroughly enjoy.

After the examinations were over the children of the factory workers went off to their pioneer camps where they had a good holiday. Now they are back at school. And once again the study room of the club offers its hospitality to the children. The mothers working at watch factory no. 1 do not have to worry about them: they know that their children will do their homework in time, and spend their leisure hours sensibly.

HELP FOR SCHOOLS FROM LENINGRAD ENTERPRISES

BY A 'TRUD' CORRESPONDENT

(*Trud*, Aug. 19, 1948)

IN less than two weeks now the new school year will be beginning. On September 1, half a million pupils in Leningrad city and province will go back to school, and more than 50,000 children will sit at school desks for the first time in their lives.

In Leningrad factories, mills, institutes and establishments have 'adopted' schools and are actively helping them in their everyday work. It was felt that their experience was bound to be of great interest to others, and a meeting was, therefore, arranged by the trade union official for Leningrad city and province, and held in the Palace of Culture [1] on Aug. 16. The meeting was attended by the province committee and by the chairmen of the district committees of the primary and secondary school teachers' union, the editors of the newspaper *Trud*, representatives from 'patron' organisations, and heads of schools. The subject under discussion was the new school year and the necessary preparations for it. Below we publish excerpts from some of the speeches made at the meeting.

A ROOM FOR FIRST-FORM PUPILS

(*From the speech made by Ya. Suser, shop foreman in the 'Progress' factory and chairman of the cultural commission of the factory committee.*)

Our trade union branch is always in contact with schools nos. 138 and 142 in the Kalinin district. More than 270 children of workers from our factory attend these schools. We keep a constant watch on

[1] A large club-house in Leningrad, run by the trade unions.

the progress and conduct of these children and, where necessary, come to their aid. The overwhelming majority of boys and girls are doing well, but I am sorry to say that 19 of our workers' children are having to sit their examinations again this autumn.[1] What did the factory committee's cultural commission do? We sent these children to pioneer camps in the first shift so as to give them time to gather strength and to prepare themselves for their examinations. At present they are all attending courses organised for them by the school and, all things considered, they should be able to pass their examinations and move up into the next form. We are looking over their work every day.

The schools are quite ready for the new year. Repairs have been finished, and they've made a really good job of them. Everything is shining white and in perfect order. The cultural commission has helped to list all boys and girls starting school this year. We visited all the homes and hostels of our factory workers, and discovered another ten girls and seven boys who ought to start school this year. We have decided to furnish a special room in our factory where the smallest of the children can be looked after when they come out of school.

THE 'PATRONS' HELPED

(From the speech made by A. Kudryasheva, deputy headmistress, school no. 341, Volodarsky district.)

There are strong ties of friendship between our school and the Thälmann works. The workers' attitude to the school is one of exceptional care and attention, and their concern for all the needs of the children is moving to see. At the beginning of the summer when the children were only just going off to their pioneer camps, our 'patrons' helped us to repair the school building. In July the repairs had already been finished and the school was given an 'excellent' grading by the government commission.

The 'patrons' do not confine themselves to our economic needs. They are also interested in the teaching process and are helping us to bring up conscious builders of the communist society. Old workers often give talks at the school telling the children about the joyless and hard life they used to live before the revolution. The works organises excursions for the schoolchildren, invites them to social evenings and

[1] Children who fail their annual school examinations in May can in many cases take them again in the following autumn, before the beginning of the new school year.

concerts and gives encouragement to outstanding pupils. None of our pupils have left school early, and no little merit for this belongs to our 'patrons'. Last year a sixth-form pupil, Tamara Smirnova, decided to leave school due to financial difficulties at home. But the trade union helped to support the family, and Tamara has now successfully moved up into the seventh form. One could mention many other examples of this kind. . . .

CHOOSING A CAREER

BY V. KOCHETOV[1]

(*Literaturnaya Gazeta*, Sept. 7, 1954)

On Aug. 19 of this year, *Literaturnaya Gazeta* published an open letter sent in by one of its readers, printing worker A. Chirikovsky, from the city of Borisov[2]. The letter was addressed to the writer V. Kochetov. Chirikovsky's son finished secondary school this spring. Together with tens of thousands like them, his parents started to discuss their son's future career seriously with him. In the course of this discussion they discovered that the boy had acquired a wrong outlook: he felt ashamed to go into industry and to be a worker at the bench. Worried by this outlook of his son's, Chirikovsky wrote to the author of *The Zhurbins*, asking him to help parents and young people to find out how a Soviet boy could come to show such contempt for physical labour—a contempt which is alien to our society.

Today we publish Kochetov's reply to this letter which was entitled 'We Are Waiting for a Heartening Word from You'.

Dear Comrade Chirikovsky,

First of all, allow me to say how deeply I respect you for the stand you have taken with regard to your son's future. . . .

Your letter did not come as a surprise at all. If you visit the long-distance telephone exchange of our city of Borisov any day during the second half of August you will find that a considerable proportion of the telephone conversations centre on the successes or failures of sons and daughters, on whether they have passed the entrance examinations for an institute and been accepted.

I mention the city of Borisov with such confidence because I think that it is in no way different from our other towns in this respect; and

[1] V. Kochetov is a famous Soviet writer. His novel, *The Zhurbins*, describes three generations of a working class family, with a tradition of shipbuilding, in Leningrad.

[2] A small town in the Belorussian Republic.

not all the parents (by far!) in these other towns would have acted as you did. Oh no, these parents plan to get their children into institutes *at all costs*; it must be an institute—which, does not matter. You can hear their frenzied voices appealing to all kinds of 'influential' friends, acquaintances and half-acquaintances hundreds of miles away: 'Get Borya in!', 'do something for Mitya!', 'take pity on Tamara!'.

The number of boys and girls who finished ten-year school this year was far greater than that which could possibly be accepted by the higher educational institutions. And surely that is only natural in a country where education has such tremendous scope—a country where *universal secondary education* is being introduced. And does every Soviet citizen have to be an engineer, a designer, a doctor or a teacher? I am told that there are almost 10,000 different professions and trades in the Soviet Union. The overwhelming majority of these can be mastered without a higher educational institution. Who is going to drive engines, smelt steel, make clothes for the Soviet people, grow corn for them and build their houses and cities—who will supply those necessities of life without which life itself is impossible, if all our Mityas, Tamaras and Victors are going to be doctors and teachers?

Some parents evade this problem altogether: 'Someone or other will supply all that,' they say. 'Others, but not our Mitya or Tamara!' What is so surprising is that very many of these parents themselves started life without any institutes. Twenty or twenty-five years ago these same fathers and mothers worked at fitters' benches and textile machines, as dockers in the ports, ploughed and sowed on the land and sang wonderful songs about blacksmiths forging the keys of happiness. And today they have suddenly taken fright that their children too might have to work at benches and machines, and to plough and sow.

Then there are those parents who send their children, as soon as they can walk and talk, to the 'groups' which still survive today, where they are looked after by age-old governesses who still remember a bit of French mixed with down-town Russian. Later the children are sent to 'English' schools where instruction is given in a foreign language—irrespective of whether the child has a flair for the English language or not.

You ask me why it is that some fathers and mothers tremble at the thought that their son or daughter might, for some reason or other, fail to enter an institute on finishing secondary school and might have to go out to work. 'Where has this attitude come from?' you ask. 'Who has sown these seeds of contempt for physical labour in the hearts of our boys and girls?'

It is a justifiable question and I can understand your asking it. You, no doubt, recalled the beginning of your own working life. As far as I could gather, that was already after the Soviet régime had come to power, about 1923. So the way lay open before you already then and you could have gone to an institute, couldn't you. But you went your own way, following your own aspirations, and became a compositor. I am sure that most of us who are between forty and fifty years old today chose our way of life according to our aspirations. We too could have gone on to a higher educational institution on leaving school. But things turned out different for many of us. The country needed young doctors, engineers and teachers, and many of us went to study in institutes. But at the same time the country also needed young turners and tractor drivers, and some of us went to work at the bench or to drive tractors. We went gladly, ready for this kind of work. Our parents despised governesses, despised idleness in every shape or form; they believed in labour—the labour of the worker and of the engineer, of the tractor driver and the teacher; they believed that labour develops and forms a man's personality. And we have inherited this sacred faith in the power of labour from our fathers and mothers. How many of us went into the factories, mills and construction works at that time, during the years of the first five-year plan!

We did not, of course, all remain workers at the bench. What has become of the comrades with whom we used to hurry to the factory gates in the mornings? One has become the chief engineer of a large factory, while another has remained a worker at the bench. But what is he, this worker at the bench? He is a most highly skilled moulder, a very great expert at his trade who lectures in higher educational institutions. Others again have become agricultural specialists, actors or generals.

All roads lie open before us. If it is your dream to be an inventor, you can be one. If you feel a longing to cure people and to fight for better health, you can be a doctor. You can be an actor, an artist or a composer, if you are willing to devote your whole life and everything that is best in you to the career of your choice.

No, my dear young friend: first of all you must find out what you want to be, what your vocation is. Some of you, spoilt by your parents, rely on your father's acquaintances (through whose help a 'two' can be changed into a redeeming 'three'), make your way through the school, graduate from it according to plan, enter an institute according to plan, and supply the country with qualified specialists of the most mediocre kind.

Some of you, I am sure, choose your career from the handbook for candidates for higher educational institutions. Some of you, for instance, probably decide on the mining institute only because it gives grants to students even if they receive a 'three', the agricultural institute only because the vice-principal there is a cousin of your mother's, or the institute of planning and economics simply because you failed the entrance examinations to all the other institutes.

A life which begins with such an unscrupulous attitude and with such indifference towards the future, often continues in that same dull world of odious and dismal mediocrity where people do not love their work and do not therefore find any satisfaction or joy in it. It is merely a duty, a job which provides you with an existence—that is all it means to you. And you cannot give anyone else any pleasure either. I know a working woman who was left with three children fifteen years ago when she lost her husband. Life was very difficult for her, but she made it possible for all three children to finish secondary school and all three, two sons and a daughter, went on to institutes. I cannot say anything against the sons. They became reasonably good engineers. But the daughter! She studied at a medical institute and is now a doctor. But she does not love her work and is no good at dealing with people. Ever since she was a child she has loved sewing. And today too she is better as a needlewoman than as a doctor. She would have made a wonderful craftsman. And why didn't she? Because mummy made her enter the medical institute, mummy insisted that her little girl must have a higher education and become a doctor.

It is a wonderful thing for a man to long for knowledge and education. And our network of higher educational institutions is very wide indeed and can satisfy this longing for millions of young boys and girls. But a higher education is not only acquired through a diploma; it means more than that. Surely our famous turners and steel smelters, who are training the best of the workers in the people's democracies and who give lectures to engineers, have higher educational status in their own particular trade.

Why is it, Comrade Chirikovsky, that some parents are nevertheless afraid to let their children work, and that children too have begun to show contempt for those careers which entail physical labour?

We are all of us to blame: you and I, millions of parents, hundreds of writers and thousands of artists, our newspapers and magazines, the wireless, the cinema, the theatre and the school.

We have been carried away by the fact that all roads really lie open to the young people of our country, carried away to such an extent that we have *only* extolled those professions which could be acquired through a higher educational institution, and have waxed enthusiastic about families where *all* the children have studied in institutes. We have repeatedly said that the difference between physical and mental labour would vanish in the communist society towards which we are moving; but our view of this process has been onesided, for we thought that physical labour would be almost entirely replaced by mental labour.

This is how many people argue: thanks to the mighty technical progress made by our country, unskilled work, which on the whole requires physical energy alone, is disappearing more and more with every year. Thus, for instance, we no longer have smiths with their sledge hammers at the factories, or people carting bricks on 'buggies' at building sites; the sledge driver and the pony putters have disappeared from the mines, and so forth. All that is quite true. But will there ever be a time when the labour now done by the worker will disappear altogether? I do not think so. His labour will be highly mechanised, but it will still exist.

We have been in a hurry to exclude the worker's labour entailing physical energy from our picture of the future, and this is why we have only extolled those professions which entail purely mental labour.

Our school children know all about the labour of outstanding designers and innovators, but they know very little indeed about the labour of those who produce material wealth themselves with their own hands. In our country the noble labour of the worker is not praised and sung in poetry. Where are the novels, stories, poems, films and plays about the working class? They are negligibly few. . . . Literature and art are not doing enough at the moment to help our young people to see and feel the beauty of the Soviet worker's skilful labour.

One of the reasons why it has not been able to do this is that it has gone out of its way to hide the labour of the worker from the eyes of our children. In many families, for instance, the wonderful tradition of handing down a trade from father to son is rarely kept up. And why? Because the sons and daughters do not know anything about their father's and mother's work and never see their parents at the bench. One of the secretaries of a province committee of the party told me recently what had made him become a worker: every day he had taken some food wrapped in a cloth to his father at the factory; every day he had seen the workshop and the machines, had watched his father at work and admired his skill; and he was absolutely certain what he wanted to be—it was his dream to master machines just like his father had done.

Which of our children can boast that he has seen his father fixing a crankshaft to a powerful diesel motor, preparing blades for gigantic turbines or assembling a combine? Institutes hold special 'open door days' to attract children into professions such as engineering, medicine and teaching. But what about 'open door days' in our wonderful factories? They could be held at the Kirov plant in Leningrad, at the Stalin motor works in Moscow, at *Uralmash* in Sverdlovsk and in hundreds of other factories which can fire the children's imagination and help them to choose a career.

During winter and early spring representatives of various institutes visit the senior forms of our schools and arouse the children's interest in the various educational establishments. But factories do not send their representatives . . .

Surely we could do something that would help our children to see more than the factory yard and the awards and medals earned by their parents—to help them also to see what their parents did to earn these awards, and to arrange frequent meetings for children with those workers at the factory who are experts at their trade.

Polytechnical education too would help to make pupils decide to become workers. But unfortunately practical polytechnical teaching does not really exist as yet in our schools. The school does not yet make it possible for the children to handle a hacksaw, a spiral drill or a plane, and to feel the wonderful power in the hands of man as master of his machines. On the contrary, some school teachers are inclined to frighten children by saying that if they, the children, go on getting a 'two' they will have to be sent into industry. People still use such stupid threats as 'you'll just be a shepherd'. The comrades who use this threat in all seriousness obviously know nothing at all about the conditions in which a shepherd works nowadays, and that a man who wants to be a good shepherd today has to take special courses and have a thorough knowledge of his animals; they obviously do not understand that shepherds become Heroes of Socialist Labour and Stalin Prize winners in our country.

We have no 'clean' and 'dirty' professions. Every kind of labour is equally honourable. It is simply a question of the motives of young people for choosing one or other profession. Some have clear, bright and honest motives. The motives of others are doubtful, determined by calculations about 'advantages' and 'disadvantages' of the various professions. You are quite right, Comrade Chirikovsky, we ought all to join forces in order to expose and destroy the myth you speak of that mental 'easy labour' has special advantages over physical 'heavy abour'. My happiest years, for instance, were spent as an ordinary worker at a factory. It was at the factory that I first learnt to know comradeship and friendship, and that I first felt the strength of the community and the nobility and beauty of working class people.

Please forgive me, Comrade Chirikovsky. You asked for a brief note, and I see that it has turned out a long one. But, despite its length, it still leaves a great deal of fundamental importance to be said in connection with the serious problem which you raised in your letter.

2. LEISURE

VOVA SEES A FILM

BY S. VESELOV

(*Komsomolskaya Pravda*, Feb. 13, 1949)

A FILM arrived at the *Dawn* cinema. It came together with a small grey piece of paper with the prosaic name of invoice. The reel was put into the projecting room, the invoice stayed in the hands of the cinema manager. The latter ran his eye down the invoice and stopped only at two points: the date by which the film must be returned and the hiring fee. He speedily underlined these points with a finger nail carefully allowed to grow long for this purpose. The other points (including instructions that the film should not be shown to children under 14) remained unnoticed, and the invoice, as a dull accompaniment of the film, was put away in a grey folder.

We thought that the point about not allowing children under 14 to see the film would probably be observed. But what we were to see later made us reproach ourselves for reaching such a hasty conclusion.

The hour at which the film was to begin drew near. The manager emerged from his office like a commander leaving his trench at the beginning of the battle, and his leather coat could be seen appearing here and there about the cinema, always ready to defend that sector where the threat was greatest.

The ticket collector had already taken up her position, an expression of severe incorruptibility on her face, and the usherettes too were at their places. The girl at the ticket office was already there threatening visitors from her box office window as if from a pill-box, and brandishing an enormous pair of scissors. The approaches to the cinema were covered by two guardians of the peace: a sergeant-major and a sergeant of the police force.

VOVA SEES A FILM

No, I thought as I walked up to the box office, nobody unauthorised will get into the cinema.

I had already bought my ticket when I noticed a little boy behind me wearing a rabbit jacket and a cap of the same material which had slid down over his eyes. He must have hidden behind me and managed to get past the policeman, I thought. But his triumph will be shortlived: he has still to get past the severe girl at the ticket office.

I learnt later that the little boy in the rabbit jacket was Vova N., a first-year pupil at the school next to the Tretyakov Gallery. Vova is very small for his age and, although he has already been going to school for half a year, he still looks like a kindergarten-age child. In the kindergarten already Vova had been given the nickname of 'chick' because he was so small. And, as often happens, the nickname had stuck to him when he went on to school. At drill Vova stands at the very left of the line. He learns well, is loyal to his friends and therefore respected by the form which good-naturedly calls him 'chick'; and this nickname even has a protective ring about it when it comes from those on the right-hand side of the line.

Vova shifted his cap back from his eyes, stood on his toes and put three rubles on to the counter.

'One please,' he tried to say in a bass voice.

The bass voice did not come off, but the girl nevertheless took his money and gave him a ticket.

I felt discouraged, Vova was triumphant. Quickly he walked past the policemen, casting them a somewhat sly glance out of the corner of his eyes.

Never mind, I calmed myself as I followed Vova into the foyer, he still has to get past the ticket collector. Vova lifted both his hands to the door handle and opened the door with some difficulty; then he set his cap aright and, with an independent air, handed his ticket to the collector. The woman with the incorruptible expression tore off her half and returned the other to Vova.

All the same he won't get in, I thought. There are still the usherettes and the manager. But the usherettes were showing people to their seats and had no time for Vova, while the manager was so busy instructing someone to 'turn on the ventilator' that he did not notice Vova although he slipped past under his very nose.

Slowly the lights went down. I was sitting next to Vova. A ray of light from the projection room was thrown on to the screen and we saw the first title. Vova spelt it our aloud: *An Indian Tomb*. The pictures of famous architecture and of Indian nature somehow managed to reconcile the adult viewer to the banal and utterly primitive theme of the film. But I could not reconcile myself to the fact that I was sitting next to a seven-year old who was spending one and a half hours watching all sorts of murders, scenes of jealousy and other chilling horrors, made up according to Hollywood recipes.

The lights went up again, and I saw my young neighbour looking upset and pale. I felt sincerely sorry for 'chick' Vova. The audience began to leave, and it was only now that I noticed that a good half consisted of schoolchildren.

I went up to the manager.

'Do you know that half your audience consists of children?' I asked him.

'Come now, not half surely, a third perhaps,' he answered.

'But why do you let them in at all?'

'It's difficult; we'd be the only cinema—all the other cinemas let them in; we're no worse than they are, anyway.'

Maybe there was some sort of peculiar logic—manager's logic—in this argument. But nevertheless the fact remains that on that day schoolchildren saw *Floria Tosca* at the *Express* cinema, *The Venetian's Travels* at the *Udarnik*, and *Elysian Nights* in the Kalinin and Krupskaya clubs, the club of the worsteds clothing factory and at other places—all at afternoon sessions.

And I do not want the *Moscow*, *Central* and *Screen of Life* cinemas or the club managers at the watch factory and the Babaev Moscow clothing factory no. 5 to feel pleased at having passed unnoticed just because I have not mentioned them specifically. The cultural establishments entrusted to them also show films to children which are not intended for them.

In our country we are concerned to give children and adolescents a harmonious upbringing. 'Chick' Vova could be protected from harmful films if policemen, girls at the ticket office, usherettes and managers started to care about him, if cinemas organised a repertoire of Sunday film shows at which the teachers and pioneer leaders of local schools were on duty, if Vova's parents knew about the sort of film their son saw with the three rubles they had given him, if the corresponding authorities took a firmer line with those cinema and club managers who are willing to use any method to make things pay, if—there are many more measures that could be taken. The most important thing is that they should be taken quickly. For while we are enumerating and discussing them, somewhere in a cinema a small boy in a rabbit jacket is going past the usherettes with a stony expression on his face, to see a film that is not intended for him.

FILM SHOWS FOR CHILDREN

BY YU. FILANOVSKY

(*Kulturno-Prosvetitelnaya Rabota*, 1955, no. 3, p. 15)

IN the summer of 1954 the Arzamass province department of culture received a letter from Nikolai Fyodorovich Kirsanov, headmaster of the Medyany village secondary school. Kirsanov was applying for a permanent projector for his school, to enable him to give regular film shows for his pupils and teachers.

Why did he write the letter? Let Nikolai Fyodorovich tell us himself....

*

For a number of years now I have seen our schoolchildren attending the film shows at the club. Unfortunately, our village does not always arrange special children's matinées. Towards evening the children's thoughts are already at the club waiting for the film to begin. Children who go to school in the second shift have sometimes left early from the last lesson in order to get to the film show in time. In our school the last lesson of the second shift finishes at eight p.m.; the film shows in the club usually begin at eight o'clock too. These shows are also frequented by young boys and girls who are not from the school, and some of them are badly brought up and rough. Our children have picked up vulgar couplets and dirty songs from these people at the club.

Film shows at the club do not start punctually, and sometimes drag on until midnight, and so the children spend three or four hours, sometimes even longer, at the cinema. This is bad for them, keeps them from doing their homework and affects their general progress at school.

Children do not always know which films are wholesome and suitable for them. Films can sometimes be unsuitable, if not harmful for the children. At the ages of 14 and 15 they are usually anxious to go to film shows together with adults, and as a result they frequently see films which ought not to be shown to adolescents.

All this made me try to find a new form of cinema service for children, and I decided to organise regular film shows for them in the school itself.

I obtained a permanent projector, and we decided to use the largest of our class-rooms as the cinema. In order to conform to the fire regulations in our 'cinema', we obtained a special fire extinguisher. A hole was made in the wall, and this served as projection room.

. . . Those who come to school in the first shift see the films in the afternoon after their lessons are over, those in the second shift see them in the evening. Our teachers' council decided that the children should see the films together with their form teacher. A rota of teachers to be on duty during the film shows was worked out, and the children are taught how to conduct themselves in the hall. . . .

Formerly the children used to rush away to the club if a film was to be shown there, afraid that it would start 'without them'. Now every child knows that the show will start on time and that everyone with a ticket will go in an organised manner to see it. These film shows have had the very important result of keeping the children away from the bad influence of the street. For our pupils the street now no longer means hanging around the club waiting for the film to begin; for them the street means skiing, skating and excursions.

The school gives two film shows a week. In addition special shows for pupils from the senior forms are put on on Sundays. I think that the pupils from the junior forms, who can see films at school twice a week, ought to spend their Sundays in the open air.

We are intending to increase our number of film shows to 12 per month in future. . . .

DO NOT PASS BY, COMRADE!

BY L. PANTELEYEV

(*Literaturnaya Gazeta*, Jan. 26, 1954)

A nine-year old boy had read a book about the civil war. 'Did you understand it all?' I asked him.

'Yes,' he replied. 'There were only two words I didn't know: what's an SR [1] and what does *besprizorny* [2] mean?'

One can of course deplore the fact that a third-year pupil should have so little general knowledge. But I preferred to be pleased. For it is indeed remarkable that the word '*besprizorny*', which was in such current usage at one time, should have become a strange and unknown word to our children, just as strange as 'SR' or 'Nepman'. What a terrible evil this child vagrancy was—a real danger and a terrible calamity for our young republic. As in other struggles, so here too the people were victorious. *Besprizornost* has long ceased to exist. We have finished with it for ever.

But I should here like to dwell on another, very serious, phenomenon, different from *besprizornost*: on what is given the vague and loose term of child neglect.[3] One cannot but be worried about this phenomenon. A battle is being waged against it daily, but for some reason we only speak about it in hushed voices. And this is quite wrong: child neglect is not just the figment of someone's imagination; it is a very real evil which leads both children and adults into trouble.

I am referring to those children who, for some reason or other, have got out of hand, have 'gone wrong'. The problem has become particularly acute since the end of the war because of the many fatherless children. But that is not the only reason. The children's conduct can also be derived from the fact that many parents are

[1] Short for Socialist Revolutionary.

[2] *Besprizornye* was the name given to the homeless waifs mentioned on p. 43 which roamed the country during the twenties.

[3] *Beznadzornost*.

extremely busy, that the educational work carried on in schools is rather muddled, and that children do not always get enough really sympathetic attention. And you and I, my dear reader, must share the blame for all this.

Komsomol, trade unions, permanent commissions,[1] police, people connected with house managements, parents' committees in schools —all these should take part in the battle against child neglect.

It would be untrue to say that none of these organisations are doing anything. An organisation consists of people, and where the people are lively and full of energy and initiative, the work too is alive. But the trouble is that there is very often no proper contact between all these institutions and organisations.

The police have to deal with the consequences of child neglect continually every day, and they are more or less systematic in their struggle against it.

Recently police officer Kruglov brought three little boys into the children's room of one of the Leningrad police stations.

This is what had happened: in broad daylight Oleg Nozhenko, Yury Martynov and Vladimir Miloserdov, sixth-form pupils [aged twelve to thirteen] from school no. 211, had set out to climb the spire of the Kazan Cathedral. Having discovered the children 'in a place not designed for ambulation', the police officer had given a few short blasts on his whistle; but the boys had either not heard him or had decided not to take any notice; at any rate they had proceeded to climb higher still.

Willy-nilly the officer had had to play the role of rock-climber—not usually part of his duties—and half an hour later the offenders were standing before the inspector at the children's room.

I wonder, incidentally, whether many people know about these children's rooms?

Children's rooms were opened at city police stations ten years ago. Their task is to fight against child neglect or, to be more exact, against the consequences of child neglect. The young 'offender' who finds himself in one of these rooms often does not even realise that he is at the police station and that the woman talking with him, who looks rather like a school mistress, is an inspector and a member of the police force. And the whole atmosphere in the children's room is such that the children will not be frightened; there are no bars, railings or creaking locks. In fact the room looks more like that of a headmaster or director of studies at school. . . .

[1] See footnote 1, p. 13 above.

Having got the three young 'rock-climbers' down from the cathedral spire, police officer Kruglov took them to the children's room. The inspector drew up a statement of the case, the children were spoken to, their parents were called and the school was informed.

In this case these measures were considered sufficient. But 'this case' is not among the worst with which the inspector has to deal. As a rule it is not enough merely to talk to the offender and to register the facts. The child may have a good heart-to-heart talk with the inspector and shed sincere and burning tears of repentance, but one must not forget that it leaves the children's room again after that and continues to play in the street. What guarantee have we that it will not be brought back again by the police a month or a week later? Are we to sit and wait for the child to come back?

It is not enough for the inspector to prepare himself for this further meeting; he must, if possible, try to *prevent* it.

A great deal is required to make this possible: the inspectors must go to the school and talk with the form master, take an interest in the child's home conditions, speak with its parents, visit the city education department and the child commission of the district soviet, see that a delapidated playground at a neighbouring block of flats is repaired, and visit the cinemas where young boys hang about in the evenings.

And sometimes they do try to do all these things. But they have not got the personnel. However hard they try, they cannot possibly get everything done. As a rule, the inspector is not a teacher, i.e., he has no special educational training, and he needs help. Unfortunately the inspector of a children's room gets no help from people with special qualifications or with technical skill. They are even without unskilled help; in fact they get no help at all—skilled or unskilled.

Once again I should like to recall the far-off twenties when our country was struggling against *besprizornost*. What a hard and passionate struggle that was and how many glorious names were connected with it: Dzerzhinsky,[1] Krupskaya, Gorky, Mayakovsky, Makarenko and Gaidar.[2] Wide sections of the public were taking an active part in this struggle and there are many unnamed komsomol heroes who distinguished themselves in this field.

Life today is very different, and the conditions of the twenties have been left far behind. But we must not leave behind our good

[1] Dzerzhinsky was a prominent revolutionary. He was *inter alia* interested in problems of education, and the famous children's colony run by Makarenko was named after him.

[2] Gaidar (1904–41) was a famous writer of children's books.

traditions, and we should ask ourselves what part the public is playing today in the complex work entailed in the upbringing of children. We cannot reconcile ourselves to the fact that the komsomol organisation does hardly anything at all to eliminate child neglect.

I do not want the komsomol comrades to take offence or to try to make excuses. I know that the central, province and city committees of the komsomol arrange conferences from time to time which pass unimpeachable resolutions about child neglect. But they put so little *heart* into this work at present and forget about it all again so quickly, while their circulars and decisions lie there gathering dust.

Last year the Leningrad city committee of the komsomol passed a very good resolution: it decided to give some real help to the police, and to attach 25 komsomol activists to each children's room. Students from the Herzen Institute of Education were attached to the room where Comrade Krayushkina is working. What could be better, you would think, than to use future teachers for this work! And, apart from everything else, what wonderful experience for them!

But what happened? A few girls from the institute did in fact turn up at the children's room. They were instructed to go to the *Saturn* cinema, a place which is greatly frequented in the evenings by young hooligans. The girls went to the *Saturn*, but never returned to the children's room.

I spoke with the secretary of the institute's komsomol committee, L. Dvoyeglazova.

'Yes, it's perfectly true,' she admitted with a sigh. 'We're to blame for having neglected this work.'

I do not want to excuse the students, but for the sake of fairness it must be said that 'this work' has not only been neglected by future teachers but also by those who are already active in the teaching profession today. The workers of children's rooms have every right to reproach the school severely in this matter.

A twelve-year old lad is hanging about the cash desk of the *Molodyozhny* cinema. With an affected and cowardly smile, he holds out a hand, pleading:

'Please uncle, give me a tanner [1] for a ticket!'

There are many kind uncles in the queue. How often, Comrade reader, do we show kindness of this sort which really amounts to nothing more than *indifference*!

The boy gets his tanner. He now has enough money for his ticket, an 'eskimo' chocolate ice-cream, a cake and some aerated water with a triple portion of fruit syrup.

[1] Literally 'a ten-kopek piece'.

The next day finds him by the cash desk once again.

'Please uncle——,' he chants in the dull voice of a professional beggar.

At last a *really* kind uncle, someone who really loves children, firmly took Yura B. by the hand and went off to the children's room with him.

Yura said that he was in the seventh form at school. His mother was called. She confirmed Yura's statement, and told the inspector at what school he was. The director of studies was rung up and some surprising things came to light: Yura B. passed his examinations in the spring of last year and had in fact been moved up into the seventh form. But he had never once been back to school since then, having stayed absent the entire first term and the beginning of the second; but neither the school—the headmaster, the director of studies and the form master—nor Yura's mother had thought it necessary to take any interest at all in where he was and how he was spending his time.

Eleven-year old Yurik V. has been in the first form for the last four (yes, four!) years now, and is once again having to stay down. Perhaps he is in some way lazy or stupid? No, all the teachers agree that he is a gifted and promising child. Then what is the matter? The school maintains that the parents are to blame.

It is true that Yurik has bad parents. One does not even want to use the word 'parent' when referring to such people. His father is a drunkard, his stepmother illtreats him. The child is badly clothed and often not properly fed. How can he be expected to do well at school under such conditions?

But how could the boy be allowed to remain in such a situation? The school to which Yurik V. has been going for the past four years must know *why* he stays absent. And of course they do know. But they may even be glad to be rid of one of their 'difficult' children—saves a lot of trouble!

Anyway, they can always put the blame on the home, and this, I should add, is very often done. As a rule, the school blames the parents if the children behave badly.

Of course very often the blame is not shifted from the guilty to the innocent, but from one guilty party to the other. There are many so-called unsatisfactory families, i.e., families which cannot or will not give their children a good upbringing. But is that any excuse? The family is unsatisfactory, the child is being brought up badly: who if not the teacher should interfere and help, teaching and prompting the parents? But as a rule these families are only visited by officials from the children's rooms who more often than not come when it is already too late, or almost too late.

I do not want to cast any aspersions on our many millions of teachers. I know very well that we have excellent and talented teachers, whole teaching staffs, who take a vital interest in the fate of *every* child entrusted to their care, no matter how 'difficult'. But it is unfortunately a fact that some of our schools try to rid themselves of the 'difficult' children.

We will find it very hard to eliminate child neglect until our schools learn to arrange their educational work properly without making distinctions in their attitude to the 'easy' and 'difficult' children, until the komsomol (and in particular its school branches) arouse themselves from their state of semi-somnolence and, finally, until we make pioneer meetings less boring.

Our chief concern should be to *prevent* child neglect. But what if the school has already made mistakes, the pioneer organisation has failed to take action, the komsomol has not helped—and the child finds itself under the influence of the street? Who is to take the responsibility then?

As I have already said, there are many people who are responsible, too many perhaps; and precisely for this reason you do not know whom to blame at all.

I feel that those organisations which, as it were, play a central and co-ordinating part in the whole struggle against child neglect, should intensify their work. Moreover, there is no need to find or to set up a central organisation of this kind. On paper it has already existed for a long time. As far back as 1942, orphan commissions were formed and attached to the city soviets. It is true that these commissions still exist today though their functions are somewhat broader now and they no longer deal solely with orphans. But the trouble is that almost all these commissions work badly, are inadequately staffed and unpopular.

I should like to make the following suggestion: it is not enough simply to intensify the work of these commissions; they need to be radically reorganised and their duties defined more precisely; they should have more rights, and representatives from all organisations which might be in any way useful should take part in them. Naturally people should not simply be assigned to work in a commission; they should only be 'assigned' if they *love children and are anxious and able to work with them.* Where a commission is really lively and active, and people do not merely hold meetings but sincerely care about the work entrusted to them, correct methods of work will, I am sure, be found.

We must not forget that the majority of city children still spend their leisure in the courtyard. The police have much less trouble with children from houses where some sort of child activity is organised, where there is a 'red corner', a sports ground or some other, similar, facility.

Commissions acting in conjunction with house managements [1] should form a nucleus around which a permanent and active group of people (not merely one consisting of honorary representatives) could be formed; this group could include teachers from the neighbouring schools, representatives from the various local enterprises, establishments and institutes as well as ordinary inhabitants, such as housewives and old-age pensioners—in short, anyone who loves children could work in one of these groups.

Facilities, such as ordinary children's rooms organised by a house management, good toy centres where toys can be borrowed, volleyball grounds or ice rinks in the yard, and amateur artists' circles mean more to the children in their normal, every-day lives than the most expensive luxury would. And the 'difficult' children need these things most of all.

The situation as regards children's rooms organised by house managements is most unsatisfactory. There are somewhat fewer in Leningrad now than there were before the war. You can, of course, put all this down to the housing shortage. But can we accept any excuse at all in a matter which concerns the vital needs of our children?

I know that there are quite a few people (probably also among those who read this article) who think:

'That's all very well, and I agree with it, but it's nothing to do with me. My Pavlik's a tomboy and doesn't do very well at school; but still, he doesn't go smashing windows or begging, and he's never been in the hands of the police, thank God!'

It is the old outlook which is unfortunately still alive and which says: 'it's no concern of mine' . . . .

Who among us has not adopted a wrong attitude in situations like the following, which appear at first sight to be of trifling significance: you go down the street and see a girl at the corner selling flowers; a nine-year old boy asks a passer-by for a light and then makes some pungent school-boy remarks behind his back. And what do you do? You frown, sigh, wax indignant—and pass by.

Do not pass by, comrade!

[1] *Domupravleniye.* The authority responsible for the administration of a dwelling house or, more often, a block of flats, in cities and industrial settlements.

IN A HOUSE MANAGEMENT

BY N. ANIKIN, MOSCOW CITY

(*Uchitelskaya Gazeta*, April 30, 1954)

IN the evenings the children used to meet in doorways or on the stairs; they would play together, argue and sometimes quarrel with one another. These meetings had a bad reputation: the children would often shock their parents with stories, expressions and bad habits even, picked up from the older children. But how, for instance, was ten-year old Slavik not to start smoking when fifteen-year old Boris, a trade school pupil, himself offered him a cigarette from his own cigarette-case! He just couldn't refuse; they'd laugh at him!

In this way the influence of the 'street' was making itself felt. When people talk about this influence, they usually think of children who have completely gone to the bad—almost like the vagrant children of the twenties. At the meetings on the stairs of block no. 26 there were no such children, but the older ones were nevertheless falling into bad habits more and more, and passing them on to others.

Slavik's mother simply would not believe that her good, obedient boy should have a bad influence on his eight-year old comrade. Others might have a bad influence on Slavik—that was a different matter entirely. But then one day she saw two little friends take turns in puffing at a cigarette-end; one of them—her Slavik—was teaching the other:

'It's only nasty at first—passes off after a bit,' he said.

The little boy frowned but put on a brave face; what else could he do in front of his comrade!

When the children's conduct was discussed at a parents' meeting, Nikolai Vasilevich Kozlov, chairman of the house management's cultural committee, said:

'The children are showing off and trying to impress one another with their daring, falling into bad habits and so forth because they're not being looked after properly. The children living in our block can't find anything serious to occupy them at present because they're not organised; and I think that we should therefore help them to get themselves organised.'

It was decided to form a club for the children. Through the joint efforts of the parents, a basement was cleaned and repaired. But then they were faced with another difficulty: how was the club to be run? After all, a house management has no funds for employing instructors for hobby circles or for any of the other expenses involved.

Comrade Protasov from the Kuibyshev district House of Pioneers found a solution. Comrade Protasov, as leader of the technology circle in the House of Pioneers, is often besieged by young boys wanting to know how to make a kite, mend a clockwork toy and so forth. At a meeting of the sponsoring committee he suggested that a 'skilful hands' circle should be formed.

This was the first and largest circle of the club and included children of all ages, from the very smallest to those in the senior forms. Then, one by one, other hobby circles were started. Many parents came of their own accord and offered their services as instructors in the hobby circles; some others were persuaded by the members of the sponsoring committee to take part in the work—everybody can spare one hour a week. In this way music, sewing and embroidery, 'native language', ballroom dancing, biology, filming and other circles came into being. These are run by musician N. T. Lyakhovsky, dancing mistress S. I. Verderevskaya, cinema operator K. I. Belozerova and others.

There were many applications to join the circles, since more than 500 children live in the area which comes under house management no. 26. Everyone wanted to learn how to operate a film projector, to do fretwork or metal work, assemble simple machines in the 'skilful hands' circle, or grow indoor plants. Gradually all the children became members of the house management club, and the former evening gatherings on staircases and in doorways stopped of their own accord.

During the day the various circles are at work; in the evenings there are films, talks and lectures on the history of Moscow, on literature and on art. And when there are no talks or lectures, the children come just to sit and play draughts and chess, or to talk with their friends.

How about the economic side of the club? The house management workshop supplied us with a few joiners' benches, vices, a planing machine, an electric whetstone, and various hand tools and materials for the technology circle. Many of the things we needed were provided by the inhabitants themselves. The factories in the district also came to our aid:

'We have never been refused anything for the children,' P. E. Sianko, chairman of the house management, told us.

The members of the sponsoring committee made the acquaintance of the directors of some of the factories and institutions in the district and were able to arouse their interest in the useful work they had begun. As a result, the club was given attractive furniture by sailors, a film projector by its 'patron', the Institute of Teaching Methods at the RSFSR Academy of Pedagogical Sciences, as well as a wireless and sports equipment. These contacts have also made it easier to find people to take charge of circles and give talks and lectures, and have given children greater opportunities to meet interesting people such as sailors, outstanding workers from local factories, and artists.

The sponsoring committee established close contact with school parents' committees and with teachers. The committee members helped schools to list all children of school age according to house managements, while the teachers in their turn are helping them towards the right methods in dealing with children.

One day the Naidenovs approached the sponsoring committee with a complaint about their children.

'We realise that our children are doing badly at school because there is nobody at home to look after them,' they said. 'But we can't do anything about it; we work as conductors on the railway and are sometimes away from home for two to three weeks on end. The children won't listen to their grandmother and do their homework carelessly.'

This gave us the idea of opening a 'quiet room' in the club where the children could do their work. The headmaster of school no. 310, Comrade Zobov, told a general meeting how to organise it, and we now have a special room in the club where schoolchildren can do their work. It has teaching appliances for geography, history, physics, chemistry and biology. A parent on duty maintains order. Twice a week it is visited by teachers with whom parents can discuss their various problems of upbringing in the home.

As a rule, the room is used by those who cannot do their work at home for some reason or other. Then there are some children for whom attendance in the room has been made compulsory; these come by decision of teachers, parents' committees of schools or the sponsoring committee of the house management, because, for various reasons, they have nobody to look after them at home. The members of the sponsoring committee estimate that about 30 of these are being catered for.

The backward among the pupils have started to do their homework better and more carefully. The parent on duty does not try to take the place of the teacher; he does not, for instance, go through the children's homework, but merely sees to it that they do it.

There are many interesting things for the children to do in the courtyards belonging to house management no. 26: each yard has its own volley-ball and *gorodki*[1] pitches, sports equipment and a sand-pit for the younger children. All this is run by the parents themselves, with the active help of their children. The house management made some special tools for them, including 20 half-size spades and crow-bars for clearing ice, buckets, wheel-barrows and shovels. Labour has a good influence on the children, and they take greater care of things they have made themselves.

The work of the club did not merely organise the children; it also—and this is just as important—helped parents to tackle problems of upbringing.

[1] A kind of skittles.

A DISTRICT HOUSE OF PIONEERS

BY YU. NOVOZHENOV

(*Molodoi Kommunist*, 1955, no. 2, p. 65)

A READER of our journal, U. Vasileva who is herself a director of a district House of Pioneers (in the city of Dolina, Stanislav province, Ukrainian SSR), has asked us for an article on a House of Pioneers. Below we publish a description of the Novozybkov House of Pioneers in the Bryansk province.

It is a large wooden house, well known to the schoolchildren of Novozybkov. For more than ten years now its welcoming lights have brought in the children in the evenings. Everyone here spends his time on his favourite hobby—planing, sawing, making models, learning to draw, sew, recite, sing, and so forth.

The House of Pioneers was opened in 1936. During the war it was ransacked and destroyed by the occupation forces. It had its second birth in 1945. The house had to be rebuilt and the workrooms to be equipped all over again. The town committee of the komsomol came to its help, and organised a few 'Sundays'. The young boys and girls went to work with a will, for many of them had attended the House of Pioneers themselves before the war. A great deal of work was also done by Afanasii Ivanovich Erokhin, who had been the director of the House of Pioneers for many years. An energetic man and an inexhaustible source of ideas, he had soon arranged interesting and attractive activities. Hobby circles for designing, making model aeroplanes, embroidery, photography, drawing, elocution, dancing, music, etc. were organised. A pioneer lecture room was opened and given the slogan, 'I want to know everything.' Afanasii Ivanovich invited engineers, teachers and agricultural specialists, from the local factory, the pedagogical institute and the agricultural college who gave interesting and varied talks and lectures to the children.

All the circles of the Novozybkov House of Pioneers work in a purposeful manner. Everything here is subordinated to the one aim of helping the school in every possible way with its work of upbringing and teaching, and to inculcate useful working habits and a love of knowledge. The House of Pioneers is also performing another important task in helping pioneer groups to improve their activities. The circles are organised with great care here.

Take for instance the drawing circle. There are 18 people in it, some of them specially gifted children. But, apart from work with these pioneers, the circle also holds seminars for young artists working on pioneer wall newspapers. At these seminars they learn to put together a wall newspaper and to write headlines, and are taught what drawings, kinds of type and ornamentation to use. The young artists acquire a great deal of useful knowledge in this circle.

Good work is also being done by the photographers' circle which is run by A. I. Dzhaly, a fourth-year student in the physics and mathematics faculty of the Novozybkov Pedagogical Institute. The House of Pioneers has a total of seven cameras. This is a modest enough 'stock' and has to be handled sensibly in order to get the maximum use out of it. There are pupils from every school in this circle, and towards the beginning of summer each pioneer group appoints a photographic correspondent who goes on excursions and trips with the other pioneers, and provides the illustrations for the group's album. During the last school year the circle trained 12 young photographers. This year it is training 11.

At the beginning of this school year physical labour was introduced into our schools. This is something new and difficult. It is particularly hard to organise in such a small town as Novozybkov. The schools are still without workshops and equipment, and the House of Pioneers and the town committee of the komsomol are therefore giving special attention to the work of the designers' circle. This circle has been sub-divided into a junior group for third- and fourth-form pupils, and a senior group for pupils in forms five to seven. In the junior group the pioneers are taught elementary work with paper, cardboard and plywood. This group is run by Comrade Petrov, a student of the physics and mathematics faculty at the Pedagogical Institute. He is teaching the children how to use simple tools. Pupils in the senior group are making model aeroplanes and ships, and are taught electrical engineering. The House of Pioneers has also started a group attended by 12 children which will work in the laboratories of the physics and mathematics faculty of the Pedagogical Institute. This group will be led by the dean of the faculty, Comrade Lavrov.

The girls in the embroidery circle are learning to sew, and to do cross stitch and satin-stitch. Their appliqué work, 'Pioneer Summer' and 'Children of the People's Democracies', and their two-colour embroidery, 'Pushkin Themes' were regarded as among the best entries at the province exhibition of children's work. The embroidery circle also has a few women students from the Novozybkov Pedagogical Institute. Soon these girls will be taking charge of school embroidery circles themselves.

Until recently the pioneer meetings in some of the schools of the town used to be dry and uninteresting. There were no gay pioneer songs to be heard at them, no interesting games to be seen. Possibly the children or the pioneer leaders would have liked to make the meetings entertaining but did not know how to. The House of Pioneers came to their help and organised an entertainers' circle. Every school in the town sent two people from each of their fifth, sixth and seventh forms to this circle to learn how to arrange 'pioneer rallies'. A. I. Erokhin himself drew up a plan for one such 'rally'. It included community singing of new songs, dancing, games and relay races. Soon now the 'entertainers' will be able to arrange 'pioneer rallies' and 'break entertainments' in the schools by themselves.

All this work would of course have been unthinkable without close contact with the town committee of the komsomol and the schools. The staff of the House of Pioneers often visit schools, talk with teachers and pioneer leaders, note their needs and requirements and take part in group and detachment meetings.

Apart from this, the House of Pioneers always invites teachers and pioneer leaders to its mass activities. Before its plan of work is approved, it is discussed with pioneer leaders and by the town committee of the komsomol. The House of Pioneers held a conference of primary school teachers on 'Lectures for Children in the Junior Forms'. During this school year there will also be conferences for directors of studies and senior pioneer leaders on problems of organising polytechnical workrooms in schools and on work with hobby circles in the pioneer group. Heads of schools and senior pioneer leaders will hear lectures on 'Pioneer Rooms—The Use of Symbols', and on 'The Importance of Traditions in Pioneer Work'. For form teachers and senior pioneer leaders there will be a lecture on 'Socially Useful Work for Pioneers'.

The House of Pioneers has a good library of books on extracurricular activities for children, and it is used by many teachers and pioneer leaders. It is continually expanding. The director visits the Houses of Pioneers, in Bryansk, Moscow and Bezhitsa, studies their work and notes down anything of interest that he might introduce at home in Novozybkov. He saw, for instance, that Moscow schoolchildren had arranged an exhibition of reproductions from the pictures in the Tretyakov Gallery, and decided to do the same in his House of Pioneers. The leader of the drawing circle, P. A. Chernyshevsky, gave pioneers a detailed account of each picture, how it came to be painted and of the artist who had produced it. And so the pioneers of Novozybkov now know a great deal about the pictures in the Tretyakov Gallery even though they have never been there.

Every year the House of Pioneers arranges a Summer Festival and a Flower Festival, a 'Round the Camp Fire' rally of young tourists, day trips, evenings of 'fairy tales' and 'science made interesting', fancy dress balls and so forth.

The 'I want to know everything' pioneer lecture room has existed for many years and is visited by dozens of children. The short talks, full of interesting facts and accompanied by films, widen the children's horizon and help them in their work at school. The polytechnical lecture room has enjoyed particularly great popularity during the past year. School teachers and lecturers from the institute, agricultural specialists and outstanding industrial workers have given lectures here. A teacher from school no. 5, Comrade Batyuk, gave a talk on 'Making New Plants', and showed the film, *Michurin*;[1] Comrade Stanyakova, a designer, spoke on 'What our Factory Makes for the New Construction Works of the USSR'. Comrade Vysotsky, a member of the all-Union Society for the Dissemination of Political and Scientific Knowledge, gave a talk on 'Science and Religion'.

The House of Pioneers is doing a great deal towards spreading a knowledge of agriculture among the children and helping pioneer leaders and teachers from the villages with their methods of work. The pioneer *aktiv* from the villages is always invited to the various mass events such as the tourists' rally and the Summer and Flower Festivals, and pioneer leaders of village schools attend the seminars. Teachers from these schools often come to the House of Pioneers for advice on various problems.

The pioneers from the villages often visit the Novozybkov House of Pioneers. The latter in its turn organises excursions and trips to collective farms and machine tractor stations for the city children. This year the children visited the Novozybkov MTS, an agricultural experimental station and the Budyonny collective farm.

The House of Pioneers is helped in these undertakings by its wide contacts with various public bodies in the town, with the agricultural college and the all-Union Society for the Dissemination of

[1] See footnote 1, p. 62 above.

Political and Scientific Knowledge. The House of Pioneers also works in close contact with the Pedagogical Institute. . . . The Institute often places its lecture rooms at the disposal of the House of Pioneers and helps to arrange evenings on scientific and technical themes. The students from the Institute do their out-of-school practical work at the House of Pioneers, where they can receive advice on problems of method, etc., and take charge of circles. . . .

As a rule, the children attending the House of Pioneers do well at school, but this does not mean that they are the only ones who can be enrolled in the circles. On the contrary, children who are getting bad marks and violating school discipline also come here.[1] The staff of the House of Pioneers try to teach them love of work, and are always able to find something of interest for them to do. . . .

Soon the children taking part in circles today will go out into life. But they will always remember their native House of Pioneers, where they spent many an interesting hour, which taught them to love and respect labour and helped them to choose their career.

[1] Some Houses of Pioneers apparently make a rule of admitting only pupils who do well at school. This practice is condemned (e.g. *Rabotnitsa*, 1955, no. 8, p. 26), since the other children are considered to stand in greater need of the special attention provided by the Houses.

PIONEERS SPEND THE SUMMER IN THE CITY

An account of comprehensive[1] pioneer groups and detachments working in the schools and dwelling houses of Leningrad

BY A. FILIPPOV, SECRETARY OF THE LENINGRAD CITY COMMITTEE OF THE KOMSOMOL FOR SCHOOLS

(*Komsomolskaya Pravda*, May 27, 1949)

WHILE the annual examinations and tests were still going on in the schools, the party, soviet, trade union and komsomol organisations had already begun on the great work of organising the children's summer holidays. This year 110,000 children —many more than last year—will spend some of their holidays in pioneer camps in the picturesque countryside around Leningrad, on the Karelian Isthmus, on the banks of the Neva and by the Gulf of Finland. In accordance with the resolutions passed at the XI Komsomol Congress,[2] the komsomol organisation of Leningrad is taking steps to improve its work among pioneers and schoolchildren in general this summer. It is trying to make the activities interesting, good for the children's health, in short, to provide a sensible holiday for them. We have estimated that about half the children of school age spend the summer in the city. It is very important that educational and health facilities should be provided for these children.

Our summer activities for children in the city are organised in conjunction with the education departments. Comprehensive pioneer groups catering for children of school age are formed in schools, dwelling houses and district Houses of Pioneers.

In the October district, for instance, eleven such groups are being formed: nine of them attached to schools, one to a group of dwelling

[1] I.e. groups catering for all children of school age, whether members of the pioneer organisation or not.

[2] Held in 1949.

houses, and one to the district House of Pioneers. In school no. 241 the garden has been widened, and a sports ground complete with equipment has already been laid out by the komsomols. The group will be led by the senior pioneer leader Arseneva and by the teacher Nazarova. The programme for the comprehensive group has been discussed at a special meeting of teachers. Apart from these groups, the October district committee of the komsomol and the education department have decided to set up 20 comprehensive detachments in dwelling houses. These detachments will be led jointly by teachers and pioneer leaders.

Comprehensive pioneer groups and detachments are being created in all the districts of Leningrad. As a rule, a group of this kind comprises between 200 and 300 people. A senior pioneer leader is in charge. The group is split up into detachments (about 50 people in each) headed by detachment leaders. Every group has a teacher, a P.T. instructor and a trained nurse.

What will these groups do during the day? Very much the same as the camps outside the town. In the morning there will be the hoisting of the flag, drill and P.T., and this will be followed by the various activities organised for the children. The main task of these groups is to improve the children's health and to give them a sensible holiday. For this reason a great deal of attention will be given to sports, outings and excursions.

Last year the camp at Chaikovsky Street, no. 2, Dzerzhinsky district, did some good work. It organised many interesting outings, excursions and sports. An *aktiv* of parents took part in the work. Another camp is being organised here this year again. A camp is also being opened in the courtyard of a large block on the Troitsky fields which houses the workers on the Neva locks. The courtyard has been equipped with swings, sand-pits and a volley-ball pitch. During the summer the children from this block will make trips to the Pulkovsky heights and to the places where Pushkin lived and worked. The camp also has its own football team.

A great deal of help in equipping playgrounds attached to schools and dwelling houses has been given by the workers in 'patron' enterprises.

But it is not enough merely to equip playgrounds, put in sand-pits, and erect volley-ball poles and a horizontal bar. The children's holidays must be made interesting, meaningful and attractive. The quality and the methods of work used with children during the summer depend on the pioneer leaders, and the city and district committees of the komsomol select them very carefully. The comprehensive groups are run by young teachers and senior pioneer leaders, detachments are run by students, senior pupils and komsomols selected by komsomol factory committees. All nominations of pioneer leaders must be approved by the bureau of the komsomol's district committees. Every group elects a pioneer *aktiv*.

The people who are entrusted with this work are given the same serious training as those who take charge of camps outside the town. The training mainly takes the form of study in the seminar held by the city for senior pioneer leaders, and in the district seminars for detachment leaders. The seminar's curriculum includes courses on the teaching of sports and nature study, and on organising excursions, games and outings in groups and detachments. The Pioneer Palace acts as a centre where experience of work with comprehensive groups and detachments is pooled. It holds special advisory meetings for pioneer leaders, and shows exhibitions of the methods used in organising the children's summer holidays. District Houses of Pioneers are also helping pioneer leaders in this way.

Leningrad is one of our country's important cultural centres. There are scores of museums, parks and gardens for the children to visit, and we intend to make wide use of all of these facilities. In this we have the co-operation of everyone in the city. A decision of the executive committee of the Leningrad city soviet has made entrance to all gardens and parks free to children.

A children's corner has been opened in the Kirov Central Park of Culture and Rest. It has a sports-ground, a swimming pool and a workshop making children's toys. There are many attractive and useful things for children to do in the young nature lovers' club, the aeroplane modelling club and the young sailors' club. These clubs are supervised by experienced teachers and instructors from the Pioneer Palace.

The Kirov Park is used as a centre for mass rallies, walks and competitions for the children. The 'Pioneer Summer' festival for the younger age groups and the fancy dress ball for the senior forms in celebration of the end of the school year are held here. The city will also hold a pioneer camp fire here in honour of the XI Komsomol Congress. In addition there will be a rally of comprehensive pioneer groups devoted to the theme, 'Up and Down my Beloved Country'.

Sports competitions will be held in all the districts of the city. The winners of these competitions will meet in the finals at the third of the traditional city sports days for Leningrad schoolchildren to be held. The winners of pioneer camp competitions will also take part in these finals.

Pioneers and schoolchildren in general show a lively interest in their parents' work and in their strivings to further the technical development of socialist industry. On excursions into the Central Park of Culture and Rest the children will meet some of the city's distinguished Stakhanovites and scholars. . . .

The komsomol organisation has made it its duty to give pioneers and schoolchildren in general a good knowledge of the sights of Leningrad, its historic monuments and its suburbs. The comprehensive groups will go on many excursions and trips, especially to the places where Pushkin lived and worked. These places will be visited by all the comprehensive groups, and every district is organising excursions to the village of Mikhailovskoye.[1]

In accordance with the decisions of the XI Komsomol Congress, the Leningrad komsomol is taking steps to ensure that those children who stay in the city during the summer should have just as attractive and useful a time as those who are away in camps, that they should have a good, healthy holiday and gather strength for their studies.

[1] Where Pushkin lived for some years.

A MOTHER'S STORY

BY S. SEMYONOVA

(*Uchitelskaya Gazeta*, Aug. 7, 1954)

EVERY year as the summer approaches, my son Alik begins to moan that he doesn't want to go to the pioneer camp.

'I don't want to, it's boring,' he complains, at the same time looking to see what impression this demonstration of his is making.

When I was a child I used to spend the summer in pioneer camps, and I remember them as something beautiful and romantic: camp fires, tents, talks, songs, and excursions into the wood to gather fir-cones and mushrooms. Day followed day in sunny sequence, and I would be sad when the leaves began to turn yellow and we had to return to the city.

And here is my son Alik who will have none of it. He sits on the settee wiping his eyes with his grubby fists, and pretends to cry. We've spoilt him. Oh, how we've spoilt him!

'Go and get on with your homework at once,' I say to him angrily. 'You're just behaving like a cheeky lordling; you don't know what you want yourself.'

Alik takes offence and, dragging one leg after the other, lazily ambles over to his table. But before he opens his books he bursts out angrily:

'All the same, I won't go.'

It cannot be said that Alik is one of those children who bring their parents nothing but joy. People often complain about him: for not doing his homework, fidgeting in class, fighting, or breaking a window-pane. . . .

When summer came I nevertheless sent my son to the camp, from where he wrote a letter to me complaining that he was bored, and asking me not to leave him there for the second holiday shift.

The camp run by our institution is a very good one, and a great deal of money and care has been expended on it. It is almost a sanatorium, with its lovely bright rooms, its excellent beds with downy covers, its carefully organised days and its large staff. There are books, games and entertainments—everything children could want. There are flower-beds, the paths are sanded, and a swimming-pool has been fenced off in the river. . . . But Alik kept asking me to take him home.

I tried to find out what was the matter. His complaints largely consisted of: 'they won't take you with them', and things that 'they won't allow', 'won't give you, and 'won't let you do' . . .

To tell the truth, I was happy to hear my son's complaints: it was obvious that the children were being looked after very well, and that meant that nothing would happen to them and that I need not worry about my child's health. But there was something else in his complaints which I had not taken into account.

This year someone invited my rebellious son to stay with him on a collective farm.

'Let him spend the summer with us,' he said, undaunted. 'I've got plenty of room in my house, and the old woman will look after him.'

Once more I warned him about Alik's character, but he waved his hands at me.

'He's getting impudent here,' he explained to me with conviction. 'But he won't be impudent once he's there.—He's quite a big lad, isn't he.'

Later, when I received a letter from Alik, I realised what the man had meant. And I realised a lot more when people from the collective farm told me how my son was getting on and how he was behaving himself. And I began to see my son and my methods of upbringing in a different light entirely when I visted the collective farm myself.

But first of all here is the complete version of the letter which Alik sent to me from the farm. It was his first and last letter that summer.

DEAR MUMMY,

I'm not going home with Anna Andreyevna. I haven't had a sore throat. Aunt Motya has hidden my shoes and says that she'll give them back to me when I go home in the autumn; she says I'll be stronger if I go barefoot. We've managed to do the garden alright. I've planted cabbages in the collective farm; at first I did it badly, but now I can do it just as well as Zinka. I'm sleeping indoors, but when we've made hay, I'm going to sleep in the hayloft together with Dmitry Zakharych. We've got 20 chickens; two got carried off by a kite—very sad. I help here and I'm not bored. Our collective farm managed the vegetable plot alright. It'll soon be time to make hay now. At first the boys used to beat me, but they don't any longer now; they take me with them to the plots and to midnight feasts. Send the books with Anna Andreyevna.

Your affectionate son,

SASHA-ALIK.

This letter was disturbing; but it also pleased me and gave me much food for thought. It was disturbing because my Alik had hardly ever gone barefoot before, had never slept in a hayloft and had never gone to a midnight feast. I was pleased by the tone of the letter. In between the maze of errors I could read real concern. The words 'our collective farm' and 'we managed' were quite new. And why had he signed himself Sasha-Alik?[1] And the 'your affectionate son' had obviously been prompted by someone. I had the feeling that some new teacher, some new school, had entered into my son's life.

That evening Anna Andreyevna Golovkina, a teacher from the *Dawn* collective farm who had brought me Alik's letter, returned, and I asked her to tell me more about my son. Anna Andreyevna sat there drinking tea and talked happily, assuring me right at the beginning that he was a good boy. This is what she told me.

It took a little time before Alik felt at home in the village. Everything—the people and the life around—was new to him. The evening he arrived he went outside the gate, and was besieged by the collective farm children. Alik showed off, lied that he was getting nothing but 'fives' at school and showed them his fountain-pen. Just then a cloud of dust could be seen along the road and whips could be heard—they were bringing in the cattle. Our hero, the city boy who had never seen cows before, flattened himself against the fence. And then suddenly a horned cow went past quite near to him and, to the great amusement of everyone else, Alik took to his heels. The children started to make fun of him, wouldn't let him play lapta[2] or knucklebones with them, and pushed him around a bit at first. Thereupon the mistress of the house, Matryona Fyodorovna, took her lodger under her wing. She was a strong, lively old woman who successfully managed her work on the collective farm as well as her allotment. And Alik would follow at her heels wherever she went, to the plot, the field or the cow shed.

[1] Both Sasha and Alik are shortened versions of Alexander, but Alik is the more sophisticated and Western of the two.

[2] A Russian ball game resembling rounders.

'Don't stand about like a pillar,' grandma Matryona said to him one day. 'Take a spade and do some digging. The two of us could get it all done by dinner-time.' And Alik began to dig a bed, trying for all he was worth. The stern old woman had won his heart and he hung on every word of hers. At midday they brought in the cows. 'Why were you afraid of the cows?' the old woman asked him. 'They're peaceful animals—won't touch you. There's only one fierce one in our heard, Ignatov's cow, and she's had her horns sawn down. Don't be afraid; go up to them.' Alik overcame his fear and went up to the mottled Krasavka who was looking at him indifferently out of large, calm eyes. He soon grew used to her, took the fork and cleaned out the cow shed and started shouting 'whoa there' in a rough voice.

Gradually he started to mix with the children. The first to accept him into their circle were the girls. He was good at telling them about Moscow and about the books he had read. Soon the boys joined the girls. The children would meet in the evenings on the logs by the school and sit there until nightfall. The moon would rise above the dark fir trees and the sharp outlines of the cottages, and shine down on a tracery of boughs like in some old fairy tale. And Alik would go on talking until the young girls and boys came with their accordions and chased the children home to bed.

Zina, the 11-year old pioneer grand-daughter of Matryona Fyodorovna, had an important influence on Alik. Barefoot, sunburnt and agile, she overtook Alik in whatever work they did, whether it was planting seedlings, gathering strawberries or weeding in the fields. Zina's hands moved with amazing speed, and she left behind her tidily weeded, thick rows of carrots. Alik was not used to the work and tired easily. He would now kneel to the work, now sit back on his haunches. 'Put your legs the way I do, look,' was Zina's friendly advice. Alik did as she said, and really found that it was easier like that. 'Weed more carefully,' Zina said severely. 'If little bits of weeds are left they grow up again and smother the carrots. Look, the way I'm doing it.' Alik looked and really began to weed better. Soon they became great friends. Zina would tell Alik all the farm news. Together with her and with the other village schoolchildren he rode to the meadow two miles away to help the collective farmers making hay.

Zina said to Alik: 'Why've you got such a funny name—Alik-Bobik? Much better call yourself Sasha.'

So that was the origin of the double signature in the letter.

Matryona Fyodorovna tried to feed her little lodger as well as she could. One day when everyone else was having roast potatoes, he was given an omelette. Alik-Sasha categorically refused to eat it.

'Let me be like everyone else, or I won't eat anything at all,' he threatened, and pushed away the frying pan.

'Alright, you're no longer small,' grandma agreed, and divided the omelette.

I saw all this with my own eyes, and I very much liked what I saw. I felt that my little son had somehow changed for the better. I thought about it all and came to the following conclusion.

On the collective farm Alik had seen that everyone around him was working: the adults were busy and the children were helping them. And so he too had wanted to work. Under the influence of this atmosphere of work he had become more serious, mature and sensible, and gradually his moods, his impudence and his pampered ways had begun to disappear of their own accord.

In the pioneer camp where Alik usually spent the summer, the children were surrounded by a wonderful holiday atmosphere, but it was like a continuous festival. And I do not know how useful such an atmosphere is. It seems to me that the educational basis of the pioneer camp ought to consist of sensibly organised and suitable work for the children to do. There is no need for a large staff. Let the pioneers keep the camp clean and beautiful by themselves. Growing vegetables, berries and flowers, picking wild berries, mushrooms, etc. —all this, and much else surely, could take up the children's leisure, help towards the success of the camp, improve the pioneers' health and teach them to be independent. They would become more sensible, agile and experienced. And they would have more fun, because they would have an aim in view, something to work for.

It should undoubtedly be part of the educational programme of pioneer camps to help neighbouring collective and state farms. Our town children only know about life in the countryside from books. In the summer, at least, let them see it for themselves. And they should not only see it; they should take part in it.

If we give children greater freedom, we must also watch over them more carefully from the educational point of view. They must not be overloaded with work, and labour should alternate with sport and leisure. But nevertheless the labour process should be the basis; not some artificial 'work for work's sake', but something connected with the normal, useful work performed by the Soviet people.

I may be wrong in some of these details, but it does seem to me that these ideas are basically correct. They have been suggested by life itself, and I have tested them out on my son.

III

YOUNG WORKER AND STUDENT

INTRODUCTION

IN this section I intend to illustrate certain aspects of the lives of young people in the USSR during the first few years after they leave school. Many young people go on to some sort of training, and I have therefore devoted a considerable part of this section to the young student or trainee. The facilities for study of various kinds are very numerous, and I have not attempted anything more than a brief outline. I shall also, however, say a little about young people in the USSR in general—their outlook, tastes and interests.

The development of specialised education since the revolution has been much the same as that of the general education described in the previous section. The universities, for instance, which had been attended by only 117,000 students before the revolution,[1] were thrown open soon after 1917 to anyone with a secondary education.[2] But, as we have already seen, very few people possessed a secondary education. Various categories of children of 'bourgeois' origin were excluded until 1935, but this ruling could be circumvented in various ways, and the class composition of students continued to be heavily weighted against the working classes for a considerable number of years.

For the time being the new government was having to make use of specialists from the pre-revolutionary intelligentsia, an unsatisfactory state of affairs since large sections of these were hostile to the new régime. The government was therefore particularly anxious to train a new generation of specialists as soon as possible, and special measures were decided upon in order to make universities and institutes accessible to children of working class and peasant origin.

The 'Workers' Faculty', the *rabfak*,[3] was instituted, and played

[1] Medynsky, *Narodnoye Obrazovaniye*, p. 161.
[2] Decree of Aug. 2, 1918.
[3] *Rabochy Fakultet*.

an important part in the next few years. The *rabfak* provided preparatory courses for people who wanted to enter a university but lacked the necessary educational qualifications. The first of these to be opened (in 1919) was attached to Moscow University and provided four-year evening courses. In 1921, full-time, three-year courses were started in Moscow and Leningrad, and by 1924 they had also been established in the national republics.[1] Access to the courses was not open to everyone. *Rabfak* students had to be 18 or over, and were sent on the recommendation of the trade union or party branch at their place of work. Conditions in these *rabfaks* were often very primitive. A contemporary article describes a *rabfak* hostel in Kostroma as a building 'absolutely devoid of all furniture where students work, eat and sleep on the bare floor'.[2]

Academic standards too were generally low at this time. Universities were largely run by the students themselves, who spent a great deal of their time in this work. According to Harper [3] they were largely responsible for the maintenance of discipline, and took part in the planning of the curriculum. In addition, university life was overshadowed by the tremendous shortage of practically everything. We have a book written at the end of the period, which gives us a vivid picture of student life under NEP.[4] There were no fees to be paid, but there were few student grants to be had either. Some students received funds for study from a state enterprise in return for an undertaking to work in its employment for a period of three to four years upon graduating.[5] Most students, however, seem to have been dependent on other grants. The hero in the book mentioned above finds that there are nine other applicants for the grant which he is hoping to obtain. But even though he does eventually secure a grant, he still has to face the urgent problem of finding food and accommodation. The book is largely a chronicle of a student's daily struggle for survival, associating with people he dislikes merely to scrounge a meal, and spending the night with a prostitute simply because he must have a roof over his head.

The book also illustrates the atmosphere prevailing among some

[1] S. Kaftanov, *Vysshee Obrazovaniye v SSSR*, 1950, p. 10.

[2] *Krasnaya Nov*, 1922, no. 3, p. 246.

[3] *Civic Training in Soviet Russia*, 1929, p. 253.

[4] Ognyov, *Diary of a Communist Student*, 1929.

[5] G. T. Grinko, *The 5 Year Plan of the Soviet Union*, 1930, pp. 262–3. This system had the advantage, from the government's point of view, of giving the enterprises in question a measure of influence over the university attended by the contracting student.

of the students. Most of them were not of working-class origin[1] and were worried about it. They were desperately keen to be 'proletarian' and to throw over the old 'bourgeois' conventions of behaviour. Quite apart from this exaggerated eagerness, the times hardly lent themselves to middle class refinement. Here, for instance, is the starving student at a party; he is eating some fish, and spitting the bones on to the floor:

A bourgeois girl: 'Can't you put the bones on a plate?'

Student: 'Why bother with such antiquated conventions? Put the bones on a plate indeed, when I've had no grub for four days!'[2]

Specialised education outside the universities was in much the same position, and students here were faced with similar difficulties. Apart from the training colleges providing what the Russians call 'specialised secondary education'—a three- or four-year course for pupils with seven-year schooling—the Soviet authorities had also set up technical training schools for future industrial workers. These were the factory apprentice or FZU schools.[3] The first of these was set up in 1920.[4] Their pupils had usually had very little, if any, previous schooling, and for the next few years, therefore, the FZU schools tended to give a prominent place to the teaching of general, elementary subjects.

It was during this time too that the Young Communist League (*komsomol*) first began to play an important part in the life of young people in the country. This organisation had been founded in 1918.[5] The first years of its existence had been marked by great heroism in the civil war,[6] but NEP had brought a period of disillusionment. This was a difficult period for everyone, and for young people in particular. The romanticism of the first years immediately after the revolution was largely spent. Capitalism, far from having been destroyed, seemed to be making a good recovery. Unemployment was

[1] According to Grinko (*op. cit.*, p. 260), the class composition of students in 1927 was:

Workers' children	25·4%
Peasants' children	23·3%
Children from the intelligentsia	41·6%
Others	9·7%

[2] Ognyov, *op. cit.*, p. 118.

[3] *Shkoly Fabrichno-Zavodskovo Uchenichestva.* [4] Medynsky, *op. cit.*, p. 140.

[5] Ostryakov, *Chto Trebuet Komsomol ot Komsomoltsa*, 1938, p. 9. The I Congress of the Union of Russian Communist Youth in October of that year is usually regarded as the foundation date of the organisation.

[6] The novel, *How the Steel was Tempered*, by N. Ostrovsky, provides an excellent picture of a komsomol of this period, in the shape of Pavel Korchagin, the hero. The book has become one of the Soviet classics.

widespread. In fact socialism seemed a long way off. The komsomol movement nevertheless continued to grow slowly during this period, although it suffered a number of temporary setbacks. In 1926 it apparently numbered 1,780,000 members, and by 1928 it had grown to 2,000,000.[1]

The educational network had grown considerably during these ten years of Soviet rule. The first five-year plan however marked the beginning of a much more rapid improvement in education. I have already described the growth of schools during this period right up to the beginning of the war. There was a similar increase of universities and other specialised schools and training colleges:

NUMBER OF PUPILS

	Univ.-level institutions	*Spec. sec.-level institutions*	*FZU type schools*
1915	124,700	48,000	—
1928	159,800	253,600	178,300
1932	394,000	754,100	975,000
1939	619,897	951,000	—

Sources: Sotsialisticheskoye Stroitelstvo, 1935, p. 616; Medynsky, *op. cit.*, pp. 150, 162.

As the educational network grew larger, student life too became much more stable, and students began to give a little more attention to their studies, and a little less to the actual running of the university or institute. FZU schools were able to become more specialised as the general level of education improved, and from 1933 onwards 80 per cent of the teaching programme consisted of technical subjects.[2]

At the end of this period, in 1940, several changes were introduced into the Soviet educational system. One of these was the institution of school and university fees which I have already mentioned elsewhere in this volume.[3] The official reason given for this measure was that the increased standard of living of the population, and the great government expenditure on education in past years had made it 'necessary to place part of the cost of education in secondary schools and university-level institutions on the shoulders of the working people themselves'. University fees were fixed somewhat higher than school fees and ranged from 300r. to 500r. a year, to be paid in two annual instalments.[4]

[1] *Bolshaya Sovetskaya Entsiklopedia*, 1951, vol. 9, pp. 336–7.

[2] Medynsky, *op. cit.*, p. 140.

[3] See p. 46 .

[4] Decree of Oct. 2, 1940 (in *Narodnoye Obrazovaniye: Osnovnye Postanovlenia, Prikazy i Instruktsii*, p. 456). In Leningrad, Moscow and other capitals of Union

There can, I think, be no doubt that the introduction of fees dealt a temporary blow at the principle of equality of opportunity and created a very real danger that the reasonably intelligent child of well-to-do parents would go on to a university almost automatically, while the child from a poorer home would only do so if it was particularly intelligent. It is important to add, however, that the government grants ranging from 130r. to 200r. per month[1] which the majority of Soviet students were apparently receiving, do not seem to have been affected by the decree.[2] It is also important to note that many categories of pupils were exempted from these fees in the next few years. In addition, the fact that wages rose while the fees stayed the same will have helped to make the latter less unsatisfactory as time passed. According to the draft of the new five-year plan (1956–60) all university fees are to be abolished.[3]

The year 1940 also saw a change in the organisation of the FZU schools. A decree 'On State Labour Reserves'[4] established three new types of school into which the old FZU schools were merged—the trade school and the railway school, both with two-year courses, and the factory or FZO[5] school with a six months' course. These schools were intended to supply the country with the increasing skilled and semi-skilled labour force it now needed, since industry had reached the level where it could no longer operate on the basis of the, almost totally, unskilled labour, largely drawn from the countryside, which it had been using so far.

The decree envisaged an annual influx of between 800,000 and 1,000,000 pupils into these schools. According to the decree, this number was to be 'called up' every year, each school having apparently to provide a certain quota from its seventh-form pupils. Except in cases where there were sufficient volunteers, the dullest of the children were apparently chosen by the selection commission, which comprised the chairman of the town or district soviet, a trade union representative and the secretary of the local komsomol branch.[6] In 1943 a decree was passed exempting pupils in forms IX and X of

---

republics fees amounted to 400r.; in other towns they were 300r.; colleges of art, drama and music charged 500r. a year.

[1] S. Kaftanov, *Soviet Students*, 1939, p. 18.

[2] E. Ashby, *Scientist in Russia*, 1947, p. 73, maintains that some 90 per cent of all students were receiving grants.

[3] *Pravda*, Jan. 15, 1956.

[4] Decree of Oct. 2, 1940 (*Pravda*, Oct. 3, 1940).

[5] *Shkola Fabrichno-Zavodskovo Obuchenia.*

[6] E. Ashby, *op. cit.*, pp. 63–4.

secondary schools from this call-up. A year later, pupils from form VIII were also exempted.[1]

The former FZU schools had been run by individual enterprises which had drawn their pupils almost exclusively from the industrial population. The new schools were to be run by a centralised authority, the newly established Ministry of Labour Reserves, and to include young people from the countryside as well. Pupils were expected to have a minimum of four years' previous schooling, and upon graduating, were to spend four years working in a government enterprise. The schools had a most important part to play almost immediately upon their inception for, as the war started, they had to supply replacements for the men who had left for the front. Tuition, food, accommodation, uniform and textbooks were all provided free, but much of this was naturally of a very low standard during the war years. One of the items in this section ('The Youngest') gives us an idea of some of the hardships endured by these young boys and girls. Their 'uniform' existed only in name, and they often arrived at school in makeshift clothes borrowed from their parents.

The war in fact played havoc with the whole educational system. It is impossible to tell, for instance, how the introduction of university fees affected the growth in the number of students, since large numbers of teachers and students soon left for the front. By 1942 only 460 of the country's 800 university-level institutions were working,[2] and the number of students had dropped down to 227,000.[3] For the next few years education and educational problems faded into the background as the whole country was caught up in the war effort.

A few years later, however, the country was again able to give some attention to education. In 1943 a new type of night school for young workers was set up.[4] A year later it was named 'Night School for Young Workers', and a similar school for 'Rural Youth' was introduced.[5] These were intended to supplement the relatively scanty education which many boys and girls had received during the war. The Schools for Young Workers tended to cater for pupils who already had a four-year education, although extra classes for those with less were apparently organised. The schools followed the teaching programme used from form V upwards in the ordinary seven- or ten-year schools. Schools for Rural Youth were run on a very similar

[1] Decrees of Feb. 3, 1943, and Feb. 25, 1944 (*Narodnoye Obrazovaniye* . . ., p. 67).

[2] Kaftanov, *Vysshee Obrazovaniye v SSSR*, p. 13.

[3] V. Zhirnov, *Razvitiye Sovetskoi Sotsialisticheskoi Kultury* (1952), p. 48.

[4] Decree of July 15, 1943 (in *Narodnoye Obrazovaniye* . . . (*op. cit.*), p. 247).

[5] Decrees of April 30, and July 6, 1944 (in *ibid.*, pp. 247, 250.)

basis, except that here no previous education was taken for granted at all, and the curriculum included that for forms I–IV in the ordinary primary schools. All tuition in both types of school was to be free. During the first three years of their existence, 158,000 pupils passed through the courses provided by the schools.[1]

As we have already seen from previous sections, the first task of the country after the war was that of repairing the tremendous devastation that the war had brought. Almost half the country's university-level institutions had been destroyed.[2] But university education appears to have recovered very rapidly, and by 1950 it had more than regained its pre-war level.

NUMBER OF UNIVERSITY-LEVEL STUDENTS
(*including extra-mural students*)

1949	774,478[3]
1950	1,230,000[4]
1951	1,356,000[5]

Special provisions were made for those returning from the armed forces whose studies had been interrupted by the war. Free preparatory courses for ex-service men without complete secondary (ten-year) education were organised, and all ex-service men with gold or silver medal Leaving Certificates[6] were admitted to university-level institutions without an entrance examination.[7] In 1947 one sixth of all university students consisted of ex-service men and women.[8]

The conditions of student life have also improved considerably. The turbulent twenties, when the students spent much of their time in the actual administration of the university, and when questions of class origin were of great importance have long been left behind. Students now spend the major part of their time on their studies. They are expected to attend 36 hours a week on the average for lectures and seminars.[9] Degree courses vary in length from four to six years, and are divided into two terms or 'semesters' per year, on

[1] Zhirnov, *op. cit.*, p. 32.
[2] Kaftanov, *op. cit.*, p. 14.
[3] Medynsky, *op. cit.*, p. 162.
[4] Kaftanov, *op. cit.*, p. 74. 400,000 of these were extra-mural students.
[5] *Results of Fulfilment of the State Plan for the Development of the National Economy of the USSR in 1951*, p. 27.
[6] See p. 47 above.
[7] *Pravda*, Sept. 17, 1945.
[8] *Izvestia*, July 4, 1947. This seems a very low percentage indeed, since demobilisation must have been in full swing by that time.
[9] Medynsky, *op. cit.*, pp. 174–5.

the continental pattern. Examinations, mostly oral, are held at the end of each semester. A certain amount of practice work, usually in the student's last year, is obligatory, and varies in length from six to sixteen weeks. Upon graduating, students must choose one of a number of posts in which they are obliged to remain for three years. They are expected to take up a post of this sort after one month's paid holiday.[1]

There are some special scholarships and grants, such as the Stalin Grants (770r. a month), for exceptionally gifted students. Apart from these, all students who receive satisfactory marks (four or five) are given a grant which varies from 220r. to 480r. a month.[2] It enables a student to live without help from his parents, and there must be many students who could not study full time at all if it were not for this grant.

One of the biggest problems is that of accommodation. The housing shortage in the towns is still very great, and students as a rule live in dormitories in special hostels. 'The Student and his House' gives us an idea of some of the difficulties in the way of students whose homes are outside the urban centres which have university-level institutions.

Universities and institutes have many hobby circles, rather like our various student clubs, attached to them. In addition to these, they have 'students' research societies'. These are intended to teach students to do independent work, to give potential university teachers something to cut their academic teeth on, and, as is shown by the item on these societies, to help prepare students for their future career.

It is impossible to write about university life in the USSR without mentioning the new Moscow University. This is a most impressive building which stands on the Lenin Hills outside Moscow. Its style is rather too ornate for the Western eye, and has also recently been criticised in the Soviet press. The building houses departmental libraries, reading rooms and laboratories on a vast scale. It also includes a students' wing with 6,000 separate and beautifully equipped bed-sitting rooms which are more or less comparable with the women's colleges in Oxford. The new building houses the science faculties only, and another, similar building is planned to house the

[1] Kaftanov, *op. cit.*, p. 87. The pay during this month is the equivalent of the monthly student grant.

[2] *Ibid.*, p. 112. In Moscow University, for instance, the grant varies from 300r. to 450r. A student pays 15r. a month for his room and about 3.50r. for his main meal of the day. In Tbilisi University, the grant varies in size from 190r. a month for first-year students, to 500r. for students in their final year.

rest of the university. Blocks of flats are going up in the district, some of them to house university staff. An underground extension to the new university is planned, and the whole quarter is envisaged as Moscow's new '*cite universitaire*'.

All this, however, cannot be regarded as typical of Soviet universities as a whole. It is rather to be regarded like the Moscow underground: as a monument to the past achievements of the country and a symbol of its ambitious aims for the future—and is so regarded in the USSR.

Specialised secondary education has continued to develop since the war.[1] Fees for these schools are the same as those for the last three years of the general secondary school,[2] but all pupils whose studies are 'satisfactory'[3] receive grants. Pupils who graduate with distinction from these schools may take the entrance examination for a higher educational establishment straight away. The rest may do so upon completing a period of three years' work in their own special field.[4]

The network of Labour Reserve Schools has also grown, and since 1948 has included special mining schools to train mining technicians.[5] It also now includes agricultural schools training tractor drivers, combine operators, etc.[6] Whatever the practice may have been during the war years, it no longer seems to be necessary to call up pupils for these schools. A school in Zlatoust, for instance, is said to have had twice the number of applications that it could accept.[7] Conditions in these schools today appear to have greatly improved since those war years when young Galya (in 'The Youngest') arrived in her father's boots. The staff of these schools now have other problems to deal with, such as the Tarzan and Nat Pinkerton crazes described in 'Pupils' Reading'. This item also serves as an example of the kind of work a school librarian is expected to do. It will be seen that the organisation of the library is the least of her duties, and that she seems to spend much of her time introducing the pupils to Russian and Soviet classics.

I have included a purely descriptive item on these schools ('Letter

[1] By the end of 1951 the number of pupils had risen to, 384,000 (Medynsky, *op. cit.*, p. 150). In 1954 the figure stood at 1,600,000 (*Pravda*, Sept. 15, 1954).

[2] See p. 46 above.

[3] '*Uspevayushchye*' (Medynsky, *op. cit.*, p. 152). The amount of the grants is not stated.

[4] *Ibid.*, p. 153.

[5] *Bolshaya Sovetskaya Entsiklopedia*, 1952, vol. 12, p. 308.

[6] Decree of Sept. 7, 1953 (*Izvestia*, Sept. 13, 1953).

[7] *Molodoi Kommunist*, 1953, no. 9, p. 7. See also *Izvestia*, Sept. 14, 1951, where a teacher complains that she cannot find a vacancy for an orphan in her care.

from a Trade School') in order to give the reader some idea of the atmosphere in one of these schools, and of the extra-curricular activities organised for the pupils. It also throws some light on the part played by the komsomol organisation. The 'Letter' describes it, both as seen through the eyes of some of the pupils, and from the point of view of the organiser himself. It will be seen that there are only boys in the school described in this item. Today, trade schools, like all other schools, are co-educational once more.

Night schools of the kind described on p.142 above still exist today.[1] There have been some complaints that pupils tend to drop out as the course becomes more advanced.[2] It is obvious that a course of study at night school will mean a period of very hard work, and the temptation for the young worker, particularly if his earnings are reasonably good, to spend his evenings enjoying himself must be very great.

'The Youngest' was no doubt written as an example of young people studying, raising their qualifications, earning high wages and enjoying a high standard of cultural life. It illustrates the opportunities open to those with sufficient energy and determination to study on top of a hard day's work at the factory. Study of this kind is becoming increasingly important with the development of industrial techniques and of education.

Night schools also provide a very important stepping stone to the young worker who hopes to go on to a university or institute. The importance of this is illustrated in 'The Path to Knowledge' (translated on p. 150), the author of which has worked his way up from the factory to the university. The style and some of the statements made in this item may well appear somewhat high-flown to the reader, but it must be remembered that the author of this article is writing about the most important achievement of his life, and that it must indeed be thrilling to become a student in a university you have built yourself.

So far I have only dealt with the young Soviet student. I should now like to say a little about the young worker in the USSR. One of the items in this section ('Why Must Shukhov Have a Signet Ring?') deals with young workers, many of them former pupils of FZO schools. It contains some interesting information on prices of various goods in 1948, shortly after the currency reform, and on the wages

[1] *Uchitelskaya Gazeta*, Oct. 16, 1954, reported some 1,300,000 pupils in Night Schools for Young Workers.

[2] An article in *Pravda* (March 2, 1955) on Schools for Young Workers in the Penza province, complained that attendance at some courses had fallen to under half its original number by the spring.

earned by young workers upon finishing their training at FZO schools.

I have included one article ('Summer Recreation for Young Workers') to illustrate the activities of the komsomol among young workers. This particular item also tells us something about the ways in which young Soviet workers spend their spare time. Their working day is usually an eight-hour one, with two weeks' paid annual holiday. Until recently young workers under 16 had a six-hour day and an annual holiday of one calendar month, while all workers above sixteen were treated as adult labour which worked an eight-hour day, with an annual paid holiday of two weeks.[1] This ruling has now been modified: workers below the age of sixteen, provided they are engaged in some form of study, will have a four-hour day; workers between the ages of sixteen and eighteen will now work a seven-hour day, and will have the same annual holiday of one calendar month as the fourteen to sixteen age group.[2] The item mentioned above does not say very much about holiday arrangements, but concentrates on the kind of facilities which the komsomol should provide for young workers in the cities. The article is obviously published as an example to be followed.

The article entitled 'A Quarrel' shows how the times have changed. Even as late as the thirties young people were sometimes anxious to be thought workers, and the komsomol had to fight against a tendency among some of them to regard ungrammatical speech and rough language as the hallmark of a true worker.[3] Today the komsomol is having to fight against snobbism of a different sort. The girl in the article above is no doubt proud of being more than an 'ordinary worker', and feels that she will be marrying 'beneath her station' unless her future husband is a white-collar worker of some sort. The article condemns this outlook, and at the same time stresses the fact that the 'ordinary worker' of tomorrow will be on an incomparably higher level than he was in the past.

Some of the other descriptions in this section deal with what the Russians call 'survivals of the past', such as alcoholism, and superstition which is classed together with religious beliefs. Judging from 'The Evil Eye', the level of religious beliefs to be combated appears to be very low, and borders on superstition. It is quite likely, however, that the authors have purposely exaggerated the crudities they describe, in order to discredit religion in general. It is a little

[1] *Sovetskoye Trudovoye Pravo*, 1949, p. 247.

[2] *Vedomosti Verkhovnovo Soveta*, Sept. 3, 1955.

[3] S. Ostryakov, *Chto Trebuet Komsomol ot Komsomoltsa*, 1938, p. 42.

doubtful, for instance, whether 32 young girls were really found to be pregnant after visiting Old Believers' cells. The absence of adequate scientific lectures in the countryside reflects a general disinclination on the part of city dwellers to work in rural areas. The article realises, however, that lectures are not enough by themselves, and that young people cannot be won away from the church if no alternative secular, emotional and artistic outlets are provided for them.

The last two items in this section describe the lives led by young people working in areas far from the large urban centres of the USSR. At the beginning of 1954 an appeal was launched for komsomols to go out into some of the most remote areas of the country and to begin cultivation of vast tracts of virgin land. The response to this appeal was very good, and thousands of komsomols are now settling in these areas. 'Meeting' and 'On the Virgin Lands' describe the kind of people who volunteered for this pioneering work, and also tell us something of the tastes and lives of these new communities.

In the introduction to the last section I mentioned the tremendous impact which full secondary education was beginning to have on the school. But its repercussions are of course far wider. The specialised secondary schools, for instance, formerly catered for pupils with seven-year schooling, and provided a *specialised* secondary education in place of the *general* secondary education provided in forms VIII–X of the ordinary school. An increasing number of pupils will now enter specialised secondary schools on completing the ten-year school,[1] and I think that it is quite likely that the level of this kind of education will gradually come to be very much closer to that of the universities than it is now.

The various trade and FZO schools will have to be altered even more radically. A new type of vocational school was in fact opened last year in order to provide a high-level technical training for pupils with a full, ten-year education who intend to go into industry.[2] By the end of 1954, 250 of these were already working.[3] These schools provide a two-year course. Tuition, meals and uniform are free. Accommodation too is provided for students from outside town. The schools, 51 of which will train agricultural specialists, provide courses for 76 different trades. The teaching programme largely consists of practical work. This new type of school may well be the prototype for the trade school of the future.

[1] In Armenia 60 per cent admitted to such schools already have a ten-year education (*Kommunist*, Jan. 5, 1955), and the proportion is likely to be higher in the RSFSR.

[2] *Uchitelskaya Gazeta*, Aug. 21, 1954.

[3] *Semya i Shkola*, 1954, no. 12, p. 21.

Industry will feel the impact of secondary education for all most forcibly. It will have a smaller labour force, but one that is likely to be more impatient with outmoded and primitive methods, and that will be better equipped to introduce more modern machines. The same holds true for agriculture, though here secondary education may also have the, equally important, effect of counteracting the age-old peasant mentality which is still very strong at the moment. I think that there can be no doubt that, if the Soviet experiment of secondary education for all is successful, its long-term benefits will more than offset the many problems which it is causing at the moment: it will provide the country with a population equipped for the new era of automation and atomic power.

THE PATH TO KNOWLEDGE

BY V. KOZLOV, FIRST YEAR GEOGRAPHY STUDENT, MOSCOW UNIVERSITY

(*Dvorets Nauki*,[1] p. 106)

IN a few months' time the lecture rooms of the new university building will be filled with thousands of students, the bell will go and the first lecture notes will be made. The light of the gold star shining out into the Moscow sky will announce the opening of this national Palace of Learning.

People of every kind of trade and profession are working on the site of the new building . . . all united by one aim—to finish it on time. They are proud in the knowledge that their country has entrusted them with the construction of this 'city' for the scholars of the communist era.

Who of our young boys and girls does not dream of studying at Moscow University, whose traditions go back to two centuries almost, at the university which forms an integral part of the achievements of our great Russian science, culture and art. But it is even more wonderful to feel, as I and some of my fellow builders did, that you are not just a student at the university but that you also helped to build it.

The path to learning is open to everyone of us, Soviet people. And when I, a former building worker, became a student, I could not help comparing my own youth with that of my father.

My father did not even finish the *zemstvo* primary school,[2] and my mother was semi-literate. But it was their most ardent

[1] This is a volume of stories and articles written by some of the workers who took part in the construction of the new university building in Moscow. It was published in 1952.

[2] The pre-revolutionary primary school mentioned in the introduction to Section II. Rural schools of this kind came under the authority of the *zemstvo*.

wish that their children should study. My father was always reminding me:

'Study, Victor. The country is giving you every opportunity; the road lies wide open before you.'

I had no difficulties at school. I was not sure yet what career I would choose, but I knew that I wanted to build beautiful houses, wide bridges and railways.

The war destroyed all my plans. After finishing at the seven-year school, I went into a factory where I soon learnt to work a lathe. But even in those hard years I never forgot to read books.

I was still wanting to study when I joined the Forces. I served in the Fleet Air Arm on the Leningrad Front, servicing aeroplanes. There was much work to be done: some days our fighters made eight or nine flights. Nevertheless I always managed to find an hour or two for reading. One day I came upon a book about the famous Russian traveller, Przhevalsky. I was fascinated by the accounts of the great discoveries of nature made by the explorer in Central Asia and of his journeys into China and Tibet. . . . Ever since then it has been my ambition to become a geographer too.

When the war ended, it did not take me long to make up my mind. I decided to go back to the factory, and to study at a Night School for young workers.

One day I happened to see the plan of the new university building on the Lenin hills[1] in a magazine. During the lunch break I read the articles about the Palace of Learning together with the other workers in the shop.

'Oh, the lucky people who'll be studying in that building,' I said.

'You might become one of the lucky ones, if you get down to your studies seriously,' the komsomol organiser of the shop answered me. 'It's a great honour to be a student at the best university in the world. You have to be worthy of it.'

His words had struck home. I started to spend whole evenings after my work reading, trying to make up what I had missed during the war.

One day I met a war-time comrade of mine, Anvar Shakirov, who told me that he was working as an electrician on the site of the new university building.

'Do you know what, Victor,' he said to me. 'Come and work with us on the site. We're short of electricians and you know the trade from your army days, don't you?' And so I began working on the site, in Torbin's brigade.

[1] Just outside Moscow.

. . . After my first shift I went home together with Torbin. We somehow started talking about the future: our work and the university. It was then that I told the brigade leader that I wanted to become a geographer. Torbin said to me:

'Well Victor, you laid your own electric cable today. We're working on the very part of the building where the geography department is going to be.'

I was walking on air, anxious to get back to work as soon as possible in order to bring nearer the day when I would enter the university, no longer a building worker but a student.

. . . In the spring of 1951 special preparatory courses for the Certificate of Maturity[1] examinations were organised on the site. It was difficult to settle down to your books after a hard day's work, and you could feel how tired you were. . . . The undergraduate and postgraduate students of the university gave us a great deal of help, and on Sundays we would spend nine or ten hours at our studies.

And then came the solemn day on which I received my certificate of maturity. But I still had to pass the university entrance examinations, and once again I sat down to my books.

It is difficult for me to describe what I felt when I saw my name among the list of students accepted for the first year course and realised that I had become a student of Moscow University . . .

We have the greatest scholars in the country to lecture to us and to supervise our practical work. As future geographers, we are receiving a very extensive training which includes mathematics, chemistry, geodesy, geology, foreign languages, the great science of Marxism-Leninism and other subjects.

After my studies at the university I often go back to the building site to see my fellow workers, who want to know all about my studies and the lectures and seminars I attend. And they do not ask out of idle curiosity. Dozens of young workers are preparing to enter higher educational establishments, such as Moscow University or architecture and building institutes. Every time I go to the site I see changes heralding the completion of the great building. . . . And I walk over the site with the pride of one who took part in it, and with the joy of one who will be a student here, I await the day when my department moves into the new building.

[1] The graduation examination of the ten-year secondary school.

STUDENTS' RESEARCH

BY Z. ROGINSKY, LECTURER AND SUPERVISER OF THE STUDENTS' RESEARCH SOCIETY, AND V. MICHURIN, LECTURER AND HEAD OF THE FACULTY OF PHYSICS, YAROSLAVL

(*Uchitelskaya Gazeta*, Oct. 20, 1954)

PUPILS' research in such subjects as physics, mathematics, biology and chemistry forms an important part of polytechnical education. There are many schools, however, in which this work is done badly or not at all. This is due to the fact that some of the teachers lack the necessary knowledge and skills. Students' research societies can do a considerable amount towards filling the serious gap which at present exists in the training of teachers of physics, mathematics, biology and chemistry.

The Yaroslavl Pedagogical Institute has had a students' research society for the past five years. At the moment it consists of 10 sections sub-divided into 35 circles, and is attended by more than 800 students.

Students' research work is improving and becoming more penetrating and thorough with every year; its pedagogical orientation too is becoming more pronounced. A few years ago we used to complain that only a few of the papers prepared in the circles dealt with problems of school teaching; but last year already more than half the papers had some connection with the school and with teaching problems. This change is also reflected by our annual students' research conferences. At the VIII students' research conference which was held recently, for instance, half the papers read had a direct bearing on our students' future profession. Many of the papers made use of the experience of the best teachers in the city and province, as well as students' own experience of teaching.

Here are a few examples: 'The Form Teacher—Planning General

Education Work' by Krutova, a fourth year student in the physics and mathematics faculty; 'Word Analysis in the Senior Forms of the Secondary School' by Makeko, a fourth year student in the faculty of modern languages; 'Geography in the Pioneer Camp' by Ivanov, a third year student in the science and geography faculty; 'Physical Culture and the Pioneer Organisation' by Khomutov, a fourth year student in the faculty of physical culture.

Circles studying methods of teaching individual subjects are of particular importance and should become the most numerous in pedagogical institutes.

The experience of the physics and mathematics section of our students' research society has shown that its work can help to give students a better training for their future career.

Take the work of the physics circle, for instance, which specialises on teaching methods in that subject. The circle has worked out a plan for an excursion of seventh form pupils to a tramway depot to illustrate the 'electric engine' and the 'transformer' which pupils study in this form. The section specialising on the teaching of mathematics has been working on 'pupils' mistakes in geometrical proofs and how to prevent them' and on 'independent work for pupils in geometry'.

The circles discussed subjects for school evenings of mathematics and physics, studied the problems involved in arranging school competitions in these subjects, and decided on suitable questions to be set in competitions.

Problems of students' training for their work as teachers has its place in other circles too. The radio engineering circle made a set of instruments to be used for demonstrating this subject in schools, and read papers on such subjects as 'making a radio network inside the village school', and 'the school radio newspaper'. During recent years heads of faculties and other members of the staff have begun to give greater attention to the organisation of students' research work. The pedagogics faculty is a disappointing exception in this respect: some of the teachers in this faculty take no interest at all in the work of students' circles.

The following facts give us reason to believe that there has been a definite improvement in the quality and standard of our students' research work: post-graduate students in most faculties of the institute usually tend to be former members of the students' research society; some members of the students' research society have gone on to do post-graduate work in other university-level institutions upon graduating from our institute, and it is no accident that many of these are doing their post-graduate research on the subjects which they studied in the student circles.

Students' research, particularly in pedagogical institutes, trains the most gifted among the students for post-graduate work; it also—and this is perhaps its chief purpose—trains them to be teachers. Students' research work in the pedagogical institute should help to produce a specialist—a teacher and educator capable of an independent and creative approach to the problems of communist upbringing and education which he finds in teaching his subject at school. We have noticed that many of our former students who took an active part in the students' research society have become successful school-teachers. . . .

It is most useful for the future teachers to help with school hobby circles, and these circles should be run by members of students' research societies. This work is doubly useful: it give students experience in handling pupils' hobby circles and provides them with a better knowledge of school life, and at the same time helps the school to develop extra-curricular activities on a mass scale.

There are some university teachers who feel that regular work in the school's extra-curricular activities takes up a great deal of the student's time and has had a bad effect on his studies at the institute. On the other hand, we have students who ran pupils' hobby circles over a long period of time and also did well at the institute.

During the summer the students do their practice work in pioneer camps where they organise radio, photography, aeroplane modelling and other circles.

. . . Once a year, usually in May, the Ministry of Education sends out a directive on the annual exhibition of students' research work. But this directive is simply a shortened version of the directive sent out by the Ministry of Higher Education a few months earlier. . . .

The Ministry of Education ought to assign funds to enable us to publish the best students' research in special volumes of collected articles. Our institute already has the material for one such volume, but has no funds for publishing it.

It would be useful if the Ministry of Education were to call an annual conference in each republic to discuss problems of students' research, pool experience of work and establish contacts between the various students' research societies. If the Ministry of Education were to establish a lively contact of this kind and provide some real leadership, students' societies would be better equipped for what is their chief task—the training of educated teachers capable of creative and independent thought.

THE STUDENT AND HIS HOUSE

BY L. LIKHODEYEV AND V. MIKHAILOV

(*Literaturnaya Gazeta*, March 25, 1950)

SOON now the windows of Moscow's great new university 'city' on the Lenin hills will be lit up.

Attractive and well-built dwelling houses are going up together with the twenty-six-storey building of the new university. Six thousand students and post-graduate workers will be housed in the six thousand comfortable, bright and cosy rooms of the university. There will be a wonderful club, several gymnasia, a swimming-pool, libraries, reading rooms and museums—all for Soviet youth, who demand a high standard in culture and scholarship as well as in living conditions.

Great Stalin concern for Soviet scholarship as the most advanced in the world and for its younger forces is evident everywhere: in the building itself of this remarkable university city on the Lenin hills, in the tremendous growth in numbers of students, in every new teaching establishment that is opened, in the achievements of students' research societies and in the government's budget which allots a colossal sum to education.

The same concern can be seen in the large sums provided by the government for building, repairing and furnishing students' hostels. There are, however, a number of cities which do not put these funds to satisfactory use. This is what sometimes happens.

Novocherkassk[1] is a city with many higher educational institutions. It has a small one-storeyed building on Committee Street, which used to house a bakery. But the sanitary requirements for baking bread are such nowadays that it can no longer be used: it has low ceilings and small rooms, and no water or drainage. And yet someone decided that this building would do for a students' hostel.

[1] An industrial town in the Rostov province, with a population of 100,000.

THE STUDENT AND HIS HOUSE

Stooping so as not to bang his head on the top of the door-post, a student from the land reclamation institute enters 'his house'—the place where he will have to live for the next five years.

People from the Volga, Siberia and the Ukraine have hung the walls with newspaper maps of the future—the Stalin Plans for Transforming Nature.[1] The students have put red pencil marks on the parts where they are hoping to work when they finish their studies.

Students do a lot of reading. There are piles of books on the floor, on the window-sills and under the beds: there are no book shelves. The students are trying to make 'their house' cosy; the beds are tidily made and the room is kept clean, but many of the beds have coats lying on them, and the fluff from the old mattresses is oozing on to the floor.

The land reclamation students often visit their neighbours, the students from the polytechnical institute who enjoy enviable living conditions. The bright rooms there are fully equipped with the 'inventory', as the bunks and chairs are called, and the atmosphere is congenial and pleasant both for study and leisure. And the students from the Novocherkassk land reclamation institute feel bitter and indignant when they think of the people who cannot be bothered to provide them with comfortable, bright and congenial rooms.

As long ago as 1947, a sum of 4,000,000 rubles was assigned for a hostel to house the students from the land reclamation institute. They even got as far as assembling the building materials, and there might have been an attractive students' hostel on Podtelkov Street by now, but——

In order to build a house of this kind you must have a plan and, for some unknown reason, an order for this was placed with the agricultural building authorities. This organisation, which has a great deal of experience in building excellent cow sheds and stables, produced a plan for something that turned out to be a cross between a sheepfold and a silo tower. And, although the 'plan' had cost 60,000r., it had to be abandoned.

The next plan was drawn up by the Novocherkassk city architect and approved by the city and province executive committees. But then a new misfortune occurred: the head of the province architecture department, Comrade Zakharov, took offence because he had not been asked to draw up the plan himself. He took offence and proceeded to prove to the committee of experts at the Architecture Administration attached to the RSFSR Council of Ministers that the

[1] See footnote 1, p. 89 above.

Novocherkassk plan was unsuitable. And so the hostel still exists only 'on paper'.

Of the 4,000,000r., 300,000 have been thrown to the winds; the remainder has been taken away from the institute. Its students, meanwhile, continue to live in an unsuitable building.

We can understand their indignation. The Novocherkassk students are not, however, only thinking about themselves. . . .

In the autumn of 1949 hundreds of young people took the competitive entrance examinations to the Geological Survey Institute in Moscow. If you want to become a student there, you must get not less than 24 marks, and only well prepared candidates get into the institute. Georgii Antashuk from the town of Melenki in the Vladimir province was one of these.

The examining committee would have liked to accept the talented young boy, but the hostel only had 14 vacancies for students such as Antashuk, who came from outside the city.

Apart from the academic contest, you also have to pass in an 'accommodation contest' to get into the institute. Antashuk had 27 marks but he failed in this second, unofficial 'contest', and his place in the institute was taken by someone with only 23 marks, but who happened to have accommodation in the capital.

In 1949 nobody from outside the city entered the editing and publishing department of the Moscow Printing Institute. Only 10 per cent of the pupils in the Chkalov Pedagogical Institute can be accommodated in the hostel. Dozens of students in the Novocherkassk Veterinary Institute have to live in makeshift conditions on the premises.

The USSR Ministry of Higher Education spends about10,000,000r. annually on 'digs' for students in private houses. The RSFSR Ministries of Education, Agriculture and Health also spend millions on these 'digs'.

All of the institutions involved are most successful in spending the millions allotted for 'digs', and there is nothing left over at the end of the year. But the millions assigned by the state for building and rebuilding hostels—these millions are used very inadequately indeed.

In 1949 the USSR Ministry of Higher Education once again failed to use all the funds assigned for this purpose. In the past three years the RSFSR Ministry of Education has barely managed to build two hostels; in 1949 the USSR Ministry of Agriculture had the greatest difficulty in providing new accommodation in one students' hostel even.

Year after year plans are left unfulfilled and year after year funds remain unused. It seems that students' hostels continue to be regarded by the heads of these ministries as 'objects of secondary importance' which 'can wait'.

We need hardly say that there is no justification whatever for such an attitude to the building and repair of hostels. Our young students want to have—and should have—comfortable, convenient and spacious hostels. It is time that it was understood that the building and furnishing of students' hostels cannot be put off any longer and that it should be regarded as something of great importance to the state.

PUPILS' READING

BY I. MAKAROVA, LIBRARIAN, TRADE SCHOOL NO. 2, KIEV

(*Komsomolskaya Pravda*, May 28, 1950)

A FEW months ago I still used to come across bulky old tattered books about to fall apart, lying on a window-sill or a bedside table in the rooms of the first-year pupils, and the uneven blue pencil on the old and greasy cover told me that the notorious Nat Pinkerton and Tarzan the ape-boy had somehow found their way into the hostel.

As a rule, these books had no owner: they belonged to 'nobody', and were passed from hand to hand. And so everyone in the room would waste time reading useless trash incapable either of enriching the reader and widening his horizon, or of stimulating great feelings and new ideas.

I did not, however, find it so very difficult to deal with trash-reading. Young boys between the ages of 14 and 16 are particularly curious, and are usually keen on books. No great effort was needed to make every pupil a regular reader in our library.

Every day dozens of children crowd into the library as soon as the last bell has gone. How different they all are, in their tastes, their breadth of vision and their interests, I think to myself as I watch the lads. And in a year's time they will all go out into the world as independent people. Does our library do all it can to provide these young boys with the kind of reading that will help them towards the breadth of vision which the young worker of our epoch, as active builder of the communist society, must have?

'At last you've started getting the sort of books I like,' Alexander Zolotarev once said to me, returning Ostrovsky's *Born of the Storm*.[1]

I liked Alexander's remark. It was good to feel that one had been able to discover some definite bent in the young readers, an interest

[1] A novel on the civil war struggles in the Ukraine.

in books on the Civil or Patriotic Wars, for instance, or in history, science or technology.

I mentioned this at one of the conferences on methods of work for trade school librarians, and aroused a heated argument.

'I don't agree,' Klavdia Igorevna Dorner, librarian of trade school no. 3, objected. 'How can we allow ourselves to be guided by a reader whose tastes are only just beginning to be formed?'

Others among my colleagues maintained that we must not allow our pupils to become in any way one-sided and that their reading should have a direct bearing on the curriculum.

And so our librarians' group began to discuss the problems involved in drawing up individual reading plans for each of our young readers and deciding on a definite compulsory minimum of literature with which every young worker should be familiar.

The criteria to use in planning a minimum of this kind were suggested by the curriculum.

Together with the trade school teachers I drew up lists of recommended literature, classified according to subject. We put up a list of supplementary books on 'The Great Past of the Soviet People', for instance, for first-year pupils studying the book, *Our Great Motherland*, at current affairs lessons. A well-drawn poster which contained a list of 'Books about People who Fought for the Soviet System' attracted general attention.

At present, library activists and members of the ornamental bookbinding circle are working on lists of books for pupils studying the history of the CPSU(B). Lists and book exhibitions divided by subject have all helped me to attract readers.

I am always having to ask myself whether the young boys really understand what they read, and what sort of impressions the books make on them.

Anatolii Zavoloka, for instance, returned *Story of a Real Man.*[1] Anatolii is a gifted lad who is doing well at school, but tends to be lazy at times. He is inclined to look through the illustrations of dozens of books and then take out the one with the brightest cover. Had Anatolii understood the penetrating images of Meresev and of commissar Vorobyov?

I asked him a few questions, and soon realised that Anatolii had

[1] A novel by Polevoi based on the life of Alexei Maresev, a Soviet pilot who lost the use of both legs during the war, but learnt to fly again. In the novel, the hero is called Meresev. Vorobyov is another character in the book.

The novel has been translated into English (Foreign Languages Publishing House, 1952).

only skimmed through this wonderful book. He had not read it because, you see, he had seen the film at the cinema and already knew the ending. So why bother to read it all?

Sasha Patsan, on the other hand, gave me a most lively account of the *Story of a Real Man*, but refused point-blank to read Likstanov's *Malyshok*.

'I know it's about boys like me, and I'd rather read about real heroes, like the ones who beat the fascists,' he tells me.

Some of the children have a narrow conception of heroism as something which must, as a rule, be bound up with military exploits. I think that this is due to the fact that we do not, as yet, give sufficient prominence to books about such heroes of today as the five-year plan fighters, and that we seldom describe the great romanticism of labour.

Readers' conferences help us to a deeper understanding of the lives led by the heroes of books and towards a penetrating analysis of what we have read. The subject of the first readers' conference we held was Ostrovsky's *How the Steel was Tempered*;[1] at the second we discussed Polevoi's *Story of a Real Man*. The speakers carefully prepared their contributions. They did not simply give an account of the story, but made a thorough analysis of the various characters. I remember how vividly Ippolit Kvitnitsky spoke about Meresev's generation, a generation reared by our party.

'Everyone of us ought to develop characters like Vorobyov and Meresev,' he said. 'You can be a hero in the most ordinary things, even in studying, for instance.'

The library has now decided to hold a 'book week' in the school, during which a discussion of Likstanov's *Malyshok* will take place. In addition, a meeting with Zbanatsky, Hero of the Soviet Union and author of *The Secret of Sokolino Forest* has been arranged.

Mass work with the pupils is an integral part of the library's activities. But experience has shown us that it can only be fruitful where there is an individual approach to every reader.

Vasilii Vysota, for instance, is a striking example of this fact: last year a shy young boy came into the library and asked whether we had anything on crystal sets. He declined my offers of works of literature, and said that he had too little time to read them. I knew that he was getting 'very good' marks in all subjects except literature. Finally, I managed to persuade him to take out Gogol's *Taras*

[1] N. A. Ostrovsky. This novel is an autobiography. It is available in English (Foreign Languages Publishing House, 1952). Most of it deals with the Civil War period.

Bulba. In a short space of time Vasilii had read Gorky's *Childhood*, and the biographies of Nekrasov, Pushkin and Gorky.

Gorky's collection of essays *On Youth* and his *Advice to Young Writers* made a big impression on the lad. Shyly he showed me his first attempts at poetry and announced that he would work hard and do a lot of reading so as to become an all-round, educated person.

Vasilii is still a wireless enthusiast, but his horizon has grown infinitely wider during the past year. The reading plan which I drew up for him has helped him to systematise his range of interests. During the past few months, for instance, he has read Lenin's speech to the III Komsomol Congress, J. V. Stalin's *On Youth*, two pamphlets—*Our Aim is Communism* and *Democratic Youth in the Struggle for Peace*—and Pavlenko's[1] *American Impressions*. His readings in contemporary literature include Pavlenko's *Happiness*, Babaevsky's *Cavalier of the Gold Star*,[2] Polevoi's short stories, *We, the Soviet People*, Kozachenko's *Leaving Certificate*, as well as poetry by Mayakovsky, Surkov and Tvardovsky. Finally, Vasilii has read a number of popular articles on the fitter's trade, on the teaching of academician Pavlov, on plant life and on the origin of the Earth.

Drawing up individual reading plans for every pupil requires a great deal of thought and work. I am still inexperienced in my job, and I must admit that I often come up against all sorts of difficulties.

It is one of our main tasks, for instance, to help our pupils to grow to love their future trade already now while they are still at school; they should dream of their future and feel proud to be workers. But the books which could help us to do this can be counted on the fingers of one hand. Our writers do not, unfortunately, give sufficient attention to the portraying of the young worker. I do not mean the large canvasses which will no doubt be eventually produced. I am referring to small sketches and stories about innovators in industry, former pupils of trade schools and labour reserve schools which would be of great help to us. I do not know why the Ukrainian *Youth* publishing house does not print collections of these sketches and stories.

We have the same criticism to make of publishers of technical literature.

Our library has about 9,000 books. Two thousand of these are

[1] A Soviet writer. *Happiness* is a novel dealing with post-war reconstruction in the Crimea.

[2] This is a novel on collective farm life immediately after war. The book was awarded a Stalin Prize, but has recently been criticised for glossing over the difficulties with which Soviet agriculture was confronted.

technical. This would seem quite sufficient for our readers; but in actual fact only 20 or 30 of these books are regularly used. The demand for Perly's *Wonderful Machines*, Kostrikov's *The Magic Lamp*, and *Aid to Young Technicians* is tremendous. All the other books are obsolete works on rate fixing or on tube rolling and steel smelting, all subjects which have no bearing on the trades taught in our school.

Both I and other librarians in the city are besieging the officials who select books for libraries with requests for popular scientific pamphlets and books and for science fiction. But we always get the same old reply: 'The existing works on these subjects are out of print, and modern authors are not writing any new ones.'

It would surely be possible to publish large separate editions of the novels and stories that appear in the magazine, *Knowledge is Strength*.

So far we have had to use the general list of literature recommended for pupils of labour reserve schools. This list was drawn up in 1946, and there are naturally many outstanding Soviet works of recent years which are not included.

And finally, one last criticism, this time of the komsomol committee. What interesting things we could do if our school komsomol committee gave as much attention to pupils' reading as it ought to. They could, for instance, hold a really interesting komsomol meeting on 'My Favourite Hero', and individual komsomols could talk to us on the books they read.

And it would help me a great deal too in my daily work if I had reports from the komsomol committee. But unfortunately the secretary, Georgii Romantsov, and the committee members rarely visit the library.

LETTER FROM A TRADE SCHOOL

BY V. CHACHIN, A. YUDINTSEVA, TRADE SCHOOL NO. 14, NOVOSIBIRSK

(*Komsomolskaya Pravda*, Nov. 16, 17, 1951)

LITTLE things even can sometimes spoil your mood completely. Andreika was given boots without metal tips and with white eyelets. Everybody else had ordinary boots, but of course he had to have ones that were worse!

The young lad went up to the foreman, hung about the store-room and tried to exchange his boots with other boys, but no one was at all willing. And so your mood is spoilt.

That evening the new boys were in the empty room sitting on the bare bunks (the mattresses had not yet been given out), and talking about their future lives.

Everything was unfamiliar, strange and unaccustomed. Studies had not yet begun, but there were already plenty of worries: the bunks had to be brought from the store-room and to be put up, and you had to go and get yourself a uniform. And that's not so easy. Just try shortening the overcoat they've given you allowing 'for growth', or turning up the sleeves of your tunic. You sit there racking your brains, and you don't really know how to hold a needle.

So they sat there racking their brains, sewing away and sighing. At first, Andreika felt like chucking the whole thing up and going back to his village. He said as much to his neighbour, Victor Borkov. The latter bit off the thread with his teeth, and frowned at Andreika in surprise.

'You are a sissy!' he said. 'And you a komsomol too.'

Andreika took offence:

'I didn't learn to sew in the komsomol.'

Victor quietly threaded the needle, smoothed out a fold in his overcoat and looked up.

'They taught you not to whine, though, didn't they?' he asked.

Andreika pulled a face at his comrade, snatched up his coat and went to sit on another bunk. Victor calmly went on sewing and did not even turn round. Andreika was furtively watching his comrade and, to be quite honest, he found he liked everything about him. . . .

Victor finished his sewing, carefully hung his coat over the end of the bed, picked up the bits of thread from the floor and turned to Andreika:

'Would you like to have my boots?' he asked.

Andreika fidgeted, embarrassed. 'No—really,' he stammered, 'I only just said that.'

A healthy-looking lad appeared in the doorway.

'Hello, chicks, any of you play football?' he asked.

Andreika got up from his bunk.

'Well, I play,' he said. 'I'm a forward.'

The lad put on an air of mock amazement and looked Andreika up and down.

'Forward, you say! Tell me, what team did you play for?' he asked.

'Oh, at home, in the collective farm,' Andreika answered a little more subdued now.

'Some team! I play for Novosibirsk,' the lad boasted.

Andreika suddenly felt that his collective farm team had been offended.

'Well, and what if it is a collective farm team. Our village footballers sometimes beat the town teams,' Victor said from his bunk. He said it quietly and with confidence. Andreika gave him a grateful look. . . .

Before going to bed, they were told to get the mattresses. Andreika was dragging his up the stairs, trying not to lag behind Victor, and panting with the effort. Come what may, he felt that he must have his bunk next to that of his new comrade.

The lights in the hostel were put out early, but the boys went on talking for a long time.

Victor was quietly telling Andreika his plans:

'First of all, as soon as I get into town, I'm going to buy a komsomol badge. And when I've bought one, I'm going to hide it.'

'But haven't you got a badge?'

'No, I'm not a komsomol.'

Andreika sat up in his bunk with surprise. Victor not a komsomol?

'You ought to go and join, you should have done it ages ago. What are you waiting for?' Andreika asked, sincerely not understanding his friend.

'No, Andryusha, you don't join the komsomol just like that. You've got to have something good to give, something great.'

Andreika now felt completely bewildered. He didn't remember being accepted into the komsomol for anything in particular he had done. He had just joined: he had read the Statute, filled in the form and been recommended by friends; then there had been a general meeting—and there he was, in the komsomol.

'But I don't want it to be like that, Andryusha,' Victor said thoughtfully. 'I remember for instance when I was still at school. Sometimes after lessons a whole crowd of us would run along the corridor, and the cleaner would hush us and tell us to be quiet because the seniors were holding a komsomol meeting. We would tiptoe to the door. You could hear the boys in the room saying some very severe things to one another. I hadn't known before how frankly, even to the point of tears, they would criticise each other. So that was what komsomols were like, I thought. I want to be a komsomol like them and have the right to discuss the affairs of the community, not just because I've got my membership card, but because I've earned the right to do that. . . .

Andreika was carefully listening to his comrade and he suddenly realised that he had never had thoughts like these. He had paid his dues and even spoken at meetings, but he had never thought the way Victor was thinking. . . . Andreika remembered how he had sometimes shirked his komsomol duties. Sometimes, too, he had not done his work at school as a komsomol should. And all that had passed off him and been forgiven. They might tell him off a bit but that would be all. Obviously Victor was not like that. The komsomol would mean a great deal to him. But surely the komsomol also meant something to Andreika. Of course it did; it was just difficult to put it into words.

After all, there had been difficulties in young Andreika's life where he had not whined. Last spring the school drama circle had put on *The Inspector General* and Andreika had been given the small part of Dobchinsky. To begin with, they had performed at the school and then they had given performances at the villages round about. It was raining and the roads were muddy, but they had walked there all the same and no-one had whined. Andreika felt happier as he remembered all this, and livened up a little. 'You know Victor, we walked 12 miles, all round the villages, putting on our show,' he said.

. . . Victor lay a long time with open eyes, thinking about the unexpected conversation he had had with his neighbour. It had been interesting. But had Andreika understood him? He had told him to join the komsomol straight away, that there was nothing to think over. As though there were nothing special about it: you just handed in your application and that was that. But surely that wasn't all? Victor had seen many komsomols, ordinary boys just like himself. Even here in the trade school, he had seen them wearing their badges, and yet quarrelling with the store-keeper about the eyelets on their boots, running to the teacher to complain that it was cold in the room or that the mattresses were too thin, and fighting with one another over some bed-side table or other. And what of the komsomols about whom Victor had heard so much, what had they been like? The same as everyone else or somehow different?

And it seemed to Victor as though he could hear the crunch of snow under felt boots: a girl in a cap with ear-flaps is quietly creeping towards the stable in which the fascists are sitting. She is carrying a bottle of petrol and some matches. On such a night, far from the village of Petrishchevo, a group of daring and desperate komsomols are cautiously creeping along in the shadows of the fences with the leaflets they have written. They are the Young Guard.[1] What sort of children had they been before the war? Were they different, or just like everyone else? Andreika had made a fuss over the boots, and yet he told me himself that he had trudged for miles in bad weather when it had to be done. . . .

Victor remembered the previous day and what had been said in the hostel. Odd that he hadn't seen the secretary of the komsomol committee yet. What was he like, he wondered, and why hadn't he been to see them?

The next morning Andreika was hurriedly getting ready for P.T. As he was doing up the accursed boots with the white eyelets and without the metal tips, he suddenly burst out laughing.

'What are you laughing about?' Victor asked him. Andreika waved his hand and said:

'I've just remembered some nonsense.'

After P.T. they made their beds together. Andreika turned to his friend:

'Come on Victor, let's go to the committee. Shall I come with you?'

Victor thought for a moment and then answered: 'All right Andryusha.'

Victor spent a long time washing himself and carefully cleaning his

[1] See footnote, p. 70, Petrishchevo is a village in the Krasnodon area where the Young Guard operated.

boots until they shone. He also wanted to make his bed particularly well today. What would the committee secretary say to him, he wondered. . . .

The secretary looked up and caught sight of a black-eyed young boy, nervously shifting from one foot to the other. He had not heard him coming in, and his head had been full with other things: the plan and the chart of the meetings to be held was being asked for, notices about the circles had to be put up, and the various jobs had to be allocated.

'So you want to join the komsomol,' he said. 'Good lad. Go to the library, take out the Komsomol Statute, read it through and then come back for your application form.'

Victor wanted to ask something or to say something. But the secretary was busy writing again. Victor felt a little offended. Everything had turned out quite differently from the way he had imagined it would. They had not turned him down, but nobody had spoken to him at all; more like joining a football team than the komsomol, he felt.

Andreika could hardly wait to hear what the secretary had said to his friend.

'Well, how did you get on?' he asked Victor.

'I thought it would all be quite different,' Victor answered. 'It was just ordinary—nothing very special about it.'

At long last Alexei Fisenko, the secretary of the trade school's komsomol committee, set out to visit the new boys in their hostel. Alexei had been very busy in the past few days and had not been able to find time to visit the boys before. If somebody had asked Alexei what he had been doing . . . he would have been at a loss for an answer. There were a great many little things he had done: he had taken chairs to the red corner, stuck up notices and posters, gone to fetch some nails, connected the radiogram and put the committee room in order. . . .

Alexei opened the door to one of the rooms. The boys were sitting round the trade school's party organiser, Ivan Vasilevich Shkreb, and were obviously having a most interesting conversation. . . .

When the party organiser had gone, Alexei went up to the boys and took a look at them:

'Well, how are you getting on?' he asked.

The boys smiled and gave their various answers. Alexei told the komsomols that they must go to the district committee for their registration checks. On previous occasions Alexei had left after that, feeling that there was nothing more for him to do. But today he very much wanted to stay and to speak with the boys as the party organiser had done.

One of the new boys, Valya Korchuganov, wanted to know whether the school had a technology circle. On previous occasions Alexei would merely have answered that there was such a circle and would then have forgotten about the boy, but today he was interested in why Valya wanted to know. Valya gave him a confused account of how, when he was still at school, he and his comrades had made a small rocket 'to fly to the moon'. On a certain day the complete rocket, made of cardboard and bits of tin, had been placed on a small runway in the school garden. It had 'To the Moon—Direct Route, no Changing' written on it in white paint. Somebody had played a flourish on the accordion. Then there had been a bang and the rocket had risen up, described an arc over the school and come down on the village shop. It had never got any farther.

'All the boys at home like inventing things,' Valya said in conclusion.

Alexei had to admit that he didn't as yet know just what the technology circle would be doing. Of course, it would be good if it could make model aeroplanes; but then the boys would have their own suggestions.

It is a great thing to be advising people. Alexei noticed how the boys had livened up, and how everyone wanted to tell him about his ideas and hopes. Alexei wanted to go on talking to them; he was beginning to get interested himself. And so he decided to talk to them about the things that were worrying him most at the moment: the new editors for the newspaper, the drama circle and the new agitators. The boys were keen to give their opinions and Alexei felt that they understood him and really wanted to help.

He left with a feeling of satisfaction. Only why had he not seen any second-year committee members visiting the new boys? Perhaps it was his own fault; he hadn't suggested to them that they ought to contact the new boys right at the beginning and to get to know them. He would have to start, not with the chairs for the club or the radiogram, but with the committee. He would call a meeting and then go to the new boys. . . .

WHY MUST SHUKHOV HAVE A SIGNET RING?

A Young Worker's Personal Budget

BY I. PIKAREVICH, STATE BALL-BEARING FACTORY NO. 4, KUIBYSHEV

(*Komsomolskaya Pravda*, April 13, 1948)

THERE were still five days to go until pay-day, but Vasilii Shukhov was already busy trying to find someone in the hostel who could give him an advance. One of the people he approached was Murashov. Murashov worked alongside him in the factory, and was surprised at his request.

'You don't earn any less than I do,' he said; 'why do you come to me for money?'

Vasilii could not explain either where all his money had gone. Nine days ago he had received 200r., and today he had nothing left to buy bread with. His friends calculated: three meals a day at the young workers' canteen cost between 7r. and 8r. daily, i.e. 72r. for nine days; the hostel doesn't cost Shukhov anything since the factory director has issued instructions that all former pupils of FZO schools are to be accommodated free; the cinema and baths too are free in the young workers' settlement. Shukhov's laundry only costs him 8r. What had happened to the other 120r.? We discovered that Vasilii had spent them quire irresponsibly: on the first few days after he had been paid, the charwoman had swept up a whole heap of sunflower husks from under Shukhov's bed every morning. Vasilii had spent more than 20r. on sunflower seeds in one week. For two days Shukhov had indulged in doughnuts. But doughnuts are no substitute for dinner, and so he had to have a meal in the canteen as well.

On the third day Shukhov had gone over to sweets. The factory shop only had the more expensive varieties costing between 35r. and 40r. per pound, and he had spent 20r. on half a pound.

Another 18r. had gone on a signet ring—a large yellow ring with a sparkling glass centre. Why did he buy it? Shukhov didn't even know himself, and was ashamed to wear it.

Add the money spent on ice-cream, and it becomes clear why Shukhov had to borrow money.

By way of contrast, here is Murashov's budget. Murashov works side by side with Shukhov and lives in the same hostel: good quality locknit underwear—70r., food, taken in the canteen—110r.

'Naturally, I should have liked to treat myself to ice-cream and sweets too,' he tells us, 'but that'll have to wait. Once I've learnt my job, I'll start earning more, and then I'll be able to afford ice-cream and sweets.'

There have been many changes in the young workers' living conditions since the currency reform and the abolition of rationing. The young worker can now afford to buy clothes, shoes and underwear already during the first few months of his working life, and many of our young people are spending their money in this way.

We have already mentioned Murashov. Since he started working here he has bought himself some underwear and a good suit. Orlov, an automatic machine operator in high precision ball-bearing shop no. 1, earns about 600r. a month: he has bought himself a pair of boots and a suit.

. . . But not all young workers know how to spend their earnings sensibly . . . Veshkina works as a puncher in the separator shop. Many of her friends studied at the FZO school together with her and now work in the same shop. They were able to make themselves attractive dresses long ago, while Veshkina barely has enough to pay for her dinner. Like all other young workers, she was given a loan of 2,000r. with which to buy clothes and footwear, when she came to the factory. Veshkina bought herself a coat, a dress and a suit, but she has sold all three now and spent the money on sweets, sunflower seeds and ice-cream . . .

The factory's average wage has risen by 25 per cent during the past year.[1] But there are still many young workers with high earnings who 'can't manage' . . .

Money likes to be counted, goes an old Russian proverb. This rule applies not only to state funds but also to the personal budget of the worker, and the komsomol ought therefore to help young people to arrange their budget properly.

[1] An increase of such magnitude is most unusual for any *one* year. On this occasion it probably occurred due to the extraordinary circumstances created by the currency reform, and was also in part intended to compensate for the abolition of food subsidies.

THE 'FASHION FIENDS'

BY G. GOGOBERIDZE

(*Sovetskaya Kultura*, Jan. 18, 1955)

IT is difficult to imagine anything more incongruous than the lives led by the young 'fashion fiends', as they are called. The fashion fiend has a special style of his own, and you will recognise him by his conversation, his manner, his loud clothes and his insolent stare. On meeting you, the fashion fiend straightens his almost blindingly garish tie with a deliberately 'elegant' gesture which allows him to show off his 'genuine' rings to you. Then, as a final touch, he takes out a packet of foreign cigarettes (which, however, only contains the most ordinary of 'Dukat' cigarettes), gives you a confidential nod with his highly brilliantined head, and tells you that they are 'terrific'.

. . . The fashion fiends have their favourite meeting places in the centre of Moscow. From there they go to restaurants, clubs and dance halls, or spend hours on end strolling along Gorky Street.[1]

. . . What is most surprising of all is that some of our students and young workers imitate this worthless bunch of empty-headed and dandified louts and the bohemianism they practise. There is the 18-yearold electrician Vladimir Fadeyev, for instance. Fadeyev has been christened 'The Floor Polisher' by the employees in the Moscow restaurants because of his passion for a shuffle-like dance to jazz music. . . .

The fashion fiends like to discuss wines or the latest scandals caused by them, and to impress one another with a knowledge of the 'finer points' of fashion. . . . They lie without any constraint whatever. On meeting a girl, the fashion fiend will introduce himself as a student at an institute of dramatic art. Perhaps he is interested in art and it is his dream to enter an institute of this kind? But no, the dreams of the fashion fiends revolve around such things as 'smart'

[1] One of the main streets in the centre of Moscow.

shoes—narrow at the toe and bought two sizes too big so that the front of the shoe curves upwards (this is regarded as particularly elegant). He regards a foreign tie with a picture of a half-naked woman on it as a most enviable possession.

How wretched the inner world of these people is, with its petty interests and primitive desires! Their reading matter consists of inferior pulp literature and of thrillers . . . obtained from some unknown source. The 'art' in which they indulge consists of the shrill cacophony of jazz, the monotonous boogie-woogie, the convulsive be-bop amateurishly recorded and sold under the counter, of vulgar post-cards depicting sickly beauties and foreign film stars.

. . . What are their amusements? First, there are film shows, with an admission fee, held at home where, instead of the films obtainable from the film hiring agency, some foreign piece of rubbish, once again, obtained from an unknown source, is put on. Secondly, there is dancing. . . . The pair dances, hardly moving their feet; their eyes are half-closed; their faces express a studied air of boredom.—They are dancing, you see!

The fashion fiend has been created by poor upbringing in the home, teaching children to be irresponsible, to despise work and to admire everything foreign, in other words, to admire the tastes and morals of the bourgeois 'gilded youth' . . . There are not many fashion fiends. They are isolated individuals, an insignificant group of people completely divorced from the varied, full and beautiful life of labour and romanticism lived by our Soviet youth. But can we remain indifferent to an ugly phenomenon, just because it is petty and isolated? The question has already been answered for us by the general public and by the komsomol, who have begun to wage an uncompromising struggle against these idlers who imitate trashy foreign 'fashions'. Recently for instance, the students at the Mining Institute, the Historical Archives Institute and the Potemkin Pedagogical Institute in Moscow debarred fashion fiends from their socials and ridiculed them. In many student wall newspapers and in newspapers with a mass circulation they have been the object of sharp satire, their tastes and morals have been shown in their true colours, and their poverty exposed. These forms of struggle against this ugly phenomenon have already brought some results.

We must provide our young people with more interesting and varied things to do in their leisure time. We must constantly, patiently and uncompromisingly develop their artistic tastes, instil a revulsion against alien, ugly 'fashions' and inculcate a love for everything truly beautiful, healthy and harmonious . . .

SUMMER RECREATION FOR YOUNG WORKERS

(*Molodoi Kommunist*, 1955, no. 6, p. 31)

THE summer, the most suitable and attractive of the seasons for recreation, has arrived at long last. It is the immediate duty of the komsomol to help young workers to spend their leisure usefully and to gather strength during this time. . . .

In Makeyevka[1] the komsomols and other young workers laid out 50 volley-ball, 20 gorodki[2] and 12 basket-ball pitches, planted over 5,000 trees and tidied up three parks during the spring. Here is an example that ought to be followed by all komsomol branches in enterprises. . . .

Outings into the countryside are one of the most popular pastimes and, as soon as the summer comes, many young workers go on these trips. Before every such outing, the komsomol and factory committees and the factory's activists get together to plan the day's activities. The komsomol activists are responsible for everything—games, amateur artists' performances, sports competitions, and so forth. All this has to be carefully prepared without 'over-organising' or in any way encroaching on the initiative of the young workers themselves. . . .

Parks and gardens require special attention from the komsomol. . . . At last year's evening of waltzes in the Sverdlovsk park, 10,000 young boys and girls took part. The series of lectures on 'Soviet Products Should be the Best in the World', and 'Muscovites on the Virgin Lands' held in the Gorky Park of Culture and Rest in Moscow were also very popular. The Kirov park in Grozny has an interesting neon 'newspaper' which gives extensive descriptions of the life of the town and the unsparing labour of the oil workers of the province. . . .

Our young people love sport. . . . This year we are preparing for the greatest event in the history of Soviet sport, the I Tournament of Peoples of the USSR, which will be held in July and August of next

[1] A small town in the Ukraine.

[2] See footnote 1, p. 119 above.

year. It will be preceded by local competitions. Preliminary light athletics, cross country, bicycle and relay races and swimming contests, as well as sports festivals in stadiums, have been going on ever since the spring and will continue into the autumn. Participants of the Tournament will be chosen during contests between sports teams of the various workshops, enterprises, towns and provinces. . . .

There are numerous sanatoria, rest homes, clubs, libraries, theatres, one-day rest homes, tourist centres and watering places where the workers of our country can spend their holidays. Komsomol branches should make sure that in issuing travel passes to these places, priority is given to those young workers who are needy or in poor health. All these facilities should be planned in close co-operation with the trade unions. . . .

A QUARREL

(*Komsomolskaya Pravda*, Aug. 20, 1950)

I am a civil engineer by profession, and until recently I was working on new building sites. At present I teach in a school. I heard of a quarrel recently, which I should like readers to know about. I am therefore sending in this extract from a letter written by a laboratory assistant to her friend. I do not know what her friend replied, but I hope that the readers of *Komsomolskaya Pravda* will explain to Galina Chalova how wrong she is.

I have omitted nothing from Galina's letter, only changing the names of the chief characters.

A. Amosov,
Tumanovo agricultural college,
Smolensk province.

OH, and Zina, I must tell you about the quarrel I had with Tolya Shchepkin. I met him at a dance in the House of Culture when he asked me for a waltz. After that we talked. He was very shy and kept blushing, and it wasn't until the end of the dance that I discovered that his name was Tolya Shchepkin. He was courteous and polite. I wanted to know who he was and where he was studying or working, so when I introduced myself I said: 'Galina Chalova, building materials tester', thinking that if I told him my profession, he'd do the same. But he just said, 'Pleased to meet you', and so I didn't find out a thing. He wasn't boring, though. We went for a walk in the gardens, and Tolya had a very interesting way of speaking about poetry, painting and new books. I'd never heard of some of the architects and sculptors he mentioned, and I still don't know who Bazhenov[1] and Klodt[2] were.

When I started to talk I somehow spent all the time just telling him

[1] An eighteenth-century Russian architect.
[2] A nineteenth-century Russian sculptor.

about myself: how I test the concrete blocks at the lab., how I get on with the other people there and what dresses I like. Tolya seemed interested alright, and even asked me whether they really tested the plaster solution as well.

Two months passed and I had become very used to having him around; to be quite honest, his friendship meant a lot to me. I thought that Shchepkin was probably an architecture student who was spending his holidays down here. You know yourself how architects are fond of painting and poetry and how many of them can even draw quite well themselves. I didn't know whether Tolya was any good at drawing, but we certainly used to talk a lot about art. Altogether he was a very interesting person to be with.

And then our friendship went to pieces. It all happened so suddenly. It was our day off and there was a volley-ball match on. 'Labour' was playing 'Bolshevik'. I happened to know some of the boys in the 'Bolshevik' team, and had invited Tolya to the match. We were strolling along and talking. Suddenly Tolya stopped opposite the House of Culture, pointed to an ornamented plaster work cornice and asked me whether I liked it. My thoughts were already in the stadium, imagining Zhenya Surikov neatly stopping the ball, with the crowd cheering him on. So I just said:

'It's nothing special, just an ordinary cornice.' And then I thought I'd better say something to cover up my absent-mindedness, and so I added: 'It's nice, very nice.'

Tolya looked pleased and squeezed my hand. I'd never seen him like this before.

'You know, Galina,' he said, 'when I made that cornice I was only in grade four.'[1]

As you can imagine, I didn't know what he was talking about. 'What do you mean—made the cornice?'I asked him. So then he told me that he'd been moved up into the fifth grade as soon as he had finished working on that building, and that he was working on the new club for the food industry workers at present. Soon, he says, he'll have a brigade of his own, and there was a special light in his eyes as he told me about it all.

'I'm going to make up my brigade from people straight from trade school,' he went on. 'It's only three years since I left there myself.'

So I asked him: 'Do you mean to say you're just an ordinary plasterer?'

I suddenly imagined what he'd look like in overalls all splashed

[1] Grade one is the lowest category of labour. But most workers now go straight into grade four upon finishing their preliminary training.

with plaster. I had another good look at Tolya, and he seemed quite different now. He was wearing a new, navy blue suit, but I kept seeing him in overalls full of white splashes.

'And I thought you were an architecture student,' I blurted out.

And you should have heard how offended he was.

'And what's wrong with being a plasterer?' he said.

I told him that that wasn't what I'd meant, but I just didn't seem to be able to make up for what I'd said. We went on in silence; neither of us could think of anything to say. Right at the entrance to the stadium he suddenly turned round and quickly walked off without saying goodbye or anything.

I tried and tried to make it up again with him, but he doesn't want to see me any more—so that's the end of our friendship.

I wish you'd tell me what I offended him with, Zina. Surely he can't hold that one careless phrase of mine against me for ever, can he?

LETTERS TO THE EDITOR

(*Komsomolskaya Pravda*, Aug. 30, 1950)

I am just an ordinary Soviet girl. I work at motor repair factory no. 1 in Moscow, and I was so shocked at Galina Chalova for scorning Tolya Shchepkin's friendship that I decided to write in.

'So you're just a plasterer,' she had said disappointedly. I can't understand what she was disappointed about. There's nothing wrong with Tolya being a plasterer: in our country every trade is respected.

I have a very ordinary trade: I am an assembler; but I love my work and I am trying very hard to become more skilled. And there are many others like me. All the young turners, fitters and electricians who work side by side with me enjoy their work and each one of them has a broad and bright road before him. Take Lida Kuznetsova, for instance. She arrived from her village quite recently. The factory helped her to become a turner. Lida worked at the bench and also studied at night school. This year she has already moved up to the night technicum . . .

Doesn't Galina Chalova know that many of the boys and girls who work as turners, plasterers or fitters today are the engineers, architects, doctors and skilled craftsmen of tomorrow? . . .

A. Mesonzhnik,
Moscow.

. . . Dear Galina,

We read the extract from your letter, and decided to tell you why we disagree with you.

You made your first mistake because you were a bad comrade. Tolya Shchepkin loved his trade. And you were friendly with him for a whole summer without once asking him about his work. You asked what his post was. That sort of question is usually asked by officials in the personnel department, not by friends. We think that that is probably why Tolya did not give you an answer. But then one day he felt particularly enthusiastic, and gave you a fascinating account of the House of Culture and the club for the food industry workers he was building. But his enthusiasm was not communicated to you, because all that interested you in this fascinating account was what his work was called, not the work itself: was he an architect or an ordinary plasterer—that's all you wanted to know. Tell us, Galina, are real comrades like that?

But you are not merely a bad comrade, Galina. You are also a very backward Soviet citizen. And that was the cause of your second mistake. Tolya is an ordinary plasterer. So what? If he had been a bad plasterer, an idler or a hack we might have sympathised with you. But he is a good plasterer, and his work is very useful; it makes our houses and clubs more beautiful. No, Galina, you're wrong. And we too find your contempt for Tolya's trade offensive. We are students of a building technicum in Riga. Many of us did our practice at construction sites where we worked together with bricklayers, painters and plasterers who had been former trade school pupils. But none of us put on airs in front of them. On the contrary, we learnt from them a lot and they in their turn were comradely and keen to help us. What does it matter if they haven't got any higher education yet today—they'll have it tomorrow. No-one is debarred from access to an institute. We are convinced that Tolya Shchepkin too will study at a higher educational establishment one day and become an excellent engineer or architect.

You were wrong to offend him. Write and apologise to him, and we are sure that you will be friends again.

Yours sincerely,

S. Tatarnikova, A. Slavutskaya,
M. Shiamovits, A. Shirya.

THE EVIL EYE

BY I. SHATUNOVSKY, GORKY

(*Komsomolskaya Pravda*, Dec. 18, 1953)

NOT so very long ago an unusual event occurred at the milling machine works in Gorky. For some time two of the girls working there had been bosom friends; then one of them suddenly 'cast an evil eye' on the other.

However, let us begin from the beginning. It all started when Katya Prokofeva, an instrument distributor in shop no. 20, had a quarrel with Galina.

'If you don't stop hanging around my Vitka, it'll be the worse for you,' Galina had said.

Soon afterwards Katya felt unwell. Nina Fyodorovna wanted to call a doctor, but Katya said:

'It's no use, mother. Galina's put the evil eye on me because of Vitka Platonov.'

'She's cast a jealousy spell on you,' was the instantaneous diagnosis of the various aunts who had gathered in the room.

They tried to remove the spell with the help of holy icons and a wedding dress. But none of this had any effect. Thereupon somebody ran off to fetch Galina.

'Release Katya from the spell,' the old women shouted at her when she arrived.

Galina felt really frightened. 'Go on with you,' she said. 'I can't cast spells. I didn't do anything.'

But nobody believed her. It was decided not to allow the 'witch' to go home until she had removed her spell. An incredible din came from the room, and hysterical wails could be heard all down the street. Hearing all this noise, the policeman, Stremov, arrived on the scene.

'What's going on here?' he asked sternly.

Taking advantage of the general confusion, Galina rushed to the door and disappeared.

'What's going on?' the old women shouted at him. 'The Antichrist has got away because of you, that's what's going on! That witch'll be on her broom-stick now, buzzing off through the sky.'

'A witch?' Stremov asked incredulously.

'The very same. Come and see what she's done to the girl here.'

The policeman scratched his head. It was his first case.—What if there really was a witch?

'She won't get away from me,' Stremov said with determination. 'I'll get her—even if she's at the bottom of the sea.'

Soon he did in fact return with Galina who was trembling with fright.

'These citizens have a claim against you,' said Stremov. 'Remove the spell, or I'll have to take you to the police station.'

On the following day the doctor visited the patient and diagnosed her trouble, and Katya now goes to the outpatients department of the hospital to receive treatment. But grandpa Erofei, a food shop watchman, sticks to his own opinion:

'Hospitals are powerless against the forces of evil. Only the holy lake Svetloyar can remove spells.'

What is this 'holy' lake? Anfisa, a former nun, but a married woman now, offers us the following explanation:

'Long ago—we do not know what year it was—these parts were invaded by infidel hordes. They trampled down the fields, took the maidens captive, and tried to profane the orthodox church. But the Lord did not allow them to desecrate the sacred faith; the house of God sank into the earth before the very eyes of the infidels, and a lake appeared in its place. People call it Svetloyar. Go to the Svetloyar lake, my dear sir, and go round it on your knees three times. If you think upon the name of the Lord, you will hear bells ringing and you will see the house of God at the bottom of the lake. At that moment all your wishes will be granted.'

Not only the watchman Erofei and the former nun Anfisa know about the 'wonder working' qualities of the lake. They are also known to the province department of culture, the various branches of the Society for the Dissemination of Political and Scientific Knowledge, and the province committee of the komsomol.

In the summer Svetloyar lake is even visited by pilgrims from other provinces. Time and again komsomol activists have seen people going round the banks of the lake on their knees. Last summer some school girls circled the lake in this manner in the hope that it would help them to pass their examinations. It cannot be denied that various public bodies have considered closing these 'holy places'. At one stage it was decided to arrange mass excursions to the lake. Booths, food stalls and kiosks were put up. Then someone tumbled to it that they were simply providing facilities for the fanatics that assembled there.

At present the province authorities are working on new plans for closing the 'holy places'. Some maintain that the best thing to do would be to send divers down into the lake who would examine the bottom and would then tell everyone that there is no church down there at all. Others suggest that it would be best if all sorts of fish were put into the lake and fisheries started, so that Svetloyar lake should become productive and normal, and cease to be 'holy'. Once fishermen have started working there, they say, no kneeling pilgrim will be tolerated, because he might frighten away the pike or carp.

But it is not simply a question of the 'holy' lake. The Gorky province also has a 'holy' well with 'healing qualities'; many church bells can be heard, and Old Believer[1] cells, baptists, seventh-day adventists, model houses of protestant Christians and other religious sects are all active.

As is well known, Soviet laws grant freedom of religious worship. But our laws also recognise freedom of anti-religious propaganda, and this is a right which the komsomols in the Gorky province make little use of.

The secretaries of the komsomol province committee, Mikhail Zimin and Boris Orlov, consider that the young people in the Gorky province are not under the influence of religious prejudices. But is this so?

Last year the sect of seventh-day adventists active in Gorky admitted five new members—all of them of komsomol age; this year the number rose to seventeen. Nineteen young boys and girls have become baptists. But the komsomol committee has remained indifferent to the fate of these young people.

A few years ago a young worker, . . . a komsomol by the name of Ivan Komarov, came under baptist influence. A contest of ideologies ensued between the komsomol on the one side and the baptists on the other—and was won by the baptist preacher! Ivan went to the komsomol committee and surrendered his membership card.

Nobody knows what has happened to Ivan Komarov or how he is getting on now.

[1] A sect which broke away from the Orthodox Church in the seventeenth century.

This year four people from the *Dawn* collective farm were expelled from the komsomol by the Smirnov district committee of the komsomol for marrying in church. The committee did right to expel them, but why did the young people feel drawn towards the church in the first place?

. . . The komsomol propagandists are silent. Not one official from the province committee lectured on an anti-religious topic this year. Moreover, the general opinion has been formed that lectures giving a straightforward account of the evils of religious prejudices, and of the reactionary nature of the various sects would somehow be out of place in so cultured a province as Gorky. Lectures tend to deal with subjects such as '"Strange" Atmospheric Phenomena'. But the people of Gorky are not worried about atmospheric phenomena; nobody remembers seeing any comets or falling stars over the province in recent years. The audience would, however, like to know about the 'strange' qualities of Svetloyar lake, but the lectures do not provide any answer.

. . . There is an orthodox church in the village of Svyatitsa which comes under the Sutyr rural soviet. It is the job of the local parish priest, Poluektov, to sow obscurantism among the villagers; it is the job of the club and the village activists to provide enlightenment and education. While the former performs his duties most efficiently, this cannot be said of the latter. . . . The church is as new, while the club (which, incidentally, has to cater for all the twelve villages which come under this rural soviet) has no permanent building. At the moment it is temporarily housed in the school hostel. The priest has a church elder and a church council to help him; there are hardly any club activists. The church has an excellent choir; the club has no musical instruments at all apart from a broken guitar. Instruments are only given out in Semenov when the club choir competes in the district House of Culture there, and must be given up again immediately after the concert is over. The priest, Poluektov, preaches one or two sermons a week to his flock; the propagandists have not given a single lecture on anti-religious subjects in the village recently.

'Oh yes, I remember,' Sergei Ivanovich Mityashin, the school head master tells us. 'We had some students from the Medical Institute in Gorky down here on a skiing tour in 1951, and they gave us some lectures. Since then we haven't had any lecturers here from Gorky. . . . '

The komsomols in Svyatitsa don't go to church, but neither they nor the district or province committees are doing anything to remove young people from the influence of the church completely. This year, for instance, 60 saints' days were celebrated in the Vetluga district. In spring many collective farmers interrupted their timber cutting to celebrate Shrove Tuesday. In Svyatitsa too they carefully celebrate 'saints' days'—the young people too. The latter do not take part because they believe in a god, but because there is nothing else for them to do. A film show is a very rare event in the village, although it is only eight miles from Semenov. Only one film was shown in the whole of the Sutyr district during November. It was put on twice in the club at Svyatitsa and then went on to Semenov. The club can just about squeeze in 50 people; the inhabitants of the district number over a thousand. Moreover, prices were rather high—2.50r. per ticket. Could they not have been a little cheaper?

Semenov is not a small town. It has a teachers' training college and a branch of the Society for the Dissemination of Political and Scientific Knowledge. The Society gives lectures on such subjects as 'Science and Religion on the Creation of the Universe', and 'The Origin and Reactionary Nature of Religious Feast Days and Rites'. But the trouble is that none of these lectures ever leave the district centre.

According to Anatolii Anatolevich Serikov, the secretary in charge at the Semenov branch of the Society, only three lectures on anti-religious subjects were given in the villages of the district during the past year. Three lectures for a district with nineteen rural soviets, each of which has at least ten villages!

Many good plans are drawn up and many beautiful speeches made in Gorky, in the Society for the Dissemination of Political and Scientific Knowledge and in the province department of culture. But what actually happens? The inhabitants of Svyatitsa, an ordinary village in the Gorky province, see one film per month. They have no lecturers, no artists, no mobile exhibitions or concerts and no wireless. One cannot help wondering what the heads of the province cultural and educational institutions are doing with their energy and time.

And the relative strength of the cultural and religious forces in the village is often to the disadvantage of the former. The village of Chupoleiko in the Vyksa district, for instance, has 260 houses. It has one reading room and fifteen Old Believer cells and *posidelki*.[1] The next village, Podlesovka, has no reading room and five cells. The young people have nowhere to go in their spare time, and so they are naturally drawn to the Old Believer cells. These, however, are centres

[1] Places for women to meet, originally to spin in the evenings.

of obscenity and depravity: thirty-two young girls who used to visit these Old Believer *posidelki* gave birth to illegitimate children.

It is a long time since the Gorky province committee discussed a single question connected with anti-religious propaganda. The secretary of the province committee of the komsomol, Mikhail Zimin, considers that this is not necessary. But perhaps it is necessary after all? Perhaps after all there is every reason for calling a meeting of leading komsomols and inviting the comrades from the province department of culture and from the local branch of the Society for the Dissemination of Political and Scientific Knowledge, in order to discuss why it is that we still have 'holy' places in the province, that some of the young people are superstitious and that priests and members of sects operate freely.

THE YOUNGEST

BY S. NARINYANI, SHCHERBAKOV COMBINE, MOSCOW

(*Komsomolskaya Pravda*, Jan. 31, 1950)

THE assistant foreman of the weaving shop, Ivan Serov, is responsible for the group of agitators working in houses no. 2–8 in Yuravlyov Square.

'Looks as though the fourth in our group will be Tanya Noskovich,' he says. 'We are going to allot her the two top flats at no. 2.'

. . . Tanya Noskovich belongs to the youngest generation of weavers, which is well represented at the Shcherbakov combine: there are over 200 in the satin shop alone. Some of them, like Tanya, have not yet reached majority; others will be voting this year for the first time in their lives.

The oldest in this generation are now about 23 years. They are those same boys and girls who left school during the Patriotic War and went into the factory to take the place of their fathers and elder brothers at the looms. They were hard years. Many of the girls came to Moscow from districts which had only just been liberated: from the Kursk region, the Ukraine and the Kuban. The girls' faces looked pinched and showed traces of suffering . . . Here is a photograph taken in 1943. The FZO school was still unable to provide its pupils with a uniform, and the girls are wearing the clothes in which they arrived: a torn padded jacket, father's boots, or mother's old coat.

About seven years have passed since the arrival of the first group of FZO pupils. What has become of the girl who came in her mother's old coat? Seven years ago Tanya Kuznetsova arrived here from the village of Krupets in the Odoyevo district of the Tula province. Her progress since then has been quite remarkable: in 1944 she graduated from the FZO school and became a weaver; that same year she entered the night school department of the textiles technicum; in 1948 she graduated from the technicum and became chief foreman of the napping shop.

The girl in the torn padded jacket is Varya Glazova, who came to Moscow from the Volokolamsk district. She attended both the FZO school and the Night School for Young Workers at the same time. Subsequently she entered the night school department of the technicum and, on graduating from it, became a shop dispatcher.

The girl who had arrived in her father's boots is Shura Lebedeva. Like her friends, she too has risen on the industrial ladder: to begin with, she graduated from the FZO school, then went on to the night department of the technicum, and now works as chief foreman of the warping shop.

. . . I made enquiries about wages in some 25 satin weaving shops: I concentrated on those people who had only graduated from the FZO school a year or two ago, not on the most highly skilled workers. I found that not one of them was earning less than 1,000r. a month. Lida Shulenina even earns as much as 1,300r. And, like Tanya Noskovich, Lida is only seventeen years old.

But it is not merely a question of guaranteed wages. Like many of our other enterprises, the Shcherbakov combine has its 'practice teams' which exist side by side with the productivity teams. Everyone at the works is given the opportunity of combining factory work with studies at the seven-year school or the textiles technicum, both of which have a good teaching staff. The studies are arranged to fit in with the factory's three-shift system, and the workers have a library and visual aids at their disposal—just come and study!

. . . Former FZO pupils now attend schools, technicums and institutes. But they are not simply becoming textile specialists. Their political horizon too is being widened. . . . Every fifth person on the list of agitators is a former FZO pupil . . . And each of them has something to tell the electorate . . .

MEETING

Letter from the Virgin Lands

BY LEONID VOLYNSKY, KUSTANAI[1]

(*Literaturnaya Gazeta*, April 17, 1954)

KUSTANAI'S central restaurant is crowded and smoky. . . . Every few minutes the door bangs as more and more new people come in, their cheeks rosy from the cold. . . .

But you can hardly call the tall, middle-aged man in the navy blue cloth tunic and white felt boots who is sitting at the table next to ours a newcomer. He is the director of the new group of state grain farms, Trofimenko, and he has already been living here for over a month now. Just at the moment he has put his elbows on the table and is running his palms over his large, shaven head as he listens to his companion, a man dressed in a similar navy blue tunic and wearing a broad army belt. I had seen them introduce themselves to each other five minutes earlier:

'My name's Nikitin; I've been appointed director of the Dzhetygara state farm. I've come for instructions.'

'Pleased to meet you. We've been waiting for you. The chief agricultural specialist has already been here four days; the chief accountant and the chief engineer arrived the day before yesterday.'

. . . Trofimenko gets up, straightening his tunic in a military fashion.

'Well, come to the trust when you've settled in.'

'Today?' asks Nikitin.

'Yes, we'll take our days off some other time,' Trofimenko answers him.

He goes out and his place is taken by a young boy wearing a jumper and brown skiing trousers tucked into rubber boots. He

[1] A small town in Kazakhstan.

nervously fingers his metal cloakroom number, looks around him and smooths a tuft of light brown hair which completely refuses to lie flat.

I take a look at his childishly round, snubnosed face, the thin neck in the rolltop of the jumper, the half-open downy lips slightly chapped from the cold wind, and at his komsomol badge.

'Cabbage soup and pilau,' he says to the waitress in a dignified, almost-bass voice. 'Oh, and a bottle of beer.'

I cannot hold back a smile. The lad notices it, and now his whole face has become rosy, only his brows and a funny little birth mark with three hairs on the, still beardless, chin stand out white.

'From Moscow?' I ask.

'Uhu,' he replies, frowning and leisurely pouring his beer into the glass.

'Well, and how do you like it here?'

'It's all right,' he answers, takes a drink from his glass and adds a mere: 'I like it.—And where are you from?'

Hearing that I am from Moscow and will soon be returning to his native city, he grows more interested.

'I'd like to ask you to do me a favour,' he says, frowning and drawing a piece of bread along the saucer. 'My mother lives in Moscow and, well, you know how it is, she cried when I left, worried how I'd get on and so forth. I've written and told her, but she doesn't believe me. Do you think you could go to see her? Praskovya Petrovna Zakharova, 15 Park Street, house 6/75, room 36. Tell her that everything is quite all right, that I'm alive and well, clothed and shod, and that I'm attending short courses for *DT* tractor drivers.'

'And what's your name?'

'Zakharov, Victor Panfilovich.'

'And how old are you?'

'Seventeen.'

*

A few days later I sought out Victor Zakharov in state farm no. 641. . . .

'What are you doing here?' he asks me.

'Seeing how you live. Otherwise, what am I to say if your mother asks me?'

'Oh.' Zakharov smiles shyly. 'Thank you very much. I'll take you there, shall I? It's our break just now.'

We go along the main road, past the office.

'Are you in a hostel?' I ask.

'No, of course not. You should have seen the welcome we had when we arrived. The people here gathered in the club, and within half an hour everybody had been found accommodation. This is where I live —past that little blue house.'

We go into a tidy clay cottage. . . . The clean little kitchen has a stove, a cupboard and a table with two jugs of milk and a loaf of bread covered with a towel.

'Here you are, this is how we live,' Zakharov says to me. 'Take off your coat; it's warm in here.'

He puts his exercise book on the table and takes off his padded jacket.

'This is where I sleep,' he says, pointing to a wooden plank bed with a new cover on it.

We sit down on the bench and, as we quietly talk with one another, the short and difficult life history of this seventeen-year old lad is unfolded before me.

His father was killed at the front in '43. 'I don't remember him very well, but for some reason I can still remember his voice.' He was a fitter. Victor's mother was a nurse in an evacuation hospital during the war, and naturally Victor was living with her; first in Kovrov and then in Shepetovka—'you know, where Pavka Korchagin was active'.[1] He went to a seven-year school there. In '51 he finished school and went to live with his elder sister in the Karelo-Finnish Republic. He became a diesel engine mechanic. After working there for a year, his mother asked him to come back—'you know how it is, she didn't want to live on her own'. So he returned, learnt another trade and started work as plasterer on a building site. 'We were given a separate room to ourselves in the hostel. I was in grade four, and we lived quite well—nothing to complain of. I studied at night school no. 20, the one attached to the electrical engineering works. I've always been interested in machines, and I'm keen on things like mechanics and maths. I'm not so good at literature, but I can do maths problems. That incidentally is something that's bad here: I've been the rounds of all the shops and stalls in Kustanai and there wasn't a single popular book on maths like *Mathematics as Entertainment*, for instance, to be had.'

'And are you thinking of studying further?'

'I went to the education department at home before I left and got

[1] The hero in Ostrovsky's *How the Steel was Tempered.*

the syllabus and textbooks for the eighth form. I suppose they'll have a school here, won't they?'

He falls silent and sits there thinking. After a while he continues:

'I have one advantage over the others. As soon as we finish sowing I can go to the building site as a plasterer. They'll have to do a lot of building here—starting with the bare steppe the way they are doing. . . .'

'And do you already know where you will be working, Victor?'

'The director arrived this morning—very intelligent type—and showed us the plan. It'll be about 100 miles from here—just steppe and lakes, that's all. . . .'

In the club we meet the others, staring at us with curiosity:

'Hullo, Vitya! Is that your brother who's come to see you?'

Then the questions begin: 'What's it like in Moscow just now? Has the multi-storey building in Insurrection Square been finished?'—'Silly, how could it have been, we've only been gone less than a month.'—'I know, I was working there myself, laying the electric wires. It was supposed to be ready in May, all except the ornamental pillars.'—'Well, it's not May yet!'

I say goodbye to everyone and receive dozens of messages to take to Moscow. . . .

We are on our way home. . . . The wet earth is steaming a little, and chestnut-coloured patches of dry ground are beginning to appear.

'It's steaming,' the driver says to me. 'That means the winter is on the way out.'

Large black and white crows fly up from under our very wheels and alight on the smooth snow surface, balancing themselves with their long tails.

'Never mind, we'll have swallows too before long. We'll soon be starting the sowing.'

ON THE VIRGIN LANDS

Pages from a Diary

BY V. LEONENKO, ACTRESS AT THE THEATRE OF LITERATURE AND DRAMA, MOSCOW

(*Krestyanka*, 1955, no. 3, p. 28)

SO here we were at the grain-growing state farm of Tobol. The first workers arrived here on May 9, 1954. They pitched their tents by the banks of the river Tobol near a thicket of reeds the height of a man. Birds were floating on the backwaters undisturbed, and fishes could be seen darting to and fro in the transparent water. . . .

We arrived on August 22. Only the pegs in the ground reminded us of the tents that had been here. There is a trim street of over 50 houses there now. A seven-year school has been built, and a girl in a white apron proudly showed us over the class rooms.

Children are crowding around the doors of the school. Many have come on bicycles, the prevailing form of transport here. The state farm has a library which has only just been transferred from a truck on wheels to its new building, a bath house, a canteen and a post office. A large shop is under construction. We were struck by the fantastic number of kittens and puppies. I asked a girl from Odessa why she had two kittens and a puppy as well.

'Makes us feel at home,' was the reply.

The people have settled down here. One has the feeling that they have brought a piece of their own homeland with them. Only three and a half months ago all this was wild steppe land. Tens of thousands of acres of virgin land have been ploughed up since then.

. . . We have a long way to go to our next point of call, but the journey is not dull. Now the outlines of enormous combine harvesters have become visible on the horizon. There are four of them.—We get out of our buses and invite the combine operators and their assistants to a concert to be given on the spot. Next we place our buses side by side in a row, unfold tables and chairs, set up wings in the shade of the buses, shield them off with screens and begin to get ourselves ready for a lunch-hour concert.

As soon as the concert is over the combine operators quickly start their motors and disperse to their sections. We too gather up our belongings and resume our journey. We are to give a performance of Schiller's *Robbers* 30 miles from here this evening.

The club holds some 200 people, but up to a thousand have gathered outside. We hang up the curtain and rope off the stage. The lights are fastened on to poles; when it is very windy and we cannot use the curtain, these lights are turned towards the audience during scene changes, and produce a wonderful 'curtain of light' effect.

Small boys have perched themselves on roofs, poles and trees like so many sparrows. The audience is standing in a solid wall. Everyone has made himself as comfortable as he can. Nothing matters as long as you can see what is happening on the stage, and not necessarily from the front: you can get quite a good view from the back too, and you can hear even better from there.

The play finishes at two o'clock in the morning. The girls have left, singing on their way home; even the indefatigable little boys have gone to bed; we too prepare ourselves for the night.

We play at a different place every day, and we rarely know where we will be spending the night. Sometimes we spend it in a new house that is still unfinished and has no windows and doors or no roof, sometimes we use a class room in an empty school. Tonight we will be staying in the club. We quickly put up our camp beds and fall asleep.

The next morning is clear and transparent; there is no dust yet. The horizon is so far away that it feels as though you could see to the 'edge of the world'. We bathe in the little stream and once again set off on our journey. Today we have two concerts to give, and we must set off early if we are to cover our difficult, 60 mile route . . .

All roads are alike in the steppe. Coming to a cross roads we often find ourselves having to guess between three different roads, rather like the heroes in fairy tales. A bullock cart, nicknamed a 'MOO-2' machine, appears in the distance. As it draws nearer we stop and ask the way, and learn that we must take the right fork of the road . . . At last we reach the livestock section of the state farm. There are flocks of sheep and goats, horses and enormous herds of milch cows. We are met by a young girl, who is the brigade leader—a 'virgin soil arrival' as the local inhabitants call the newcomers. She is surprised and glad to see us. 'But surely you knew we were coming,' we ask her

'Yes,' she answers, 'we did. But we thought that that was just a promise, and that you wouldn't really come. After all, nobody's ever visited us yet.—Never mind, we'll have everyone together in no time.'

She quickly mounts her horse and gallops off into the steppe. We look on and marvel at her agility: she comes from Moscow; how beautifully she has learnt to ride in these few months! We will long remember the practical efficiency of this twenty-year old brigade leader who was obeyed by everybody and with whom every problem was discussed.

We met many very young doctors, teachers, agricultural specialists and local government officials on the virgin lands. They have a most commendable seriousness and severity: they know that a tremendous responsibility rests on their shoulders—the doctor, a twenty-three-year-old girl, is the only one for the hundred-odd people who live in the new settlement, and the school teacher is a nineteen-year old girl.

But now clouds of dust have risen over the steppe, and a truck with some of our audience comes into sight. A few minutes later others arrive on horseback, followed by a 'MOO–2' drawing an enormous araba full of women. The sun beats down mercilessly. For the comfort of the audience we sit them with their backs to the sun, while we play directly into its blinding rays. Eagles are circling above our 'theatre'; inquisitive geese crane their necks and cackle whenever the audience laughs; the bullocks are lazily chewing the cud.

It is an unusual setting, but that does not worry us. The show is put on in the normal way. The costumes have been ironed, the women are wearing evening dress. The artists always try to do everything in full costume: they are, after all, from Moscow! And there are people in the audience who have never been to the capital and have never seen a real theatre. We must always remember that when we have to face such difficulties as heat, rain, dust storms, overcrowding and tiredness.

In the evening we give a concert in the village of New-Orenburg. About 2,000 people have come, including guests from the neighbouring Chelyabinsk and Aktyubinsk provinces. The concert lasts two hours and is listened to with unflagging attention. And then at the end there are cries of 'encore'. . . .

*

We worked very hard (we gave 60 performances and travelled 3,000 miles in a period of 50 days), but the tremendous interest which we met everywhere has been most stimulating for us.

We saw the deep impression we left with these people who live far from the great cultural centres; we saw how much they needed us. . . . I can never forget the young people with burning eyes sitting in front of our curtain. But there is no need for me to say anything about our young people, and the majority out there are young. Wherever we went we were always asked to 'come again soon' . . .

IV

MARRIAGE AND AFTER

INTRODUCTION

THIS section will conclude the volume, and is intended to take us back again to some of the problems discussed in Section I, thus completing the circle. With this aim in view I have focused my attention on questions concerning the *young* couple rather than on problems of family life in general, although the two naturally tend to overlap. I have narrowed my subject down still further, however, concentrating my attention on the young married woman. I feel quite justified in doing this, because it does seem to me that the woman tends to be far more directly affected by many of the problems involved than the man is.

Such an approach is bound, however, to be somewhat onesided. The Marxist classics had always regarded the emancipation of women as an integral part of building socialism. Women, they had maintained, could only regain equality with men in a new, socialist society, while such a society could only be built with the participation of women. Women had therefore to be freed from the general work involved in housekeeping and be enabled to take their place in modern industry with its demand for female labour. This development would, in its turn, transform the old domestic work into a 'public industry'.[1] They spoke of the deadening effect of woman's drudgery in the home and of the need for transferring 'the economic and educational functions of the separate household to society'.[2]

But they did not see the emancipation of women purely in terms of transforming domestic work into a public industry. They also stressed the need for a change in the attitude of the husband. And this did not simply mean that he should allow his wife to go out to work; it also meant that he should be prepared to do his share of the housework:

> So few men—even among the proletariat—realise how much

[1] Engels, *Origin of the Family* (Chicago, 1902), p. 196.
[2] K. Zetkin, *Reminiscences of Lenin* (London, 1929), p. 69.

> effort and trouble they could save women, even quite do away with, if they were to lend a hand in 'women's work'. But no, that is contrary to the 'right and dignity of a man'. They want their peace and comfort. The home life of the woman is a daily sacrifice to a thousand unimportant trivialities. The old master right of the man still lives in secret. His slave takes her revenge, also secretly. The backwardness of women, their lack of understanding for the revolutionary ideals of the man decrease his joy and determination in fighting. They are like the little worms which, unseen, slowly but surely, rot and corrode. I know the life of the worker, and not only from books. Our communist work among women, our political work, embraces a great deal of educational work among men.[1]

This aspect is almost completely ignored by the Soviet press today, not, I fear, because all Soviet men now do their share of the housework; all the articles that I have seen appear to take it for granted that the washing and cleaning is done by the mother, possibly with the help of her children. And this has more or less forced my hand. I should have preferred to give *most* of my attention to women but, in the absence of any material on the re-education of men, I have been obliged to give women *all* my attention, except for the items on the Far East, which are not strictly comparable in this connection.

It is, however, in the sphere of women's lives that the USSR has achieved some of its greatest successes and that, at the same time, it still has some of its most difficult problems to solve, and I shall try to illustrate some of these achievements and problems in this section. So far I have treated the USSR as one uniform whole. But while the trends I have described are perfectly valid for all parts of the country, the rate at which these trends have developed and the level to which they have developed in the various parts of the country have been very different. This is, of course, to be expected. Russia as a whole had been a backward country compared with her European neighbours, but some regions of the Russian Empire, notably the Eastern and Far Eastern provinces, had been at a very much lower level still. In addition, these regions came under effective Soviet rule rather later than European Russia did. Much of the Eastern territory had been under strong Muslim influence, and the woman in this territory was in a particularly backward position. Here again, the trend towards emancipation has been one and the same for the whole

[1] K. Zetkin, *Reminiscences of Lenin* (London, 1929), p. 68.

country but, as we shall see, the East has not yet achieved this to the degree already attained in the European parts of the country.

Any description of the position of Soviet women today must be drawn against the background of pre-revolutionary Russia. Like many other European countries at that time, the Russian Empire was, I believe, fairly backward as regards women's rights. Marriage and divorce laws were formulated to the woman's disadvantage, most of the more skilled trades and professions were inaccessible to her, and among the working classes drunkenness and wife beating were common. A small number of working class women were employed in industry but, in the absence of adequate facilities for the children, this could hardly be regarded as a form of emancipation. The illiteracy rate which was already very high for the population as a whole, was greater still for the female half.[1]

In the Eastern territories of the Russian Empire conditions were very much worse: polygamy was common, women were forced to wear the yashmak—a thick veil covering the head completely—they could be bought and sold in return for so many head of cattle and, once married, they were more or less kept a prisoner in the house—in fact their position was little better than that of a slave.

The revolutionary government was pledged to grant women equal rights with men and to free them from the various types of slavery condemned by the Marxist classics. The former was accomplished with relative ease, on paper at any rate. Women were granted equal rights with men in the statute book, and most of the trades and professions open to men were made accessible to women too. For the first time in history they were granted equal pay with men.

Ideas about the woman and about the role of the family were also beginning to undergo a radical change. They in fact tended at times to take on rather extreme forms during the first few years after the revolution, no doubt coloured by the fact that these ideas about the new family were in revolt against the old, patriarchal kind of family. The Marxist classics had advocated that education should become the responsibility of the state and that, as I have already mentioned, domestic work should be turned into a 'public industry'. But some people now went still further and began to argue against the entire institution of the family, which, they maintained, had been outlived. And the conditions of the civil war period, when many homes had been broken up, certainly helped to make this view appear plausible.

[1] G. N. Serebrennikov, *The Position of Women in the U.S.S.R.*, 1937, p. 192.

Some sections among the communist youth of the time advocated the notorious 'glass of water' theory, which placed sexual desire on a par with physical hunger and thirst, 'love' being distrusted as something 'bourgeois'. The theory was, however, never officially approved of or encouraged. Lenin, for instance, condemned it in no uncertain terms, and complained that the youth movement was attacked by what he called 'the disease of modernity in its attitude towards sexual questions'.[1]

The NEP period saw a greater degree of stabilisation, but it was nevertheless a time of great hardships for the bulk of the population and, in particular, for the woman. She had been granted equal rights with men in the statute book, but this equality often existed only on paper. In industry, for instance, women continued to be employed for unskilled work, if indeed they could find any employment at all, and although equal pay for equal work had been introduced, the average female wage still tended to be much lower than the wage earned by men.[2] The woman was free now, according to the law, to leave her husband if she wanted to, but in actual fact this was often impossible because she could find no employment for herself and remained dependent on her husband.[3]

The countryside had been almost untouched by the extremist ideas described above, which had been so popular with certain sections of the younger generation in the towns. The peasant household had remained much the same, and the old patriarchal structure was apparently being upheld by the peasant, *inter alia*, for economic reasons.[4] Many women therefore continued to live in much the same way as they had done before. I have already mentioned the sway of religion in the countryside. The women in particular maintained a deeply religious outlook on life. A foreign observer visiting Russia at the time found that there were villages where the local atheist would walk in fear of his life, and that the average peasant girl looked forward to a church wedding.[5] Krupskaya too mentions this religious outlook. She advocates more art, theatres and clubs in the hope that these will satisfy the emotional and aesthetic needs which the church

[1] Zetkin, *op. cit.*, p. 55.

[2] Price, *Labour Protection in Soviet Russia*, 1928, p. 72, gives it as 60 per cent of the average male wage.

[3] One of the stories in A. Kollontai's book, *Lyubov Pchol Trudovykh*, 1923, raises this problem and links it with that of prostitution.

[4] Report by Kursky, then Commissar of Justice, to the RSFSR Central Executive Committee in 1926 (translated in R. Schlesinger, *Changing Attitudes in Soviet Russia: The Family*, p. 121).

[5] M. Hindus, *Humanity Uprooted*, 1929, pp. 27–8.

had hitherto filled.[1] These measures by themselves can, however, hardly be expected to wean the population away from religion. A religious outlook probably still exists fairly strongly in the countryside, and to a lesser extent in the towns, today. 'A Komsomol Should Be Principled' would not have been published if church weddings were not a very common occurrence. The statement contained in it that *all* the letters condemned komsomol M.'s conduct is simply an indication of the type of people who write to the papers on a subject of this kind.

Propaganda work, whether in the town or the village, must have been extremely difficult during the first few years, and in 1919 special 'women's departments' were set up for this work. Here is a description of the sort of tasks which these departments were having to tackle:

> We had first to gain their confidence and then to say to them: 'Look, you have children and are tied down; would it not be a good thing if we had crèches for the children?'—The working women are interested in that kind of thing, but they are not at all interested in communism. And they will put up with us Bolsheviks only if we give them practical help.[2]

During most of this period the individual household was officially regarded as a temporary evil. Lenin, for instance, attached great importance to this point:

> Even with the fullest equality, women are still in an actual position of inferiority because all housework is thrust upon them. Most of this housework is the most unproductive, most barbarous and most arduous work that women perform. This labour is extremely petty and contains nothing that facilitates the development of women.
>
> . . . In order to achieve the complete emancipation of women and to make them really equal with men, we must have social economy, and the participation of women in general productive labour. Then women will occupy the same position as men.[3]

The Soviet authorities have always continued to insist on the importance of lightening the woman's work in the home. During a

[1] N. Krupskaya, *Zhenshchina Strany Sovetov—Ravnopravny Grazhdanin*, 1938. This particular article on religion is reprinted from *Kommunistka*, 1922, no. 3–5.

[2] A. Kollontai, *Rabotnitsa i Krestyanka v Sovetskoi Rossii*, p. 32.

[3] Speech at a non-party conference of women workers, held in 1919 (in *Selected Works*, 1937, vol. 9, p. 496).

period such as NEP, however, the opportunities for putting the necessary measures into practice were very small indeed; insistence of this kind tended to be couched in the vaguest of terms, and could only be regarded as something that might be achieved in the distant future.

The thirties saw a tremendous improvement in the position of women. The five-year plan put an end to unemployment, and women began to be drawn into industry and to acquire skilled work. By 1935 women already formed 33·4 per cent of the total labour force.[1] In the field of education too women were making great strides, and by that same year 46 per cent of the students in universities and higher educational institutions were women.[2]

The revolution in family relations was also beginning to become more stabilised. The new family law of 1936[3] made abortion illegal, and divorce proceedings much more formal and expensive. This decree marked the beginning of a new stage. The first period, when the emphasis had been on the *destruction* of the old, patriarchal family structure, was at an end, and the emphasis now changed to one of *construction*, of strengthening the new, socialist family which had to be protected both from the old patriarchal family concepts as well as from the remnants of the 'glass of water' and similar theories. Although women were still encouraged to go out to work, the housewife was now no longer regarded as either an exploited underdog or a parasite. The Soviet housewife, unlike the housewife of previous times, it was now maintained, would no longer confine her activities to housework, but would take an active interest in the life around her.[4]

This general trend was taken a stage further in the legislation of 1944.[5] The decree of 1936 had officially rehabilitated marriage as an institution. The decree of 1944 seems to me to have gone much further than that. Certain of its features, such as the titles of 'Heroine Mother' for women who had given birth to and brought up 10 children, 'Motherhood Glory', 1st, 2nd and 3rd class, for mothers of 9, 8 and 7 children respectively, and 'Motherhood Medal' for mothers of 5 or 6 children, must have served to rehabilitate motherhood as a profession. It has been suggested that these measures were intended to encourage larger families. In the countryside, however, where families

[1] S. Wolffson, 'Socialism and the Family', in *Pod Znamenem Marxizma*, 1936 (translated in Schlesinger, *op. cit.*, p. 286).

[2] *Ibid.*, p. 285. In 1929 the percentage had been 39.

[3] English translation in *ibid.*, pp. 269 ff.

[4] Krupskaya, *op. cit.*, p. 86.

[5] July 8, 1944, translated in Schlesinger, *op. cit.*, pp. 367 ff.

were no doubt already fairly large, this measure must have been unnecessary. And I very much doubt whether these medals, and the money payments that went with them, were really sufficiently enticing to overcome the disincentives for city dwellers to have large families. I doubt, for instance, whether an urban couple living in one room with very little prospect of anything better in the near future, would have been attracted by these incentives into having a large family, especially if this meant that the wife would have to leave her work and settle down to undiluted motherhood, with the consequent loss of her earnings. What the decree will have succeeded in doing is to increase the kudos of the kind of woman who already regarded motherhood and 'home making' as a profession in themselves. In the absence of any figures on the proportion of married women who were engaged in full-time jobs, it is, however, difficult to assess the effect which the decree actually had.

The decree went a certain way towards restoring the old 'a woman's place is in the home' ideas. It did not in any way imply that the woman's place ought to be exclusively in the home, but merely included the home once again as one of the many places where a woman could perform useful work. 'The Noble Work of a Mother' reflects this attitude, and I have therefore included it, even though its style is rather pompous and it belongs to a phase which is now probably on the way out. In assessing this decree, it is important to guard against exaggerating its 'conservative' implications. It is true that divorce was now made very much more difficult to obtain. But the decree also contained measures designed to help the working mother: pregnancy leave was extended, and the need for more kindergartens and crèches was stressed.

In the light of these considerations, it is wrong to regard the Soviet family today as exactly the same as the family in this country, for instance, although at first sight there appears to be little difference. In speaking of the features which they have in common, it is important not to overlook the very real differences between the socialist family and its counterpart under capitalism. And the chief difference, despite the 1944 decree, still lies in the attitude towards women, which I have already described in the introduction to Section I.

It is, I think, true to say that Soviet legislation[1] and the attitude

[1] I have already mentioned equal pay. Other important features of legislation concerning women are that pregnancy may never be used as grounds for dismissal or refusal of employment, and that pregnant women may not be employed on night shift. They receive 35 days' paid leave before the birth of the child, and 42 days' paid leave after its birth (*Sovetskoye Trudovoye Pravo*, 1949, p. 245).

officially adopted have in fact provided the foundation for the establishment of sex equality in the USSR. Many Soviet women have a trade or profession, and trade and vocational schools are open to both sexes, so that women need not necessarily fill the lower paid jobs. Unfortunately no exact figures of female labour are available, but we do know that women are beginning to predominate in some fields, such as medicine, for instance.[1] But it is important to distinguish between this foundation which is a *sine qua non* for emancipation, and the actual achieving of sex equality. There are three main factors involved here: first, a feeling on the part of the woman herself (and of the man) that marriage is not *in itself* the sole and natural career for her to follow; secondly, the co-operation of the man in the home, which I have already dealt with above; and thirdly, sufficient household devices, good shops, kindergartens and crèches. How easy is it in fact for the Soviet woman to carry on a full-time job and to look after her family as well? What labour-saving devices does she use? What is her home like? What is her husband's attitude to the whole problem? These are some of the questions that one must ask oneself in studying the position of the Soviet woman today.

I think that it is probably true to say that the average urban family lives in one or two rooms, though some of course live in the large, newly built, blocks of flats. This means that there is a correspondingly small amount of cleaning to be done and that, in addition to the economic incentive, Soviet women will tend to be less anxious than their counterparts over here to stay at home all day. Most families probably eat out at their place of work in the middle of the day, and the wife merely has to cook an evening meal when she arrives home after her work. As against this, one has to mention the scarcity of modern household amenities. Many Soviet women do their cooking on a primus stove, for instance, although gas has come to be used very much more in recent years. In Moscow, for instance, 68,000 flats were using gas in 1946; by 1955 the number had increased to over 470,000—almost eight times as many as in 1940. According to

[1] Medynsky, *Narodnoye Obrazovaniye v SSSR*, p. 163. The medical profession is, however, by and large not a very highly paid one in the USSR. This may in part be due to the fact that it is coming to be regarded as a women's profession and that women still command lower wages than men.

It is important, though, to bear in mind that the Soviet medical profession as such is bound to be depressed in comparison with its counterpart over here: in Britain the doctor enjoys a privileged social position, possibly due to the expensive training he has had, and to the fact that, until the introduction of the health service, practices were only accessible to those who could afford to buy them.

the five-year plan (1956–60) gas is to be fully laid on in 132 cities of the country by 1960, 56 of them in the RSFSR.[1] There are still very few washing machines, refrigerators and vacuum cleaners.[2] There are few laundries,[3] and food shops are only just beginning to have a delivery service, though the housewife's task is made easier by the fact that the shops are open on Sundays and until late in the evening on week days. Milk still has to be fetched from the shop. In addition, ready-made clothes have in the past tended to be rather unattractive and of poor quality, and since there is still a shortage of tailoring and dressmaking establishments, 'Soviet women are in many cases obliged to make their clothing at home'.[4]

All these difficulties and shortages may be details, but in their sum-total they mean a lot of extra work to be done at the end of a full day at the factory. The extra work and the difficulties involved are illustrated in 'The Housewife', where the woman who continues with her work is beginning to age prematurely, while the housewife who stays at home to look after the children feels frustrated. A maid is impracticable[5] and, it seems, taboo with working class people. In this case, as in most stories and sketches of this kind, the husband is blamed for his wife's stagnation. There must, however, be many cases where it is the wife who prefers to take the line of least resistance and to stay at home. And 'The Noble Work of the Mother', though implying a preference for the woman with a profession or trade, throws a sop to her, provided she engages in part-time voluntary activities, in fact, provided she does not lead a life confined to the immediate interests and cares of her family.

It is, however, an encouraging sign that the Soviet people themselves are acutely aware of the defects described above. 'It is her Right' contains a very frank and realistic discussion of the problems involved—both in terms of consumer goods and of attitudes. The speech by Mikoyan which I have already mentioned, once again stresses the need for public dining rooms, and quotes Lenin's dictum

[1] *Bloknot Agitatora*, 1955, no. 31, pp. 27–8.

[2] Only 62,000 refrigerators were manufactured in 1954 (Mikoyan, *Measures for the Further Expansion of Trade and for Improving the Organisation of State, Co-operative and Collective-Farm Trade*, 1954, p. 49).

[3] In the city of Gorky (700,000 inhabitants) there was only one laundry in 1951 which accepted orders from private individuals (*Literaturnaya Gazeta*, July 24, 1951).

[4] Mikoyan, *op. cit.*, p. 53.

[5] I was told during my visit to the USSR in 1954 that maids are usually young girls straight from the countryside who tend to stay for a very short time only: after a few months in the city they find that there are far better jobs to be had elsewhere, and so they leave.

that 'the real emancipation of women, real communism, will begin only where and when the mass struggle . . . against the petty domestic economy, or rather when its wholesale transformation into large-scale socialist economy, begins'.[1] When Lenin made this statement it had simply been part of a long-term plan, of something that a socialist society would regard as desirable. I have already mentioned the fact that statements of this kind tended to be made in general terms only. It is only now when the USSR has become industrialised that it has become possible to talk about this general aim in the more specific terms of output of washing machines, vacuum cleaners, etc. Mikoyan speaks of the need to mechanise housework, and draws attention to the fact that this has *now* become a practical possibility.

Until such time as all these goods and services, as well as the kindergartens and crèches mentioned elsewhere are really plentiful, the emancipation of the Soviet woman cannot be said to be complete. But apart from these material requirements, the so-called 'survivals of capitalism in people's minds' are an important factor to be reckoned with: many Soviet men no doubt still feel that 'a woman's place is in the home', and there must be many women who regard marriage and rearing a family as the woman's natural profession. In addition, the komsomol and other organisations too, no doubt, sometimes adopt the attitude that married women are so busy that they have no time for any outside activities and can therefore be ignored. Despite all these obstacles, the foundations for sex equality are there: women are encouraged to acquire skills and the financial and social independence which they bring, and the general social atmosphere is becoming increasingly favourable for the working woman in the USSR with every year.

The change in the status of women has been particularly marked in the Eastern regions of the country which, as I have already mentioned, had been very much more backward in every respect, than the European parts of Russia.

The new government was confronted with the, often painful, task of transforming these regions into part of a modern industrialised state. It was often a slow process, especially during the years of the civil war and NEP. An article on Turkmenia written during this period[2] complains that there has been little change since 1917, and that you can still hear people in the markets talking about 'the price of women falling'. The article quotes a typical letter from a Turmenian woman, appealing to the Soviet authorities for help:

[1] Mikoyan, *op. cit.*, p. 48.

[2] *Izvestia*, Oct. 15, 1924.

> I was five years old when I was betrothed. At 13 I was married in exchange for 8,000 Soviet money tokens. I could not live with my husband for long since he beat me and offended me; so I went to live with my uncle, my parents being dead. A few days later my uncle sold me to a bey . . . Four months later I left him, but he demands that I return the bride money and the wedding expenses. I have not enough money to buy myself free, and I turn to the Soviet government for help and protection against the bey.

Great progress has been made since that time but, compared with her Russian sister, the woman of the Soviet East still has some leeway to make up. In Uzbekistan, for instance, the percentage of women students at higher educational establishments is still very low, although there are signs that it is now beginning to increase more quickly.[1] The Central Asian newspapers also contain many complaints that girls leave school early to get married,[2] many of them, no doubt, without their consent. I should have liked to include an item on these defects, but I have unfortunately not been able to find anything suitable. Articles such as 'The Woman in the Yashmak', which describe rather extreme cases, are more plentiful. In these cases the blame is usually put on the men who, as in 'Appendix to a Membership Report', are said to retain the old attitude towards women.

But these cases should not blind one to the general progress which has been made. Before the revolution the illiterate woman was the rule; now she is the exception. For the woman to have a secondary education was an almost unheard of thing. Today it is becoming compulsory, and in Turkmenia has already been fully introduced in six towns.[3] Central Asia had no university level institutions at all, and the growth of these institutions has been remarkable (see Table on next page).

There are today many thousands of women in the Eastern republics with a university or other specialist education. In Kazakhstan, for instance, they make up 42 per cent of the republic's specialists with a university or secondary level training.[4] Before the revolution child

[1] Medynsky, *op. cit.*, p. 33, gives a total of 29,281 Uzbek students for 1949. The number is said to have increased since then. In 1952 there were, however, only 3,750 women students in Uzbekistan. By 1954 the figure had apparently doubled (*Pravda Vostoka*, Dec. 31, 1954).

[2] E.g., *Literaturnaya Gazeta*, Dec. 10, 1953, on a province in Uzbekistan where the majority of the girls did not stay to the seventh form, and *Kommunist Tadzhikistana*, Feb. 20, 1955, which has the same story to tell.

[3] *Turkmenskaya Iskra*, Feb. 25, 1955.

[4] *Kazakhstanskaya Pravda*, March 8, 1955.

	Population in 1939 in thous.	*No. of higher educ. inst. in 1949*	*Nos. of students in 1949*	*Per 1,000 of population in 1952*
Azerbaidzhan	3,210	18	17,361	93
Georgia	3,542	19	24,745	
Armenia	1,282	14	10,124	
Turkmenia	1,254	5	3,390	60
Uzbekistan	6,282	35	29,281	71
Tadzhikistan	1,485	9	4,247	58
Kazakhstan	6,146	23	18,117	
Kirghizia	1,459	7	5,257	64

Sources: Medynsky, *op. cit.*, p. 33; Lorimer, *The Population of the Soviet Union: History and Prospects*, p. 162; Beria's speech at the XIX Congress (in *Izvestia*, Oct. 9, 1952).

marriages were regarded as normal; they are illegal nowadays. When they do occur, they stand a good chance of being exposed in the local, if not the national newspapers. The 'Appendix to a Membership Report' translated below is an exposure of this kind. And the very fact that such an incident is publicised in the national press (the names of the culprits being given in full) is in itself an indication of the general trend towards emancipation.

WHERE TO GET MARRIED

BY V. DYKHOVICHNY AND M. SLOBODSKOI

(*Literaturnaya Gazeta*, April 1, 1950)

THE question of whom to marry is usually decided individually, and this method has so far justified itself. But where to be married? That is another question altogether. It appears that great care is needed in choosing your registry office, and in this connection some comradely advice is not at all out of place.

If, for instance, you want to enter into a lawfully wedded state in a friendly and festive atmosphere, get an assignment in Molotov and register yourself and your beloved at the office of the Lenin district of that city. We can guarantee that you will have pleasant and happy memories of the event, and that you will remember it all your life. You will find beauty, attention, comfort and care—in short, go and see for yourself.

Please forgive us, dear Lidia Grigoreva Lubova, if this increases the number of clients in your Lenin district registry, but you really do arrange weddings beautifully in your office.

We have good registry offices where weddings leave happy, if slightly sentimental memories, for many years. If you are about to be married, get yourself sent to Lvov on business.—Unfortunately however, marriages do not always coincide with business trips. More often than not people fall in love in the town where they live, propose there, and are married there too. And spring—that season of love —not only comes to Lvov. It also visits Tomsk, Archangel and Kurgan.[1]

In Kurgan too nightingales break into song during the nights, and pairs of lovers walk the city like sentries of love. And then, finally, there comes the anxious moment when the young lover hears the long-awaited, simple but all-important 'yes' from the woman of his

[1] A small town in Western Siberia.

choice. This marks the end of the nightingale period and the beginning of the registration period.

A little nervous and very solemn, bride and bridegroom set out to the registry office. (We must be quite honest here: we do not know whether there are in fact nightingales in Kurgan, but we do know that it has a registry office.)

It exists, but it is difficult to find. The way there is not marked by arrows of love saying 'Road to Happiness—Round the Corner on the Right', as the young lovers would like. Nor is it marked with more prosaic arrows. It is obvious that the officials here rely on love itself to lead our lovers to the city executive committee,[1] take them through the unsightly courtyard at the back of the building and, finally, to the end of the long queue outside the locked door of the registry office.

The queue takes the lovers into a narrow little corridor, and from there into the coveted holiest of holies itself. The holiest of holies turns out to be a crowded, dingy little room cluttered with office tables and crammed with visitors. A sweaty registry official quickly makes out the marriage certificate, hurriedly jumps up and, with almost indecent haste, reels off the solemn words:

'May I congratulate you on entering into a legally wedded state; I wish you a long and happy life together; next please, take a seat.'

That is how weddings are celebrated in the city of Kurgan. And not only in Kurgan. The union of loving hearts is formalised in much the same way in the Tomsk city registry office, and in the registry offices of the Upper Mully and Cherdyn districts, both in the Molotov province.

In many city and district registry offices wedding ceremonies are still badly arranged. The investigation made by the central committee of state institution trade union workers provides an eloquent witness in this connection:

In the Kungur, Chernovskoye and Elovo districts you cannot be married in winter: the buildings are not heated. The Tomsk building is heated, but there are some days, both in winter and summer, on which you cannot be married there. On days when the city registry office does not want to be bothered with clients, the following notice appears on the door: 'Open only for the registration of deaths.' You can be married in the Vereshchagino district, but not on Mondays, Tuesdays, Wednesdays, Thursdays, Saturdays or Sundays. Marriages are only registered on Fridays.

[1] See footnote 1, p. 13 above.

. . . The registry officials ought to remember that a marriage is not simply a civic act, but a *happy* civic act, and that no one has the right to cast a shadow over it.

With that remark we will close this jubilee article—jubilee, because it is the hundredth, perhaps even the two hundredth written on the subject. More than enough! . . .

A KOMSOMOL SHOULD BE PRINCIPLED

(*Komsomolskaya Pravda*, April 27, 1950)

RECENTLY Comrade M., a komsomol from the city of Chernakhovsk in the Kalinin province, asked the editors whether in their opinion he was justified in marrying in church since his fiancée wanted a church wedding, or whether he would be violating the ruling contained in the Komsomol Statute if he went ahead with this course of action. The editors explained to Comrade M. in an open letter published in this paper that such a course of action would be unprincipled and incompatible with membership of the komsomol, representing as it did, an organisation of the advanced sections of Soviet youth. They added, moreover, that it was the duty of every komsomol to carry on an uncompromising struggle against survivals of religious prejudices and superstitions, to explain to young people how harmful these were, and to spread scientific knowledge.

Our 'Reply to Komsomol M.' aroused lively comment among the readers. Many letters to the editor were sent in, all of them agreeing with the attitude taken by the 'Reply'. These letters consider that komsomol M.'s question showed a lack of principle and determination.

'We wholeheartedly agree with the editors' reply to komsomol M.,' write Comrades Oleinik, Verzuvov and Novikov, representing a komsomol meeting of service-men. 'We should have regarded him as unprincipled and spineless if he had agreed to be married in church. In doing so he would have placed himself outside the ranks of the komsomol, for it is his duty as a komsomol to explain to his fiancée and to any other non-komsomol comrades of his how harmful religious prejudices are. We decided to arrange for a talk on "Science and Religion" to be given to the service-men here, in which we intend to demonstrate the harmfulness of religion on the one hand, and on the other, the immense role played in our lives by science.'

V. Nabatov (Kharkov), a student, writes the following:

'. . . Comrade M. cannot have understood the spirit of the Statute or have been really clear as to the implications of his proposed course of action.' He urges that Comrade M., with the aid of his fellow komsomols, should explain to the girl that she is wrong, and help her to understand that a church wedding is no guarantee for a happy marriage.

Some readers' letters put the following, perfectly justified, question: what had been the attitude of M.'s komsomol branch? Did it put its point of view or did it stand aside?

Service-men Nichkovich and Alexandrovich, for instance, consider M.'s ignorance of a komsomol's duties and obligations as evidence of a serious defect of the branch and of its secretary. 'One may well conclude,' they write, 'that educational work in the branch is poor, that komsomol duties are not explained and that there are problems on which the members are not at all clear. . . .'

Readers Comrades Shutylev (Novozybkov, Bryansk province), Kovalevich and a few others, while condemning the conduct of komsomol M., ask what they should do in cases where the parents insist on a church wedding and where they do not want to hurt their feelings. There can only be one reply to this question—the same as that to komsomol M.: without in any way offending or wounding these older people, komsomols must patiently and carefully explain to them that young Soviet people, and in particular komsomols, cannot go against their basic convictions, convictions which they have formed from their knowledge of modern science and from our Bolshevik outlook on life.

THE NOBLE WORK OF THE MOTHER

BY I. TYURIN

(*Trud*, Sept. 5, 1950)

We had a discussion at the Kamenka sugar plant on the role played by women in building the communist society. At this meeting two distinct views emerged. Some people maintained that a woman must work in industry, agriculture, or in some institution, i.e. that she must contribute to the national economy with her labour, if she is to take part in the building of communism. Others considered that the housewife who stays at home bringing up her children and helping to create pleasant living conditions for her working husband, also participates in the building of communism.

We should like to know what you think.

I. Maglyovany, Kamenka, Kirovograd province.
(On behalf of a group of workers from the factory.)

WE can see from your letter, Comrade Maglyovany, that despite the difference of opinion you mention, everyone was agreed on the tremendous role which women play in the struggle to build a communist society.

. . . In our country all the conditions necessary for the woman's active participation, both as worker and mother, in the administration of the state have been created, and women are able to do great work both in the economic and cultural fields. It is the constant concern of the Communist Party and the Soviet Government to lighten the woman's labour in the home. The number of auxiliary communal establishments, such as dining-rooms, laundries, dressmaking centres and shoes repair shops, as well as the network of kindergarten and crèches, are growing with every year. The more such establishments we have and the more efficient they are, the easier it will be for the working mother to bring up her children while also taking part in the political and cultural life of the society. . . .

But what about the housewife who is bringing up her children and helping to make a good home for her husband, the family's bread-winner? Does she contribute nothing to society? Yes, she does. People who deny this, fail to see the fundamental difference between the family in a socialist society and in a capitalist society, and do not realise that the upbringing of children, including their upbringing in the home, *has acquired a social importance under socialism which it did not and could not have under capitalism.*

. . . In our country motherhood is surrounded with respect and nation-wide honour. Over 30,000 women, having given birth to and brought up 10 or more children, possess the 'Heroine Mother' gold star. About 2,800,000 Soviet women have been awarded the 'Motherhood Glory' and 'Motherhood Medal' decorations. These awards are tokens of a nation-wide recognition of the great social importance of motherhood.

. . . Hundreds of thousands of women use the services of the extensive network of kindergartens and crèches and are successfully working in industry in the towns, and in the countryside. All our public authorities hold out a helping hand to those mothers who want to be in the vanguard of the builders of communism.

But in our country women who are not employed in the national economy can nevertheless take part in the life of the society. . . Many Soviet housewives who work in their homes are also active public workers. . . . The wives of the oil workers in the village of Akhtyrsky in the Krasnodar region, for instance, are now regarded as the driving force behind the campaign to improve the general appearance of the village. Every enterprise knows of women, wives of workers and employees, who take an active part in public inspections of dining rooms and shops, and who help to organise pioneer camps and kindergartens. These women bring up their children and devote their leisure to voluntary public work.

Tens of millions of Soviet women live and work for the great patriotic goal of building communism. These are the working women who are employed in factories, collective farms and other institutions, most of them also bringing up a family. But mothers who for some reason or other are unable to work in factories or institutions and who are bringing up their children in the great Soviet family, also participate in the struggle for communism. . . .

THE HOUSEWIFE

FROM THE NOVEL *Ferrous Metallurgy* BY A. FADEYEV

(*Ogonyok*, 1954, no. 43, p. 3)

IT was morning—the beginning of another day which, just like hundreds of days before it and thousands of days to come, would be filled with all the bitterness and boredom of endless, terribly petty and soul-destroying work, all the things which filled the life of a housewife, the life of millions and millions of women.

. . . Tina recalled the past when, as a nineteen-year old girl, she had been independent, full of hope, esteemed and respected; and she realised that she would not have lost all this if she had not herself dropped everything for the sake of her husband and children. She had lost touch with her friends. Her best friend now spent her time with others who were travelling along the great highway of life with her. Meanwhile she, Christina Boroznova, spent her time clearing up after her father-in-law and her brother-in-law, Zakhar.

. . . Tina went back into the kitchen, removed the boiling kettle and put the frying-pan in its place, took off the cooked cabbage soup and put on the milk; then she measured out some semolina for the children and began to fry the meat. While the food was cooking, she set the kitchen table for Pavlusha[1] and poured out a full glass of wine for him.

Tina could hear how Pavlusha dressed and washed, tinkling with the cup which he used for shaving; and she kept remembering that he must hurry to get to work in time for Musa's smelting. But when he came into the kitchen, still without his jacket and in his slippers, a little preoccupied, but fresh and talkative as usual, Tina suddenly asked him:

'Do you think you could find out for me whether Rubtsov is on holiday? I'd like to see him.'

[1] Her husband.

Rubtsov was the head of the recently formed metal working shop where Vassa now was.

Pavlusha understood at once why Tina had mentioned Rubtsov. He looked at her moodily, drank his wine and began to eat his soup in silence.

'I know what you're afraid of,' Tina said.

'It's not what you think at all,' he answered. 'It's just that I'm concerned about you: I don't want you to look like Shura Krasovskaya.'

Krasovsky's wife Shura was the secretary of her shop komsomol branch. She worked as a dispatcher in the coke processing shop and also kept house for the whole Krasovsky family. She had to look after her little girl—a baby of eight months, her husband's mother who had now been a cripple for a year and a half, and her younger sister, a school girl in the fourth form who also lived with them. The Krasovskys had only been married two years, but Shura had noticeably aged during that time. . . . And wo whenever Tina said that she wanted to go out to work again, Pavlusha would bring up Shura Krasovskaya. But this time he received an unexpected reply:

'Of course, you'd rather I was like Zakhar's Dunka,' Tina said. 'You Kuznetsovs seem to prefer that!'

It was the first time that she had criticised Pavlusha's family.

'And aren't you a Kuznetsov too?' he asked with a sly smile.

'The Kuznetsovs' servant! If we were both working we'd be able to take on a nursemaid.'

'And be laughed at? We're both working people. It's not right for us to have nursemaids. And anyway, try getting a nursemaid here in Bolshegorsk!'

'You've got such a good reputation, they might even take them in the kindergarten.'

'And would you let them go?'

And so their quarrel had begun.—Never before had Tina experienced such an aching feeling of love towards her husband as now when she saw him going down the crowded street together with Vassa and Sonya Novikova. And never before had she been conscious of such a strong and terrible feeling of despair and defeat. In the street below Tina saw people going to their day's work, a perfectly ordinary sight, but one which typified for her a right enjoyed by everyone else, but now denied to her. It was not simply that she, who had been one of the best workers in her time, was no longer an equal with these women. It also seemed to her that all these men and women going to their work with her husband were somehow closer to him than she was herself, that, having sacrificed herself and subordinated herself to him, she could no longer be as close to him as people who were his equals and who were independent of him.

Tina went back into the dining-room, separated the bickering children and took them into the kitchen. But she did not see how they were eating, she did not hear their chatter.

'How had it all happened?' she asked herself. 'How did I come to this? How did it start?'—And she felt ashamed and frightened to answer these questions. . . .

IT IS HER RIGHT

BY E. MAXIMOVA, SPECIAL CORRESPONDENT, KALININ[1]

(*Literaturnaya Gazeta*, July 27, 1954)

THE conversation which took place in the Kalinin city executive committee is really worth quoting verbatim. The chairman of the city planning commission was speaking about the fact that some houses were still without piped water, that there were too few laundries and that women were not always anxious to use them even where they did exist. He could not understand why this was so. From behind his back a self-assured voice said:

'They're used to washing at home. It's a custom.'

A middle-aged man came up to the table. 'Yes,' he repeated with conviction, 'it's a custom, a tradition, if you like.'

'So, according to you, women enjoy doing the washing when they come home from work.'

'What do you mean? They're women, aren't they? Anyway, physical labour is good for you.' There was a frankly cynical note in his voice.

'But, tell me, when are they to go to the cinema or to do some reading?'

'Oh, they'll find time.'

By a strange coincidence Pavel Ivanovich Nerobeyev, the man who had so unceremoniously joined in the conversation, works as chief municipal engineer. Of course you do not often meet a *Domostroi*[2] type of man like this in a responsible post in the city executive committee. But in subsequent conversations here in Kalinin, with the director of a large factory, with officials from the city's trading

[1] A city of some 200,000 inhabitants in central Russia.

[2] A sixteenth-century Russian manuscript which contains rules of family behaviour and places the woman in a position of complete subjection. The *Domostroi* has now become a byword for conservatism and obscurantism.

authorities and with the manager of a dressmaking establishment, I was time and again reminded of Nerobeyev's 'they're women, aren't they?'

The skill of women's hands has been praised in song and poetry. How much these hands produce here in Kalinin: silk and excavators, cloth and all-metal carriages. They plant apple orchards, drive trams and correct schoolchildren's compositions. And it is one of the most important and noble duties of the city soviet and other public authorities and organisations to do everything in their power so that these hands should hold a book instead of a ladle, and a volley-ball instead of a washing board.

From the very first days of the revolution Lenin constantly asserted this right of women to liberation from domestic slavery. 'We are faced,' he wrote, 'with a long struggle which demands a fundamental change both in our attitude to household duties and in the tools used for these duties'.

A tremendous amount has been done since these words were said. Formerly illiterate and crushed by kitchen and housework, the woman now has full rights as a Soviet citizen. Her circle of interests has grown to an extraordinary degree, and the part played by her in science, culture and industry and in the administration of the country has become incomparably more important. But she has also begun to make greater demands. Things which only ten years ago she would have borne without protest have now become intolerable, things to which she reconciled herself yesterday arouse her indignation today. Our new household and communal facilities do not always help the woman as much as they could. And often the reason for this is a tacit conviction (not all are as frank as Nerobeyev) that women are decreed by birth to spend the greater part of their free time in doing housework.

*

A slim little woman in a blue overall is going through the workshop, a piece of artificial leather, smooth and polished like lacquer, in her hands; it has only just come from the press. The experimental shop of the artificial leather combine was only started two years ago, and these are the first results. There is great scope for the shop and, consequently, for Natalia Mikhailovna Obukhovskaya, its superintendent. The eight hours which she spends in the shop are filled with important and interesting work. Between six and seven in the evening Natalia Mikhailovna leaves the shop, but not the factory. There are many important affairs connected with her public activities to be attended to: she is secretary of the factory's party branch, member of the combine's party bureau and candidate member of the district committee; in addition she attends evening courses at the institute of Marxism-Leninism.

In the shop, at meetings of the party committee and at lectures, Obukhovskaya is in every way equal with the men—the same demands are made on her, she is respected and recognised. The right to work, to participate in public life and receive education, all these have become the inalienable and inviolate rights of Obukhovskaya and, indeed, of all Soviet women, and because they have become an integral part of our lives, they often pass unnoticed.

But then Obukhovskaya arrives home late at night, and here she has duties which the male colleagues with whom she has just left the factory do not have. There is her family: her ten-year old daughter and an invalid brother; not a large family, but nevertheless one for whom she must cook, wash and sew. Where is she to find time for all that?

'How I could do with two or three hours added to the twenty-four to sit down quietly and read a newspaper, or to go to the cinema,' Natalia Mikhailovna tells me. 'Sometimes Zinochka reminds me: "Oh, mummy, when are we going to go out? You've promised so often." I know that it is my duty and, indeed, my right and joy to go out with her, but I simply can't manage it.'

And indeed how can she get everything done when there are no baths in the suburb where the Obukhovskaya family lives, when wash day is a problem (lack of facilities for heating water quickly and for drying the clothes), when the market is at the other end o the city, and when Sunday is in no way a day of rest.

Brigade leader, Maria Mikhailovna Danshina works next to Obukhovskaya, operating a rolling machine in shop no. 4. This week she is on the second shift and arrives at the factory at 3.30 p.m. She prefers working in the evenings, because you don't have any meetings to attend and can get home as soon as the siren goes. She has a son and a daughter to look after.

For two years now Danshina has been trying unsuccessfully to get her small daughter into a crèche; and during this time she has never known a moment's peace: she might be standing at the bench, but her thoughts would be at home wondering whether everything was alright; after all the little girl had been left in the care of her six-year old brother. Like Natalia Mikhailovna, Maria Mikhailovna manages to do a surprising amount during the day; but as she goes to sleep late at night, her mind is full of things for which she has had no time and which will have to be done in the morning.

What are the city authorities doing to help Obukhovskaya, Danshina and thousands of other women in Kalinin? I do not want to know what they might be able to do in the future, but what they can do now, today. This city, which is growing rapidly and has spread far along the Volga, has only one laundry, one knitwear establishment and one for children's clothes, the latter taking five orders per day. The Zavolzhe district spreads for many miles along the Volga, but it only has one shop where paraffin can be bought. And the Novo-Promyshlenny district has no laundry or dressmaking establishment at all: you have to do your washing and sewing at home or go to another district. Ordinary daily tasks, such as buying paraffin or potatoes and taking a primus stove or a pair of shoes to be mended, are very time-consuming and mean long journeys and unnecessary worries for the woman.

Surely a big province centre like Kalinin (which, incidentally, has a large railway carriage works) could have a few trucks with petrol tanks so that housewives would not have to carry their paraffin over long distances. Why are the two new factories producing household goods, which should have been begun last year, still under—very slow—construction? It is ridiculous that a city with so great a housing programme should have been unable to provide buildings, not even one for each suburb, which could serve as laundry reception points, so that women should not have to take their washing through the whole city. Since last year the dry cleaning shop has not been functioning.

Why are many of these problems left unsolved? Is it not because some of the people responsible for the communal services of Kalinin are neglecting their duties? It is, of course, impossible to change *everything at once*, but even in the conditions of today much more could be done. There are many examples of an attentive attitude to the 'details' of everyday life to be seen, provided you want to see them. And it is usually not a question of money but of a will to imitate these examples. No immense capital outlays are required for the shops selling household goods, which the citizens of Riga have organised; or for the laundries, equipped with one or two washing machines, which they have in Kiev; these laundries are attached to blocks of flats and serve all the housewives living in the area; or for the dining rooms they have in Kharkov where you can buy a cooked dinner to take home with you.

But let us return to the Novo-Promyshlenny district of Kalinin.

A good half of the inhabitants of this suburb are workers at the artificial leather combine and their families. There are new houses here, ornamental iron railings, stone flower pots and pillars. Not long ago this was a wilderness, and the little township of attractive small houses has grown up in the last five or six years. But surely the architects and directors of the combine must have known that the people who settled here would immediately need a laundry and a shoe repair shop, neither of which exist.

A dusty street full of pot-holes leads through the suburb to the bus stop. Early in the morning, long before work starts at the combine, you can see women walking along carrying children in their arms; they are mothers taking their children to the crèche. The child has to be woken at dawn, carried to the bus stop, and then taken a mile or so further at the other end, a journey of at least two hours for the mothers. And all because the factory crèche was not repaired last summer while the children were on holiday in the country, and so had to be closed for repairs this winter, which meant that the children had to be split up and sent to other crèches—some of them near, others far away. . . .

We must not forget the mother's great and responsible social duty of bringing up her children. She must be given time for it, because bringing up children does not simply mean feeding them and keeping their clothes clean; a mother should take them out for walks, read to them, take them to the cinema, and, finally, simply talk with them and reply to all their childish 'hows' and 'whys'. Children often learn respect for the worker and for the wealth created by labour through the personal examples of their mothers. And for this reason the working mother tends to be the better pedagogue, even though she can give less time to the child than the housewife who stays at home.

Women ought to have time to read books, go to lectures and listen to music. Kalinin is growing as a cultural as well as an industrial centre. Quite recently the drama theatre gave its first performance in the wonderful many-tiered hall of its new building. A large, spacious building has been allotted to the philharmonic orchestra for concerts and lectures. In a few days the white-columned house of the new province library on the banks of the Volga will be opened. But there are many women in Kalinin who do not avail themselves of these rich cultural opportunities.

It was not easy for the inspector of the province bank, Nina Bubnova, to carry on her studies in the extramural department of the technicum; it meant working, studying and looking after her small daughter as well, since she simply could not find a place for her in a crèche. I asked Bubnova whether she was going to continue her studies.

'Out of the question,' was her reply. 'It's no good my even thinking of going on to the institute now.'

Here is something for the members of the Kalinin city soviet and for trade union officials to think about: a young woman at the height of her powers who wants to study and has the qualifications for any higher educational establishment in Kalinin, Moscow or Leningrad, and who is debarred from a higher education because her family takes up all her free time. . . .

*

I should imagine that the heads of the Kalinin city executive committee will inform the editor of the measures that have been taken as a result of this article. But I hope that the matter will not rest there. For it is not only a question of opening laundries and workshops, but also of changing the outlook of some of the officials in Kalinin. I am not interested in spasmodic campaigns; what is needed is that a sensitive, tactful and attentive attitude towards working mothers should become the rule in the activities of the leading officials of the city.

APPENDIX TO A MEMBERSHIP REPORT

BY S. NARINYANI

(*Komsomolskaya Pravda*, Aug. 8, 1950)

KHAMID ERKAKHODZHAEV'S indignation was quite justified. This was the third membership report in the last 18 months from the secretary of the Karasu district committee of the komsomol that had had to be sent to the province committee at Tashkent, and for the third time Erkakhodzhaev had to record a decrease in the number of girls belonging to the komsomol.

Khamid Erkakhodzhaev's patience was now, finally, exhausted; instead of signing the report, he decided to call a special meeting of the bureau of the district committee. We must give him his due: Erkakhodzhaev, as komsomol secretary of the Karasu district, did not embark on long, edifying and platitudinous speeches. He was a man of action. Armed with a pencil, he decided which of the komsomol activists were to blame for this serious state of affairs.

The first to be asked was the komsomol secretary of the Stalin collective farm.

'Sagimbek Karzhubaev,' the district committee secretary said to him, 'tell the bureau how many girls have joined the komsomol.'

Sagimbek Karzhubaev got up, blushed and raised his hands in dismay.

'None at all this year,' he replied.

'And last year?'

Sagimbek Karzhubaev blushed a second time.

'And none last year either.'

'And how many women left?'

'Five.'

'And why?'

'They got married.'

'And why didn't you explain to the women that there's no law against married people being in the komsomol?'

'There's no point in talking to the women,' Sagimbek Karzhubaev replied. 'They don't ever leave because they want to. It's the husbands that are the trouble. We still have that sort, with old-fashioned ideas about women.'

'Could you not expose at least one of them?'

'And how am I to expose him? In his public life he's an excellent man, sometimes he's even a komsomol.'

'Act irrespective of personalities,' the district committee secretary said severely. 'What is he, this komsomol: a friend and comrade to his young wife, or a tyrannical khan. I don't suppose you went to see any of them at home, did you?'

And for the third time that day the secretary of the collective farm branch had to blush.

'No, I didn't,' he uncomfortably admitted.

'In that case I'll come with you myself,' the district committee secretary announced with determination. 'I'll be an example to you of how a komsomol activist should behave. He has no right to make excuses for anyone. Any survivals of feudalism he sees he must expose and bring before the court of youth.'

And so as not to draw the matter out any further, Khamid Erkakhodzhaev asked for the membership cards of those girls who had simply lapsed to be brought. When they were on the table, he asked the komsomol in charge of registrations to read out the names.

'With whom shall I begin?' the latter asked.

'It doesn't matter,' the secretary answered. 'Whoever it is, we'll go to her home and take her under our protection.'

It is difficult to say whether it was a coincidence or whether it had been done on purpose, but the first name to be read out was that of Zainab Erkakhodzhaeva.

'Who, did you say?' Khamid Erkakhodzhaev interrupted and reached for the folder. There could be no doubt: uppermost in the file lay the card belonging to Zainab, the wife of the secretary of the district committee.

It was now Khamid Erkakhodzhaev's turn to blush. And he did blush, but not for long. He quickly regained his composure and, throwing a sidelong glance at the komsomol with the registration files, said severely:

'Next one!'

'The next one?' Sagimbek Karzhubaev asked in surprise. 'What about Zainab?'

'We will not visit Zainab,' Erkakhodzhaev answered.

'And why not?'

'It's not convenient.'

'Not convenient? Not convenient to criticise the secretary, you mean. But didn't this same secretary only five minutes ago call upon activists to do their work irrespective of personalities? Or didn't I hear right?' Sagimbek Karzhubaev asked, not without irony.

Khamid Erkakhodzhaev nervously paced the room.

'You must understand that I'm not only district committee secretary,' he said. 'I am also a husband. You want to visit my home and make your investigations. But what sort of authority will I have left in the eyes of my relatives if you do that? My in-laws, aunts and all sorts of women folk live near us.'

'Well, invite us to some pilau,' one of the komsomols suggested, 'and your mother-in-law will even be pleased, seeing that her son-in-law is so hospitable.'

There was really nothing the district committee secretary could do, but as they reached his house he nevertheless made one last attempt to dissuade them from going through with it.

'Look here, boys, you're quite wrong to worry about all this,' he said. 'This isn't the kind of case that needs inspecting. There's nothing typical about it.'

It transpired later that the boys were quite right to be worried. They saw many curious things in Khamid Erkakhodzhaev's home. It was a clean and tidy little house. As is customary in old, patriarchal Uzbek families, the rooms were fitted with recesses containing teapots of all sizes. There were more teapots than one household could use, but not a single table.

'Where do you have your meals?' the guests asked their host.

'Take a seat,' the latter answered and threw some cushions on to the carpet.

'That's dreadful,' Sagimbek Karzhubaev remarked. 'In our village even the old men prefer to use chairs and to eat at a table, and don't squat on the ground any more.'

The district committee secretary agreed that chairs were more comfortable. 'But,' he added, 'I don't want to quarrel with my relatives over every little detail.'

While the master of the house was thus entertaining the guests, his wife Zainab had prepared the pilau and came into the room with the food.

'Help yourselves,' she said, standing by the wall.

'And what about you, Zainab,' Sagimbek Karzhubaev asked. 'Come and sit down with us.'

Zainab did not answer, but one of her relatives said:

'It's no use asking her; she won't sit down.'

'Why not?'

'When the husband has guests, his wife should eat in the kitchen.'

Karzhubaev looked at the husband in surprise. The latter had nothing to say and guiltily fixed his eyes on the rich pilau. He did not seem to want Zainab to sit down beside him either. And why? Was it perhaps that he was embarrassed by his wife's presence? Khamid Erkakhodzhaev should be proud, not embarrassed, to have a wife such as Zainab. Young and attractive, she was not only a good housewife, but had also been considered a keen activist in the komsomol. She had even taken part in a physical culture parade in Moscow. But all that was before she had married. After their marriage, Khamid Erkakhodzhaev had stopped going to the stadium with her, and did not even take her to cinemas, theatres, social evenings or walks in the park any more. And why?

'It's awkward; my relatives are against it,' was the reply.

The relatives had not wanted Zainab to go to komsomol meetings and political classes or to continue her physical culture. And her husband did not even try to take her part.

'What am I to do? Do you want me to quarrel with my relatives?' he asked, trying to justify his conduct. 'You know yourself, they're old and backward.'

It became obvious that Zainab's husband, like his relatives, was also distinguished by backward ideas. On those rare occasions when Khamid Erkakhodzhaev appeared in the street together with his wife, he did not walk on the pavement by her side but two paces in front, as the man and the head of the family. And this 'head' humiliated Zainab not only as a woman but also as a mother.

'Two children, and both of them girls,' he said unhappily. 'If she could have borne me one boy, at least!'

The komsomols left Khamid Erkakhodzhaev's house with heavy hearts. They felt ashamed and uncomfortable for their secretary. Their secretary, after all, knew how alien and out-of-place feudal customs were today, and that he must wage an uncompromising struggle against such customs; the one thing he had not realised was that he must first of all struggle to discard these customs himself.

Khamid Erkakhodzhaev's appointment as secretary of the district committee was, of course, a mistaken one. And although his case, as he says himself, is not typical, we nevertheless regard it as most instructive, and we hope that this account will serve as an appendix to the membership report sent to the Tashkent province committee of the komsomol from the Karasu district. It will help the officials in the Uzbek Central Committee of the komsomol to understand why some married komsomol women leave the organisation.

THE WOMAN IN THE YASHMAK

BY ZULFIA, TASHKENT

(*Literaturnaya Gazeta*, April 19, 1950)

ABOVE Navoi[1] street the sun is rising in a clear, blue sky, shining on the young town with its light-coloured blocks of new buildings, many of them still surrounded with scaffolding.

As I look down the street I realise how much it has grown before our very eyes. We are its coevals and we cannot but feel tenderness as we see the new buildings—the province executive committee, the central telegraph office, the Mukimi[2] theatre, the *Motherland* and *Sredazugol* cinemas, the House of Specialists and the House of *Chirchikstroi* Workers.

At one time the old city used to begin down by the banks of the river Ankhor. I remember the low clay huts without windows and the narrow, dusty lanes from my childhood. In place of the tall House of Specialists there was a flat-roofed clay hut. This is where Khabiba Usupova, now a Merited Teacher of the Republic and holder of the Order of Lenin, used to live, teaching, and fighting for the emancipation of women. Her clay hut was the centre of enlightenment. From there she went out to the illiteracy elimination classes at which hundreds and thousands of young Uzbek women studied—first the ordinary ABC, and then the ABC of Leninism. It was there that she wrote her famous speech at the trial of the enemies of the revolution who had murdered the first two girls, Tursunai and Nurkham, to discard the yashmak.

Khabiba Usupova has just gone past in her new car. As before, she hurries to her school, and she now teaches our daughters, girls whose mothers too were her pupils. Outside the school she is met by children for whom the yashmak—the ancient woman's garb with a

[1] Alisher Navoi (1441–1501) was an Uzbek poet and philosopher.
[2] An Uzbek revolutionary poet of the last century.

heavy net which covered the face, and the *ichkaria*—a closed building where women used to be kept in the Uzbek household, are things from old oriental tales.

It is difficult to say which is the younger: the new street of our ancient city or we, its inhabitants and Khabiba Usupova's first pupils, we, the women of Soviet Uzbekistan who have become engineers, scholars, artists, and experts in the factories and collective farms.

Zulfia Umidova, doctor of medical sciences whose research has shed new light on the activity of the heart; Zarifa Saidnasyrov, candidate of chemical sciences; Israilova, a famous weaver in the Stalin textile combine; Lola Irbutaeva, a Hero of Socialist Labour[1] who has grown and harvested more than five tons of cotton from the newly cultivated lands in the Hunger Steppe[2]—these are only a few of the many names that spring to my mind.

It gives great joy to me, a poetess of Soviet Uzbekistan, to go along this street, named after Alisher Navoi who sang of the beauty and spiritual wealth of women five centuries ago. . . .

The figure of a woman hidden beneath a yashmak flits across sunlit Navoi street like a dark shadow, an incongruous and offensive sight on this new street of a Soviet town. Why is this woman in a yashmak? Who forces her to wear it?

To answer these puzzling questions, certain isolated, but nevertheless disgraceful, facts must be brought to the notice of the public. And I consider it my duty as a citizen to do this.

Zumrad Mukhamedova was forced by her husband, a worker on the Tashkent railway, to live the life of a recluse. Is this what she had been to a Soviet school for—to wear the yashmak and be kept a prisoner at home? Oguldzhan graduated from school with honours, but now that she has married the head of the education department (what a cruel joke!) in Yangi-Kurgan, she is locked away in the *ichkaria*. The headmaster of a seven-year school which comes under the Palandar rural soviet (Kitab district, Kashkadarya province) is a man called Gusinov. A considerable number of girls have been dropping out from the school. But, far from fighting against this evil, Gusinov actually helps to give his pupils away in marriage, even though they are not yet of age! That is what happened to Ulasha Kurbanova, Koisuna Dusmatova and to four of their friends. In the Khaturcha district, Samad Akhmedov, a married man and father of three children, married two more wives. The district authorities

[1] See footnote 1, p. 83 above.

[2] *Golodnaya Step*. A large tract of desert land. The reclamation of this land was begun in 1949.

were informed of this disgraceful event but they say that the sowing is in full swing and that they are too busy to bother about such 'trifles' as polygamy just at the moment.

. . . Never in the history of mankind has there been a spiritual revolution such as our Stalin era is witnessing among the peoples of Soviet Central Asia. What tremendous flowering of socialist culture it has brought! But it is wrong for people to indulge in unwarranted complacency, and to behave as though we had nothing more to achieve. . . . .

The position of women in our republic has changed beyond all recognition: Soviet power has endowed women with every right, women have now become a tremendous force in our collective farms, and there are thousands of heroes like Lola Irbutaeva, who stand in the forefront of the struggle for more cotton; thousands of Uzbek women are komsomol and trade union officials or deputies to local soviets. . . .

I quicken my steps and catch up with the woman in the yashmak as she stops in front of the monument to Alisher Navoi, the immortal bard of Shirin, Leila and Dilaram.

Yes, lift your yashmak and take a good look! The woman has thrown back her yashmak. Her beautiful face expresses sadness and timidity. She gives me a frank smile, and I feel as though a hidden treasure is suddenly sparkling before me.

'Who is your husband?' I ask her.

No reply.

'Can you read?'

She shakes her head.—We walk along side by side. *Gulsara*, I read on the notice outside the theatre. 'Have you seen the opera? It's on at the new Navoi theatre. Have you seen the theatre?'

'From a distance.'

'You go and see *Gulsara*. It's about a girl who discarded the yashmak as long as twenty years ago. And it was more difficult for her than it is for you: there were beys, *ishans*[1] and *basmachs*[2] in those days, but she had glimpsed the light of the future, and she broke away to freedom.'

. . . We go past the new, still unfinished, building which will house the printing works. A swarthy Uzbek girl, a small cap on her black hair, is directing an immense excavator. What strength and confidence there is in her small hand as she guides this large and skilful machine!

At the corner I part with my unknown acquaintance in the yashmak. 'Until we meet again!' . . .

[1] Moslem priests. [2] Counter-revolutionary bandits.

DURSUN ANNAEVA'S CHILDREN

BY IVAN GORELOV, ASHKHABAD[1]

(*Ogonyok*, 1955, no. 41, p. 23)

SHE is sitting cross legged on a low wooden platform placed on the carpet. . . .

'Good morning, mother Dursun.'

Dursun nods her head, shields her eyes against the merciless sun, gives me her welcoming 'salaam' and asks me to sit down with her.

I sit down on the edge of the platform, inquire about her health and tell her of the purpose of my visit.

'I've come to find out more about your three daughters, Surai, Sona and Nabat, and how they all became actresses.'

'Have you asked them?'

'Yes, I had long talks with them, but they said that you would be better still at telling me, particularly about their childhood.'

There is a short pause while she seems to be recalling the past to her mind. Then, agitatedly running her hands over her sunburnt face covered in wrinkles, she dreamily looks into the distance where, beyond the garden, the huge brown humps of the Kopet-Dag mountains stand out in the purple haze of the heat.

'Yes, Surai, Sona and Nabat—all three are my children. Do you know what "Nabat" means in Turkmenian? It means candy, sweetmeat. That was the name I gave to my youngest daughter. She was born later, during a happy time when I was already in Ashkhabad.—How much we have been through! Ours is a terrible past, and the very sun grows dim when you remember it.'

*

One spring day in 1919, Memed Murad died in the mountain village of Errik-Kala. He was a poor peasant who had inherited

[1] The capital of the Turkmenian SSR.

nothing but a home-made spade and a dilapidated cloth tent. . . . He died of tuberculosis, leaving a family of six: his widow Dursun, a tall woman, strong and courageous, four children and a half-blind old woman.

Two years after her husband's death . . . Dursun's elder brother, Klych Murad, unexpectedly arrived from the village of Kypchak which lies right at the foot of the Kopet-Dag mountains. He came late one evening on a dusty black horse. He walked across the courtyard as though he owned it, his eyes grasping like an eagle's and his weather-beaten face set in angry folds. He drank some tea and helped to mend the tent. But then, when the children had gone to sleep, he began the following conversation:

'Sister, there is a man in our village, a very good man, my neighbour Aman Sopar. He is already old, about 60, but he has sheep and money. He is a widower and he wants to marry you.'

'No,' Dursun interrupted him with firmness.

'Now don't get heated, sister. Sopar will pay a good price: a lot of green tea, a horse, four sheep and two silk gowns. Nobody could ask more for you.—Only, the children will have to stay here in the tent.'

'No, Klych, I shall never abandon my little children, never. And now, go away; you and your black horse have brought me bad tidings.'

'But I have the right of an older brother,' Klych angrily hissed. 'If you won't come of your own free will, I'll take you by force. Don't you forget the law of our ancestors!'

He left without even saying goodbye, mounted his horse in silence, rode off and vanished into the twilight haze, leaving a cloud of dust behind him.

Not a week had passed when four horsemen rode up to Dursun's tent one night. The children were already asleep and Dursun was outside pounding grain. The horsemen dismounted by the wall. One of them stayed with the horses, the other three went up to Dursun. She recognised Klych and her cousin Kuvonch. The third, a tall man, was unknown to her.

'Get ready, sister,' Klych commanded in a peremptory voice.

. . . In the darkness someone caught hold of her arm . . ., the tall stranger gagged her, and she was taken out to the wall to be tied to the saddle . . .

When Dursun regained consciousness she found herself in a low clay hut which she recognised as that of Klych. She had been here with her late husband during the first spring of their marriage. . . . Towards evening they brought her some food.

A week later her brother brought Sopar, wearing a new gown and a clean shirt. He silently inspected Dursun as though she were a horse at a market, thought for a minute, stroked his beard and sighed.

. . . Forty days later Dursun's younger brother, Alisher, arrived from Ashkhabad where he lived in a hostel, studying. He did not dare to criticise his older brother, but went about the house silent and gloomy. In the evening he brought Dursun water and burst into tears.

'You must run away to Ashkhabad where they have a women's department,' he told her. 'Nobody is allowed to beat women any more now or to sell them for bride money. Lenin said so. . . .'

That night Dursun stole out of the tent . . . Alisher was waiting for her by the water tank. They took one another by the hand and, keeping to the back gardens, made for the camel road which was barely visible in the darkness. . . . In the distance the whistle of a steamer could be heard and it seemed to Dursun that it was calling her with its bold, iron voice. There in Ashkhabad were people who would save her children. And they quickened their steps, going farther and farther away from the village.

In the women's department in Ashkhabad she was overcome by tears, and it was a long time before she was able to speak. Two women calmed her: Maria Petrovna, a fair-haired Russian, and Ogultach, a young Turkmenian woman. Eventually Dursun managed to control herself sufficiently to ask Ogultach to save her children who had been left in the village by themselves. And at the thought of her children the tears began to flow again.

She was accommodated in Peasant House.[1] The door was guarded by a tall man in a military tunic and with a pistol in his belt. He would protect her from Sopar or Klych.

On the following day this man went to her village with a cart and brought back three of her children, Surai, Sona and Niaz, emaciated and black with dirt. Little Teshli had died of starvation.

A new life now began for Dursun Annaeva. The children were put into an orphanage, she herself was given work at Peasant House. On Sundays they would all meet and have pilau together, Surai and Sona eagerly telling their mother how they were learning to read and write, studying Russian, singing the *International* and other revolutionary songs, learning to dance a Ukrainian *hopak* and rehearsing for a big concert to be given during the October celebrations at which Surai was going to dance, and Sona, to read poetry . . .

*

[1] 'Peasant Houses' exist in many large cities. They are club houses for new arrivals from the countryside, who may obtain accommodation there overnight.

'And that's the whole story,' Dursun concluded.

Steps could be heard coming from the gate . . . and Sona Muradova, Dursun's second daughter, came in. Sona is a People's Artist of the Turkmenian SSR and the director of the drama theatre.

'Let Sona tell you the rest. She remembers those happy days very well.'

Sona insists that she is not too tired. She has a quiet, serious face with bright, intelligent eyes. She gives us an enthusiastic account of the rehearsal for *Othello* from which she has just come . . . She tells us about her own role, that of Emilia, in the play . . . and about her life.

She grew up in an orphanage in Ashkhabad together with Surai, and their neat little white beds always stood next to one another. In the large stone 'tent' life was far more pleasant than it had been in the cloth tent she had left behind in Errik-Kala.

She remembers their patient teacher, the former nurse Nina Prokofevna, who taught them needlework, made them learn their multiplication tables and showed them how to write. . . .

Surai left the teachers' training college where both girls were studying in her third year and transferred to the studio attached to the Turkmenian drama theatre; Sona became a teacher and went to work in the village of Bezmein. One autumn night *basmachi* attacked the village, and Sona was hidden by an old farm watchman who saved the young teacher's life at the risk of his own. Sona returned to Ashkhabad with a visiting caravan, went to see her mother and brother, and spent long hours talking with her beloved Surai.

One day when she came to the theatre to fetch her sister, the rehearsal was still in progress. Sona sat down and watched with growing impatience: she did not like the way the girls were playing the various characters, and felt that they ought to be portrayed quite differently. At last she could stand it no longer and went up herself to show them how they ought to act a conversation between a village school teacher and an old shepherd. After all, she knew what village teachers were like.

After that Sona was asked to see the producer and to read him some poetry. She read shyly and uncertainly, feeling very nervous. Once outside in the corridor, she collapsed on to a chair and almost wept.

A young broad-shouldered actor came past, took her by the hand and gave her a sympathetic look.

'What are you afraid of?' he asked. 'We're ordinary people like everyone else. We didn't fall from heaven. We're sons and daughters of peasants. Take me, for instance; I'm from the Geok-Tepe district in the Karakum, the son of a shepherd. So why be afraid of us? . . .

'I'd like to congratulate you on your first success. Apart from your nervousness, you passed your audition very well. You have great talent, and if you work very hard indeed, you will become an actress one day. . . .'

In 1940 Sona joined the party. In 1942 she was awarded the title of Merited Actress of the Republic, and seven years later both she and Surai became People's Artists of the Turkmenian SSR.

*

On Sunday evening the whole family gathered at mother Dursun's.

. . . 'And do you know who the youngest participant in the festival[1] will be?' slim and black-eyed Nabat asks us with a sly smile as she cuts herself a large slice of melon. 'The heroine is called Maral—"mountain eagle", and the hero, Baram—"welcome holiday". Would you like to see them?'

I expect her to show me some photographs of young artists. Instead she returns holding two babies in her arms.

'Surai's twins—eight months old,' she says. 'They're going to Moscow too.'

Nabat sits down by Dursun and tenderly puts her arms round her mother's shoulders.

'It's her fault that we all became actresses.'

'Alisher's fault too,' Surai remarks. 'He showed mother the way to Ashkhabad.' And they mention more names of teachers and producers.

Dursun is deep in thought, cutting small pieces of melon with her knife.

'No, my children,' she says quietly. 'Neither my fault nor Alisher's. I'll show you whose fault it is.' She bends down, takes a large book from the shelf and opens it at a page bearing the portrait of Lenin.

[1] Of Turkmenian literature and art, held in Moscow in 1955.

APPENDIX

PERIODICALS AND NEWSPAPERS

Doshkolnoye Vospitaniye—'Pre-School Education'.
A monthly periodical published by the RSFSR Ministry of Education.

Izvestia—'News'.
One of the two most important central newspapers in the country.

Komsomolskaya Pravda—'Young Communist League Pravda'.
A daily newspaper published by the Central Committee of the Young Communist League.

Krestyanka—'Peasant Woman'.
A popular, monthly illustrated magazine.

Kulturno-Prosvetitelnaya Rabota—'Cultural and Educational Work'.
A monthly magazine published by the RSFSR Ministry of Culture.

Literaturnaya Gazeta—'Literary Gazette'.
A newspaper published by the Board of the USSR Union of Soviet Writers. The paper appears three times a week, and is by no means confined to matters of purely literary interest.

Molodoi Kommunist—'Young Communist'.
The monthly journal of the Central Committee of the Young Communist League.

Ogonyok
A weekly popular illustrated magazine.

Rabotnitsa—'Woman Worker'.
A popular monthly illustrated magazine.

Semya i Shkola—'Family and School'.
A monthly journal published by the RSFSR Academy of Pedagogical Sciences.

APPENDIX

Sovetskaya Kultura—'Soviet Culture'.
A newspaper published by the USSR Ministry of Culture.

Trud—'Labour'.
The central trade union newspaper.

Uchitelskaya Gazeta—'Teachers' Gazette'.
A newspaper published jointly by the Ministries of Education of the various Republics and the Central Committee of the primary and secondary school teachers' trade union.

INDEX

INDEX

INDEX

INDEX

INDEX

INDEX

INDEX